TERTIUM ORGANUM

Tertium Organum

THE THIRD CANON OF THOUGHT

A KEY TO

The Enigmas of the World

P. D. OUSPENSKY

TRANSLATED FROM THE RUSSIAN
BY NICHOLAS BESSARABOFF AND CLAUDE BRAGDON
WITH AN INTRODUCTION BY CLAUDE BRAGDON

The Mystery of Space and Time
Occultism and Love
Voices of the Stones
The Logic of Ecstasy
Cosmic Consciousness
Shadows and Reality
Animated Nature
Mathematics of the Infinite
Mystical Theosophy
The New Morality
Birth of the Superman

VINTAGE BOOKS
A Division of Random House
New York

VINTAGE BOOKS EDITION, SEPTEMBER 1970

Library of Congress Catalog Card Number: 76-128440

AND SWARE . . . THAT THERE SHOULD
BE TIME NO LONGER.

Revelations, X. 6

THAT YE, BEING ROOTED AND GROUND-
ED IN LOVE, MAY BE ABLE TO COM-
PREHEND WITH ALL SAINTS WHAT
IS THE BREADTH, AND LENGTH, AND
DEPTH, AND HEIGHT.

Paul the Apostle

The Epistle to the Ephesians, III. 17–18

"*I have called this system of higher logic* TERTIUM ORGANUM *because* for us *it is* the third canon — *third instrument* — of thought *after those of Aristotle and Bacon. The first was* Organon, *the second*, Novum Organum. *But* the third *existed earlier than the first.*"

TERTIUM ORGANUM (*page* 236)

CONTENTS

Contents

Contents

Contents

Contents

Contents

AUTHOR'S PREFACE

In revising *Tertium Organum* for the second edition in English my chief concern has been to co-ordinate its terminology with the more developed terminology of those of my books written after the publication of the second Russian edition of *Tertium Organum*, from which the English translation was made.

Such a unity of terminology is the more necessary because I am obliged to lead the reader into regions of thought and knowledge where boundaries have not been clearly established, and where different authors — and often one and the same author, in different works and during different periods of his activity — have called the same thing by different names, or different things by the same name.

It must be admitted that language is a weak and inadequate vehicle even for the expression of our usual understanding of things, to say nothing of those moments when the understanding unexpectedly expands and becomes deeper, and we see revealed an entire series of facts and relations for the description of which we have neither words nor expressions. But quite aside from this, in ordinary conditions of thinking and feeling, we are frequently at a loss for words, and we use one word at different times to describe different things.

On the other hand, it is no merit in an author to invent new words, or to use old words in new meanings which have nothing in common with the accepted ones — to create, in other words, a special terminology. I have always considered that it is necessary to write in the language which men commonly speak, and I have endeavoured to do this, although in some cases it has been necessary to make some additions to and corrections of that language for the sake of exactness and lucidity.

In due time I shall separately consider the subject of language and the methods of its adaptation for the transmission of exact thought. For the present I have reference only to the language of *Tertium Organum*.

The first word demanding a more careful use is "consciousness."

In conversational language and in every-day psychology, even in psychology purporting to be scientific, the word *consciousness* is often used as a term for the designation of a complex of all psychic functions in general, or for their separate manifestations. At present I have not access to the necessary books — I abandoned them all in Petrograd, four years

Author's Preface

ago — but to the best of my recollection Prof. William James defined thought as "a moment of consciousness."

From my standpoint, which I shall elucidate in works now being prepared for the press, it is necessary to regard consciousness as distinct from the commonly understood psychic functions: thought, feeling and sensation. Over and above all this, consciousness has several exactly definable forms or phases, in each one of which thoughts, feelings and sensations can function, giving in each different results. Thus consciousness (be it this or something other) is a background upon which thoughts, feelings and sensations reveal themselves. This background can be more or less bright. But as thoughts, feelings and sensations have their own separate life, and can be regarded independently of this background, so can it be regarded and studied independently of them. For the present I shall not insist too strongly upon the idea of this *ground* as something separate in its substance from psychic functions. The practical result is the same if we say that thoughts, feelings and sensations may have *a different character,* and that thoughts, feelings and sensations of this or that character create this or that state of consciousness. It is important only to establish the fact that thoughts, feelings and sensations, i.e., psychic functions, are not *consciousness,* and that this or that state of consciousness is something pertaining to them, but separate from them, and in some cases capable of being separately observed.

In the early editions of *Tertium Organum* I have used the word consciousness in its generally accepted meaning, i.e., as a complex of psychic functions, or in the sense of their indication and contents. But as in my future works it will be necessary for me to use the word consciousness in its real and true meaning, I have tried in this revised text of *Tertium Organum* to substitute for the word consciousness (wherever it is used in the sense of a complex of psychic functions) such other words as psyche, or psychic life, which perfectly express my meaning in such cases.

Furthermore, in my work of revision, I have found numerous instances of illustrations, examples, etc., having no direct connection with the main theme. I have found also that some of these introduced themes vitiate the correctness of the main line of thought, creating associations which lead too far away. Other themes also, accidentally touched upon, demand a considerably more extended treatment than can be given them within the limits of this book, but being inadequately developed they leave a wrong impression.

In such cases I consider it necessary to eliminate this extraneous matter in order to elucidate the principal thought more clearly and di-

Author's Preface

rectly, particularly as some of the questions touched upon demanding more or different exposition are discussed at length in my forthcoming books.

In conclusion, let me express to Mr. Nicholas Bessaraboff and to Mr. Claude Bragdon my deep appreciation of their labours on the translation of my book into English. This translation, made without my knowledge and participation, at a time when I was cut off by war and revolution from the civilized world, transmits my thought so exactly that after a very attentive review of the book I could find only one word to correct. Such a result could be achieved only because Mr. Bessaraboff and Mr. Bragdon were not translating *words* merely, but were grasping directly *the thoughts* back of them. Also, it is especially pleasant for me to remember that a number of years ago Mr. Bragdon's *Man the Square* reached me in Petrograd, and that I, not knowing Mr. Bragdon's other works at all, selected this little book from a whole series received from abroad, as one which carried the message of a common thought, a common understanding.

P. OUSPENSKY

Constantinople,
June 1921

TERTIUM ORGANUM

INTRODUCTION

IN NAMING his book *Tertium Organum* Ouspensky reveals at a stroke that astounding audacity which characterizes his thought throughout — an audacity which we are accustomed to associate with the Russian mind in all its phases. Such a title says, in effect: "Here is a book which will reorganize all knowledge. The *Organon* of Aristotle formulated the laws under which the subject thinks; the *Novum Organum* of Bacon, the laws under which the object may be known; but *The Third Canon of Thought* existed before these two, and ignorance of its laws does not justify their violation. *Tertium Organum* shall guide and govern human thought henceforth."

How passing strange, in this era of negative thinking, of timid philosophizing, does such a challenge sound! And yet it has the echo in it of something heard before — what but the title of another volume, Hinton's *A New Era of Thought?*

Ouspensky's *Tertium Organum* and Hinton's *A New Era of Thought* present substantially the same philosophy (though Hinton's book only sketchily), arrived at by the same route — mathematics.

Here is food for thought. In the words of Philip Henry Wynne, "Mathematics possesses the most potent and perfect symbolism the intellect knows; and this symbolism has offered for generations certain concepts (of which hyper-dimensionality is only one) whose naming and envisagement by the human intellect is perhaps its loftiest achievement. Mathematics presents the highest certitudes known to the intellect, and is becoming more and more the final arbiter and interpreter in physics, chemistry and astronomy. Like Aaron's rod it threatens to swallow all other knowledges as fast as they assume organized form. Mathematics has already taken possession of great provinces of logic and psychology — will it embrace ethics, religion and philosophy?"

In *Tertium Organum* mathematics enters and pervades the field of philosophy; but so adroitly, so silently as it were, that one hardly knows that it is there. It dwells more in Ouspensky's method than in his matter, because for the most part the mathematical ideas necessary for an understanding of his thesis are such as any intelligent high school student can comprehend. The author puts to himself and to the reader certain questions, propounds certain problems, which have baffled the human mind for thousands of years — the problems of space, time, motion, caus-

Tertium Organum

ality, of free will and determination — and he deals with them according to the mathematical method: that is all. He has sensed the truth that the problem of mathematics is the problem of *the world order*, and as such must deal with every aspect of human life.

Mathematics is a terrible word to those whose taste and training have led them into other fields, so lest the non-mathematical reader should be turned back at the very threshold, deciding too hastily that the book is not for him, let me dwell rather on its richly humanistic aspect.

To such as ask no "key to the enigmas of the world," but only some light to live by, some mitigation of the daily grind, some glimpse of some more enlightened polity than that which rules the world today, this book should have an appeal. The author has thrown overboard all the jargon of all the schools; he uses the language of common sense, and of every day; his illustrations and figures of speech are homely, taken from the life of every day. He simply says to the reader, "Come let us reason together," and leads him away from the haunted jungle of philosophical systems and metaphysical theories, out into the light of day, there to contemplate and to endeavor to understand those primal mysteries which puzzle the mind of a child or of a savage no less than that of the sophisticated and super-subtle ponderer on the enigmas of the world. Not that Ouspensky is a trafficker in the obvious — far from it: those who know most, think most, feel most, will get most out of his book — but a great sanity pervades his pages, and he never leads away into labyrinths where guide and follower alike lose their way and fail to come to any end.

Leaving the average reader out of account for the moment, there are certain others whom the book should particularly interest — if only in the way of repulsion.

First of all come the mathematicians and the theoretical physicists, for they already, without knowing it, have invaded that "dark backward and abysm of time" which the Ouspenskian philosophy lights up — and are by way of losing themselves there.

That is to say, in certain of their calculations, they are employing four mutually interchangeable coördinates, three of space and one of time. In other words, they use *time* as though it were a dimension of space. Ouspensky tells them the reason they are able to do this. Time *is* the fourth dimension of space imperfectly sensed — apprehended by consciousness successively, and thereby creating the temporal illusion.

2

Introduction

Moreover, mathematicians are perforce concerning themselves with magnitudes to which the ordinary logic no longer applies. Ouspensky presents a new logic, or rather, he presents anew an ancient logic — the logic of intuition — removing at a stroke all of the nightmare aspects, the preposterous paradoxes of the new mathematics, which by reason of its extraordinary development has shattered the old logic, as a growing oak shatters the containing jar.

It is from the philosophic camp, no doubt, that the book will receive its sharpest criticism, on account of the author's lèse-majesté toward so many of the crowned kings of philosophic thought, and his devastating assault on positivism — that inevitable by-product of our materialistic way of looking at the world. His attempt to prove the Kantian problem — the subjectivity of space and time — doubtless will be acutely challenged, and with some chance of success, because the two chapters devoted to this are perhaps the least convincing of the book. But no one heretofore has even attempted to demonstrate absolutely or successfully to controvert the staggering proposition advanced by Kant regarding space and time as forms of consciousness.

Whatever the verdict of the philosophical pundits of the day and hour, whether favorable or otherwise, Ouspensky is sure of a place in the hierarchy of philosophers, for he has essayed to solve the most profound problems of human existence by the aid of the binocular vision of the mathematician and the mystic. Starting from the irreducible minimum of knowledge, he has carried philosophy into regions not hitherto explored.

To persons of an artistic or devotional bent the book will be as water in the desert. These, always at a disadvantage among the purely practical-minded, by whom they are overwhelmingly outnumbered, will find in Ouspensky a champion whose weapon is mathematical certitude, the very thing by which the practical-minded swear. These he puts to rout, holds up to ridicule, and applauds every effort to escape into the "world of the wondrous."

But most of all Ouspensky will be loved by all true lovers, for his chapter on the subject of love. We have had Schopenhauer on love, and Freud on love, but what dusty answers do they give to the soul of a lover! Edward Carpenter comes much nearer the mark, but Ouspensky penetrates to its very center. It is because our loves are so dampened by our egotisms, our cynicisms and our cowardices that we rot and smoulder instead of bursting into purifying flame. Just as Goethe's *Werther*, with its sex-sentimentality, is said to have provoked an epidemic of suicides, so may *Tertium Organum* — which restores love to that high heaven from whence descend every beauty and benison — inaugurate a renascence of love and joy.

From one point of view this is a terrible book: there is a revolution in it — a revolution of the very poles of thought. Some it will rob of their dearest illusions, it will cut the very ground from beneath their feet, it will consign them to the Abyss. It is a great destroyer of complacency. Yes, this is a dangerous book — but then, life is like that.

It is beyond the province of this Introduction either to outline the Ouspenskian philosophy at any length, or to discuss it critically; but some slight indication of its drift may be of assistance to the reader.

The book might have appropriately been called A *Study of Consciousness*, for Ouspensky comes early to the conclusion that all other methods of approach to an understanding of the "enigmas of the world" are vain. Chapters I to VII, inclusive, deal with the problem of the world-order by the objective method. The author erects an elaborate scaffolding for his future edifice, and after it has served its purpose, throws it down. Aware of the deficiencies of the objective method and having made the reader conscious of them too, he suddenly alters his system of attack. From chapter VIII onward, he undertakes the study of the world-order from the standpoint of subjectivity — of consciousness.

By a method both ingenious and new he correlates the different grades of consciousness observable in nature — those of vegetable-animal, animal and man — with the space sense, showing that as consciousness changes and develops, the sense of space changes and develops too. That is to say, the dimensionality of the world depends on the development of consciousness. Man, having reached the third stage in that development, has a sense of three-dimensional space — and for no other reason.

Ouspensky concludes that nothing except consciousness unfolds, develops, and as there appears to be no limit to this development, he conceives of space as the multi-dimensional mirror of consciousness and of time and motion as illusion — what appears to be time and motion being in reality only the movement of consciousness upon a higher space.

The problem of superior states of consciousness in which "there shall be time no longer" is thus directly opened up, and in discussing their nature and method of attainment, he quotes freely from the rich literature of mysticism. Instead of attempting to rationalize these higher states of consciousness, as some authors do, he applies to them the *logic*

4

of intuition — "Tertium Organum" — paradoxical from the standpoint of ordinary reason, but true in relation to the *noumenal* world.

Joseph Conrad and Ford Madox Hueffer once wrote a novel called *The Inheritors* and by this they meant the people of the fourth dimension. Though there is small resemblance between Ouspensky's "superman" and theirs, it is his idea also that those of this world who succeed in developing higher-dimensional, or "cosmic" consciousness will indeed inherit — will control and regulate human affairs by reason of their superior wisdom and power. In this, and in this alone, dwells the "salvation" of the world. His superman is the "just man made perfect" of the Evangelist. The struggle for mastery between the blind and unconscious forces of materialism on the one hand, and the spiritually illumined on the other, is already upon us, and all conflicts between nations, peoples and classes must now be interpreted in terms of this greater warfare between "two races" of men, in which the superior minority will either conquer or disappear.

These people of the fourth dimension are in the world but not of it: their range is far wider than this slum of space. In them dormant faculties are alert. Like birds of the air, their fitting symbol, they are at home in realms which others cannot enter, even though already "there." Nor are these heavenly eagles confined to the narrow prison of the breast. Their bodies are as tools which they may take up or lay aside at will. This phenomenal world, which seems so real, is to them as insubstantial as the image of a landscape in a lake. Such is the Ouspenskian superman.

The entire book is founded upon a new generalization — new, that is, in philosophy, but already familiar to mathematicians and theoretical physicists. This generalization involves startling and revolutionary ideas in regard to space, time and motion far removed from those of Euclidian geometry and classical physics.

Ouspensky handles these new ideas in an absolutely original way, making them the basis of an entire philosophy of life. To the timid and purblind this philosophy will be nothing short of terrifying, but to the clear-eyed and steadfast watcher, shipwrecked on this shoal of time, these vistas, overflowing with beauty, strangeness, doubt, terror and divinity, will be more welcome than anything in life.

Fear not the new generalization.

Ouspensky's clearness of thought is mirrored in a corresponding clarity of expression. He sometimes repeats the difficult and important passages in an altered form of words, he uses short sentences and short paragraphs, and italicizes *significant phrases* and *significant words*. He defines where definition is needed, and suggests collateral trains of thought with a skill which makes the reader who is intuitive a creator on his own account. Schopenhauer has said that it is always a sign of genius to treat difficult matters simply, as it is a sign of dullness to make simple matters appear recondite. Ouspensky exhibits this order of genius, and that other, mentioned by Schopenhauer, which consists in choosing always the apt illustration, the illuminating simile.

The translators have tried to be rigidly true to the Russian original, and they have been at great pains to verify every English quotation so far as has been possible. It is therefore a source of great gratification to them that their efforts should have received the unqualified endorsement of the author himself.

Rochester, N. Y.   CLAUDE BRAGDON
  January 31, 1922

CHAPTER I

THE VOICE OF THE SILENCE
H. P. B.

THE MOST difficult thing is to know what we do know, and what we do not know.

Therefore, desiring to know anything, we shall before all else determine WHAT we accept as *given*, and WHAT as demanding definition and proof; that is, determine WHAT we know already, and WHAT we wish to know.

In relation to the knowledge of the world and of ourselves, the conditions would be ideal could we venture to accept *nothing* as given, and count *all* as demanding definition and proof. In other words, it would be best to assume that we know *nothing*, and make this our point of departure.

But unfortunately such conditions are impossible to create. Knowledge must start from some foundation, something must be recognized as known; otherwise we shall be obliged always to define one unknown by means of another.

Looking at the matter from another point of view, we shall hesitate to accept as the known things — as the *given* ones — those in the main completely unknown, only presupposed, and therefore *the things sought for*. Should we do this, we are likely to fall into such a dilemma as that in which positive philosophy now finds itself — and by positive philosophy I mean a general trend of thought based on the data of those sciences which are now accepted as experimental and positive. This philosophy is founded on the existence of *matter* (materialism) or *energy*: that is, of a

7

force, or *motion*, (energeticism); though in reality matter and motion were always the unknown x and y, and were defined by means of one another.

It must be perfectly clear to everyone that it is impossible to accept *the thing sought* as *the given*; and impossible to define one unknown by means of another. The result is nothing but the identity of the unknown: x = y, y = x.

This *identity of the unknown* is the ultimate conclusion to which positive philosophy comes.

Matter is that in which proceed the changes called motion: and motions are those changes which proceed in matter.

But what do we know?

We know that with the very first awakening of knowledge, man is confronted with two obvious facts:

The existence of the world in which he lives; and the existence of psychic life in himself.

Neither of these can he prove or disprove, but they are *facts*: they constitute *reality* for him.

It is possible to meditate upon the mutual correlation of these two facts. It is possible to try to reduce them to one; that is, to regard the psychic or inner world as a part, reflection, or function of the world, or the world as a part, reflection, or function of that inner world. But such a procedure constitutes a departure from facts, and all such considerations of the world and of the self, to the ordinary non-philosophical mind, will not have the character of obviousness. On the contrary the sole *obvious fact* remains the antithesis of *I* and *Not-I* — our inner psychic life and the outer world.

Further on we shall return to this fundamental thesis. But thus far we have no basis on which to found a contradiction of the obvious fact of the existence of *ourselves* — i.e., of our inner life — and of *the world* in which we live. This we shall therefore accept as *the given*.

This however is the only thing that we have the right to accept as given: all the rest demands proof and definition in terms of these two given data.

Space, with its extension; *time*, with the idea of *before, now, after*; quantity, mass, substantiality; number, equality and inequality; identity and difference; cause and effect; the ether, atoms, electrons, energy, life,

Subjective and Objective

death — all things that form the foundation of our so-called knowledge: *these are the unknown things.*

The existence in us of psychic life, i.e., of sensations, perceptions, conceptions, reasoning, feeling, desires, etc., and the existence of the world outside of us — from these two fundamental data immediately proceed our common and clearly understood division of everything that we know into *subjective* and *objective.*

Everything that we accept as a property of the world, we call objective; and everything that we accept as a property of our psyche, we call subjective.

The subjective world we recognize *directly:* it is in ourselves — we are one with it.

The objective world we picture to ourselves as existing somewhere outside of us — we and it are different things.

It seems to us that if we should close our eyes, then the objective world would continue to exist, such as we just saw it; and if our inner life were to disappear, so would the subjective world disappear — yet the objective world would exist as before, as it existed at the time when we were not; when our subjective world was not.

Our relation to the objective world is most exactly defined by the fact that we perceive it as existing in *time* and *space;* otherwise, out of these conditions, we can neither conceive nor imagine it. In general, we say that the objective world consists of things and phenomena, i.e., things and changes in states of things. The PHENOMENA exist for us in time; the THINGS, in space.

But such a division of the subjective and the objective world does not satisfy us.

By means of reasoning we can establish the fact that in reality we know only our own sensations, perceptions and conceptions, and we cognize the objective world by projecting outside of ourselves the causes of our sensations, presupposing them to contain these causes.

Then we find that our knowledge of the subjective world, and of the objective world also, can be *true* and *false,* correct and incorrect.

The criterion for the definition of correctness or incorrectness of our knowledge of the subjective world is the *form* of the relations of one sensation to others, and the *force* and character of the *sensation itself.* In other words, the correctness of one sensation is verified by the comparison of it with another of which we are more sure, or *by the intensity and "taste" of a given sensation.*

9

Tertium Organum

The criterion for the definition of correctness or incorrectness of our knowledge of the objective world *is the very same*. It seems to us that we define the things and phenomena of the objective world by means of comparing them among themselves; and we think we find the laws of their existence *outside of us*, and independent of our perception of them. But it is an illusion. We know nothing about things *separately from us*; and we have no other means of verifying the correctness of our knowledge of the objective world than BY SENSATIONS.

Since the remotest antiquity the question of our relation to the true causes of our sensations has constituted the main subject of philosophical research. Men have always felt that they should have some solution for this question, some answer for it. And these answers have vacillated between two poles, from the full negation of the causes themselves, and the assertion that the causes of sensations are contained within ourselves and not in anything outside of us — up to the recognition that we know these causes, that they are embodied in the phenomena of the outer world, that these phenomena constitute the cause of sensations; and that the cause of all observed phenomena lies in the movement of "atoms," and the oscillations of the "ether." It is believed that if we cannot observe these motions ond oscillations it is only because we have not sufficiently powerful instruments, and that when such instruments are at our disposal we shall be able to see the movements of atoms as well as we see, through powerful telescopes, stars the very existence of which were never guessed.

In modern philosophy Kant's system occupies a middle position in relation to this problem of the causes of sensations, not sharing either of these extreme views. Kant proved that the causes of our sensations are in the outside world, but that we cannot know these causes through any sensuous approach — that is, by such means as we know phenomena — and that we *cannot know* these causes, and *shall never know them*.

Kant established the fact that everything that is known through the senses is known in terms of time and space, and that out of time and space we cannot know anything by way of the senses; that time and space are necessary conditions of sensuous receptivity (i.e., receptivity by means of the five organs of sense). Moreover, what is most important, he established the fact that extension in space and existence in time are not properties *appertaining to things,* but just the properties of our sensuous receptivity; that in reality, apart from our sensuous knowledge of them, things exist independently of time and space; but we can never perceive them out of time and space, and perceiving things and phenomena thus sensuously, by virtue of it we *impose* upon them the conditions of time and space, as belonging to *our* form of perception.

Thus space and time, defining everything that we cognize by sensuous means, are in themselves just forms of our receptivity, categories of our intellect, the prism through which we regard the world — or in other words, space and time do not represent properties of the world, but just properties of our *knowledge* of the world gained through our sensuous organism. From this it follows that the world, apart from our knowledge of it, has neither extension in space nor existence in time; these are properties which we add to it.

Cognitions of space and time arise *in our intellect* during its touch with the external world by means of the organs of sense, and do not exist in the external world apart from our contact with it.

Space and time are *categories of intellect,* i.e., properties which are *ascribed* by us to the external world. They are signal posts, signs put up by ourselves because we cannot picture the external world without their help. They are *graphics* by which we represent the world to ourselves. Projecting outside of ourselves the causes of our sensations, we are designing those causes in space, and we picture continuous reality to ourselves as a series of moments of time following one another. This is necessary for us because a thing having no definite extension in space, not occupying a certain part of space and not lasting a certain length of time, does not exist for us at all. That is, a thing not in space, divorced from the idea of space, and not included in the category of space, will not differ from some other thing in any particular; it will occupy the very same place, will coincide with it. Also, all *phenomena* not in time, divorced from the idea of time, not taken in this or that fashion from the standpoint of *before, now, after,* would co-exist for us simultaneously, and all mixed up with one another, and our weak mind would not be able to distinguish *one moment* in the infinite variety.

Therefore our consciousness segregates, out of a chaos of impressions, separate groups, and we construct in space and time the perceptions of things according to these groups of impressions.

It is necessary for us to divide things *somehow,* and we divide them into the categories of space and time.

But we should remember that these divisions exist only in us, in our knowledge of things and not in the things themselves; that we do not know the true relations of things among themselves, and the real things we do not know, but only phantoms, visions of things — we do not know the relation existing among the things in reality. At the same time we quite definitely know that *our* division of things into the categories of space and time does not at all correspond to the division of *things in themselves*, independently of our receptivity of them; and we quite definitely know that if there exist any division at all among *things in themselves*, it will in no case be a division in terms of space and time according to our usual understanding of these words, because such a division is not a property of things, but of our knowledge of things gained through the senses. Moreover, we do not know if it is even possible to distinguish *those divisions which we see*, i.e., in space and time, if things are looked at not through human eyes, not from the human standpoint. In point of fact we do not know but that our world would present an entirely different aspect for a differently built organism.

We cannot *perceive* things as *images* outside of the categories of space and time, but we constantly *think* of them outside of space and time.

When we say *that table*, we picture the table to ourselves in space and time; but when we say *an object made of wood*, not meaning any definite thing, but speaking generally, it will relate to all things made of wood throughout the world, and in all ages. An imaginative person could conceive that we are referring to some great thing made of wood, composed of all objects whenever and wherever *wooden* things existed, these forming its constituent *atoms*, as it were.

We do not comprehend all these matters quite clearly, but in general it is plain that we think in space and time by perceptions only; but by concepts we think independently of space and time.

Kant named his views *critical idealism*, in contradiction to *dogmatic idealism*, of which Berkeley was a representative.

According to dogmatic idealism, all the world, all things — i.e., the true causes of our sensations — do not exist except in our consciousness: they *exist* only so far as we know them. The entire world perceived by us is just a reflection of ourselves.

Kantian idealism recognizes a world of causes outside of us, but asserts that we cannot know the world by means of sensuous perception, and everything that we perceive, generally speaking, is of our own crea-tion — *the product of a cognizing being.*

So, according to Kant, everything that we find in things is put in them by ourselves. Independently of ourselves we do not know what the world is like. And our cognition of things has nothing in common with the things as they are outside of us — that is, in themselves. Furthermore, and most important, our ignorance of things in themselves does not depend upon our *insufficient knowledge,* but is due to the fact that by means of sensuous perception we cannot know the world correctly *at all.* That is to say, we cannot truly declare that although now we perhaps know little, presently we shall know more, and at length shall come to a correct un-derstanding of the world. It is not true because our experimental knowl-edge is not a *confused* perception of a *real world.* It is *a very acute* per-ception of *an entirely unreal world* appearing round about us at the moment of our contact with the world of true causes, to which we can-not find the way because we are lost in an unreal "material" world. For this reason the extension of the objective sciences does not bring us any nearer to the knowledge of *things in themselves,* or of *true causes.*

In A *Critique of Pure Reason* Kant affirms that:

Nothing which is intuited in space is a thing in itself, and space is not a form which belongs as a property to things; but objects are quite unknown to us in themselves, and what we call outward objects are nothing else but mere representations of our sensibility, whose form is space, but whose real corre-lated thing in itself is not known by means of these representations, nor ever can be, but respecting which, in experience, no inquiry is ever made.

The things which we intuit are not in themselves the same as our repre-sentation of them in intuition, nor are their relations in themselves so consti-tuted as they appear to us; and if we take away the subject, or even only the subjective constitution of our senses in general, then not only the nature and relations of objects in space and time disappear, but even space and time them-selves.

What may be the nature of objects considered as things in themselves and without reference to the receptivity of our sensibility is quite unknown to us. We know nothing more than our own *mode* of perceiving them, which is pe-culiar to us and which though not of necessity pertaining to every animated being, is so to the whole human race.

Supposing that we should carry our empirical intuition even to the very highest degree of clearness we should not thereby advance one step nearer to the constitution of objects as things in themselves.

To say then that our sensibility is nothing but the confused representation of things containing exclusively that which belongs to them as things in themselves, and this under an accumulation of characteristic marks and partial representations which we cannot distinguish in consciousness, is a falsification of the conception of sensibility and phenomenization, which renders our whole doctrine thereof empty and useless. The difference between a confused and a clear representation is merely logical, and has nothing to do with content.

Up to the present time Kant's propositions have remained in the very form that he left them. Despite the multiplicity of new philosophical systems which appeared during the nineteenth century, and despite the number of philosophers who have particularly studied, commented upon, and interpreted Kant's writings, Kant's principal propositions have remained quite undeveloped, primarily because most people do not know how to read Kant at all, and they therefore dwell upon the unimportant and nonessential, ignoring the substance.

Yet really Kant simply put the question, threw to the world the problem, demanding the solution but not pointing the way toward it.

This fact is usually omitted when speaking of Kant. He propounded the riddle, but did not give the solution of it.

And to the present day we repeat Kant's propositions, we consider them incontrovertible, but in the main we represent them to our understanding very badly, and they are not correlated with other departments of our knowledge. *All our positive science — physics (with chemistry) and biology — is built upon hypotheses* CONTRADICTORY *to Kant's propositions.*

Moreover, we do not realize how we ourselves impose upon the world the properties of space, i.e., extension; nor do we realize how the world — earth, sea, trees, men — *cannot possess* such extension.

We do not understand how we can see and *measure* that extension *if it does not exist* — nor what the world represents in itself, if it does not possess extension.

But does the world really exist? Or, as a logical conclusion from Kant's ideas, shall we recognize the validity of Berkeley's idea, and deny the existence of the world itself except in imagination?

Positive philosophy stands in a very ambiguous relation to Kant's views. It accepts them and it does not accept them: it accepts, and considers them correct in their relation to the direct experience of the organs of

The Positivists

sense — what we see, hear, touch. That is, positive philosophy recognizes the subjectivity of our receptivity, and recognizes everything that we perceive in objects as imposed upon them by ourselves — but this in relation to the direct experience of the senses only.

When it concerns itself with "scientific experience" however, in which precise instruments and calculations are used, positive philosophy evidently considers Kant's view in relation to that invalid, assuming that "scientific experience" makes known to us the very substance of things, the true causes of our sensations — or if it does not do so now, it brings us closer to the truth of things, and can inform us later.

Contrary to Kant, the positivists are sure that "more clear knowledge of phenomena makes them acquainted with things in themselves." They think that in looking upon physical phenomena as the motions of the ether, or as electrical or magnetic phenomena, and calculating their motions, they begin to know the very substance of things, i.e., the causes of phenomena; in other words, they *believe* exactly in the possibility of what Kant denied — the comprehension of the true substance of things by means of the investigation of phenomena. Moreover many physicists do not consider it necessary even to know Kant; and they could not themselves exactly define in what relation they stand toward him. Of course it is possible not to know Kant, but it is impossible to controvert him. Every description of physical phenomena, by its every word, is related to the problems set forth by Kant — remains in this or that relation to them.

In general, the position of "science" in regard to this question of *"subjectively imposed"* or *"objectively cognized"* is more than tottering, and in order to form its conclusions "science" is forced to accept many purely hypothetical suppositions as things known — as indubitable *data*, not demanding proof.

Moreover, physicists forget one very significant fact: in his book, *Analysis of Sensations*, Mach says:

In the investigation of purely physical processes we generally employ concepts of so abstract a character that as a rule we think only cursorily, or not at all, of the sensations (elements) that lie at their base. . . . The foundation of all purely physical operations is based upon an almost unending series of sensations, particularly if we take into consideration the adjustment of the apparatus which must precede the actual experiment. Now it can easily happen to the *physicist* who does not study the *psychology* of his operations, that he does not (to reverse a well-known saying) see the trees for the wood, that he overlooks the sensory element at the foundation of his work. . . . Psychological analysis has taught us that this is not surprising, since the physicist is *always* operating with sensations.*

Mach here calls attention to a very important thing. Physicists do not consider it necessary to know psychology and to deal with it in their conclusions.

But when they are more or less acquainted with psychology, with that part of it which treats of the forms of receptivity, and take it into consideration, then they hold the most fantastic duality of opinion, as in the case of the man of orthodox belief who tries to reconcile the dogmas of faith with the arguments of reason, and who is obliged to believe simultaneously in the creation of the world in seven days, seven thousand years ago, and in geological periods hundreds of thousands of years long, and in the evolutionary theory. He is thus forced to resort to sophisms, and demonstrate that by *seven days* is meant *seven periods*. But why seven, exactly, he is unable to explain. For physicists the rôle of the "creation of the world" is played by the atomic theory and the ether, with its wave-like vibrations, and further by the electrons, and the energetic, or electromagnetic theory of the world.

Or sometimes it is even worse, for the physicist in the depth of his soul feels the falsity of all old and new scientific theories but fears to hang in the air, as it were; to take refuge in mere negation. He has no system in place of that whose falsity he already feels; he is afraid to make a plunge into mere emptiness. Lacking sufficient courage to declare *that he believes in nothing at all*, he accoutres himself in all contradictory theories, as in an official uniform, only because with this uniform are bound up certain rights and privileges, outer as well as inner, consisting of a certain confidence in himself and in his surroundings, to forego which he has no strength and determination. The unbelieving positivist — this is the tragic figure of our times, analogous to the atheist or unbelieving priest of the times of Voltaire.

Out of this abhorrence of a vacuum come all dualistic theories which recognize "spirit" and "matter" existing simultaneously and independently of one another.

In general, to a disinterested observer, the state of our contemporary science should be of great psychological interest. In all branches of scientific knowledge we are absorbing an enormous number of facts destructive

* Open Court Publishing Co.'s edition of Mach's work. 1914, pages 41, 42, and 43.

of the harmony of existing systems. And these systems can maintain themselves only by reason of the heroic attempts of scientific men who are trying to close their eyes to a long series of new facts which threatens to submerge everything in an irresistible stream. If in reality we were to collect these system-destroying facts they would be so numerous in every department of knowledge as to exceed those upon which existing systems are founded. The systematization of *that which we do not know* may yield us more for the true understanding of the world and the self than the systematization of that which in the opinion of "exact science" we do know.

CHAPTER II

As already stated, Kant propounded the problem, but gave no solution of it, nor did he point the way to a solution. And not one of the known commentators, interpreters, followers or adversaries of Kant has found a solution, or the way to it.

I find the first flashes of a right understanding of the Kantian problem, and the first suggestions in regard to a possible way toward its solution, in the attempts at a new treatment of the problem of space and time, involving the concept of the "fourth dimension" and higher dimensions in general. An interesting synopsis of many things developed in this direction is that of C. H. Hinton, author of the books, *A New Era of Thought*, and *The Fourth Dimension*.

Hinton notes, among other things, that in commenting upon Kantian ideas, only their negative side is usually insisted upon, namely, the fact that we can cognize things in a sensuous way, in terms of space and time only, is regarded *as an obstacle*, hindering us from seeing what things in themselves really are, preventing the possibility of cognizing them as they are, imposing upon them that which is not inherent in them, shutting them off from us.

But [says Hinton] if we take Kant's statement simply as it is — not seeing in the spatial conception a *hindrance* to right receptivity — that we *apprehend things by means of space* — then it is equally allowable to consider our space sense not as a negative condition, *hindering* our perception of the world, but as a positive means *by which* the mind grasps its experiences, i.e., by which we cognize the world.

There is, in so many books in which the subject is treated, a certain air of despondency — as if this space apprehension were a kind of veil which shuts us off from nature. But there is no need to adopt this feeling. The first postulate of this book is a full recognition of the fact that it is by means of space that we apprehend what is.

Hinton on Dimensionality

Space is the instrument of the mind.

Very often a statement which seems to be most deep and abstruse and hard to grasp, is simply the form into which deep thinkers have thrown a very simple and practical observation. And for the present let us look on Kant's great doctrine of space from a practical point of view, and it comes to this — it is important to develop the space sense, for it is the means by which we think about real things.

Now according to Kant [Hinton goes on to say] the space sense, or the intuition of space, is the most fundamental power of the mind. But I do not find anywhere a systematic and thorough-going education of the space sense. It is left to be organized by accident. Yet the special development of the space sense makes us acquainted with a whole series of new conceptions.

Fichte, Schelling, Hegel, have developed certain tendencies and have written remarkable books, but the true successors of Kant are Gauss and Lobachevsky.

For if our intuition of space is the means whereby we apprehend, then it follows that there may be different kinds of intuitions of space. Who can tell what the absolute space intuition is? This intuition of space must be colored, so to speak, by the conditions (of psychical activity) of the being which uses it.

By a remarkable analysis the great geometers above mentioned have shown that space is not limited as ordinary experience would seem to informs us, but that we are quite capable of conceiving different kinds of space.

(A *New Era of Thought.*)

Hinton invented a complicated system for the education and development of the space sense by means of exercises with groups of cubes of different colors. The books above mentioned are devoted to the exposition of this system. In my opinion Hinton's exercises are interesting from a theoretical standpoint, but they are practically valuable only for such as have the same turn of mind as Hinton's own.

Exercises of the mind according to his system must first of all lead to the development of the ability to *imagine objects,* not as the eye sees them, i.e., in perspective, but as they are geometrically — to learn to imagine the cube, for example, simultaneously from all sides. Moreover such a development of the imagination as overcomes the illusions of perspective results in the expansion of the limits of consciousness, thus creating *new conceptions* and augmenting *the faculty for perceiving analogies.*

Tertium Organum

Kant established the fact that the development of knowledge under the existing conditions of receptivity will not bring us any closer to things in themselves. But there are theories asserting that it is possible, if desired, to change the very conditions of receptivity, and thus to approach the true substance of things. In the books above referred to, Hinton tries to unite the scientific foundations of such theories.

Our space as we ordinarily think of it is conceived as limited — not in extent, but in a certain way which can only be realized when we think of our ways of measuring space objects. It is found that there are only three independent directions in which a body can be measured — it must have height, length and breadth, but it has no more than these dimensions, if any other measurement be taken in it, this new measurement will be found to be compounded of the old measurements.

It is impossible to find a point in the body which could not be arrived at by travelling in combinations of the three directions already taken.

But why should space be limited to three independent directions?

Geometers have found that there is no reason why bodies which we can measure are thus limited. As a matter of fact all the bodies which we can measure are thus limited. So we come to this conclusion, that the space which we use for conceiving ordinary objects in the world is limited to three dimensions. *But it might be possible for there to be beings living in a world such that they would conceive a space of four dimensions.**

It is possible to say a great deal about space of higher dimensions than our own, and to work out analytically many problems which suggest themselves. But can we conceive four-dimensional space in the same way in which we can conceive our own space? Can we think of a body in four dimensions as a unit having properties in the same way as we think of a body having a definite shape in the space with which we are familiar?

There is really no more difficulty in conceiving four-dimensional shapes, when we go about it in the right way, than in conceiving the idea of solid shapes, nor is there any mystery at all about it.

When the faculty to apprehend in four dimensions is acquired — or rather when it is brought into consciousness — for it exists in every one in imperfect form — a new horizon opens. The mind acquires a development of power, and in this use of ampler space as a mode of thought, a path is opened by using that very truth which, when first stated by Kant, seemed to close the mind within such fast limits. Our perception is subject to the conditions of being in space. But space is not limited as we at first think.

The next step after having formed this power of conception in ampler space, is to investigate nature and see what phenomena are to be explained by four-dimensional relations.

* Italics by P. D. Ouspensky. *Transl.*

Four-Dimensional Space

The thought of past ages has used the conception of a three-dimensional space, and by that means has classified many phenomena and has obtained rules for dealing with matters of great practical utility. The path which opens immediately before us in the future is that of applying the conception of four-dimensional space to the phenomena of nature, and of investigating what can be found out by this new means of apprehension. . . .

For development of knowledge it is necessary to separate the *self-elements*, i.e., the personal elements which we put in everything cognized by us, from *that which is cognized*, in order that our attention may not be distracted (upon ourselves) from the properties which we, in substance, perceive.

Only by getting rid of the *self-elements* in our receptivity do we put ourselves in a position in which we can propound sensible questions. Only by getting rid of the notion of a circular motion of the sun around the earth (i.e., around *us — self-element*) do we prepare our way to study the sun as it really is.

But the worst about a self-element is that its presence is never dreamed of till it is got rid of.

In order to understand what the *self-element* in our receptivity means, imagine ourselves to be translated suddenly to another part of the universe, and to find there intelligent beings and to hold conversation with them. If we told them that we came from this world, and were to describe the sun to them, saying that it was a bright, hot body which moved around us, they would reply: "*You have told us something about the sun, but you have also told us something about yourselves.*". . .

Therefore, desiring to tell something about the sun, we shall first of all get rid of the *self-element* which is introduced into our knowledge of the sun by the movement of the earth, upon which we are, round it. . . .

One of our serious pieces of work will be to get rid of the self-elements *in the knowledge of the arrangement of objects*.

The relations of our universe or our space with regard to the wider universe of four-dimensional space are altogether undetermined. The real relationship will require a great deal of study to apprehend, and when apprehended *will seem as natural to us as the position of the earth among the other planets seems to us now*. . . .

I would divide studies of arrangement into two classes: those which create the faculty of arrangement, and those which use it and exercise it. Mathematics exercises it, but I do not think it creates it; and unfortunately, in mathematics as it is now often taught, the pupil is launched into a vast system of symbols: the whole use and meaning of symbols (namely, as means to acquire a clear grasp of facts) is lost to him. . . .

Of the possible units which will serve for the study of arrangement, I take the cube; and I have found that whenever I took any other unit I got wrong, puzzled, and lost my way. With the cube one does not get along very fast,

21

but everything is perfectly obvious and simple, and builds up into a whole of which every part is evident. . . .

Our work then will be this: a study, by means of cubes, of the facts of arrangement; and the process of learning will be an active one of actually putting up the cubes. Thus we will bring our minds into contact with nature.

(*A New Era of Thought.*)

Taking all these things into consideration, we should try to define clearly our understanding of those sides of our receptivity dealt with by Kant.

What is space?

Taken as object, that is, perceived by our consciousness, space is for us *the form of the universe* or the form of the matter in the universe.

Space possesses an infinite extension in all directions. But it can be measured in only three directions independent of one another — in length, breadth, and height; these directions we call the dimensions of space, and we say that our space has three dimensions: it is three-dimensional.

By *independent direction* we mean in this case a line at right angles to another line.

Our geometry (or the science of measurement of *the earth*, or matter in space) knows *only three* such lines, which are mutually at right angles to one another and not parallel among themselves.

But why three only, and not ten or fifteen?

This we do not know.

And here is another very significant fact: either because of some mysterious property of the universe, or because of some mental limitation, we cannot even imagine to ourselves more than three independent directions.

But we speak of the universe as infinite, and because the first condition of infinity is infinity *in all directions* and in all possible relations, so we must presuppose in space an infinite number of dimensions: that is, we must presuppose an infinite number of lines perpendicular and not parallel to each other; and yet out of these lines we know, *for some reason*, only three.

It is usually in some such guise that the question of higher dimensionality appears to normal human consciousness.

Since we cannot construct more than three mutually independent perpendiculars, and if the three-dimensionality of our space is conditional upon this, we are forced to admit the indubitable fact of the limitedness of our space in relation to geometrical possibilities: though of course if the properties of space are created by some limitation of consciousness, then the limitedness lies in ourselves.

No matter what this limitedness depends on, it is a fact that it exists.

A given point can be the vertex of only *eight* independent tetrahedrons. Through a given point it is possible to draw only three perpendicular and not parallel straight lines.

Upon this as a basis, we define the *dimensionality* of space by the number of lines it is possible to draw in it which are mutually at right angles one with another.

The line upon which there cannot be a perpendicular, that is, *another line*, constitutes linear, or one-dimensional space.

Upon the surface two perpendiculars are possible. This is superficial, or two-dimensional space.

In "space" three perpendiculars are possible. This is solid, or three-dimensional space.

The idea of the *fourth dimension* arose from the assumption that in addition to the three dimensions known to our geometry there exists still a fourth, for some reason unknown and inaccessible to us, i.e., that in addition to the three known to us, a mysterious fourth perpendicular is possible.

This assumption is practically founded on the consideration that there are things and phenomena in the world undoubtedly *really existing*, but quite incommensurable in terms of length, breadth and thickness, and lying as it were outside of three-dimensional space.

By *really existing* we understand that which produces definite action, which possesses certain functions, which appears to be the cause of something else.

That which *does not exist* cannot produce any action, has no function, cannot be a cause.

But there are different modes of existence. There is *physical* existence, recognized by certain sorts of actions and functions, and there is *metaphysical* existence, recognized by its actions and its functions.

A *house exists*, and the *idea of good and evil* exists. But they do not exist in like manner. One and the same method of proof of existence does not suffice for the proof of the existence of a house and for the proof of the existence of an idea. A house is a *physical fact*, an idea is a *metaphysical fact*. Physical and metaphysical facts *exist*, but they exist differently

In order to prove the idea of a division into good and evil, i.e., a metaphysical fact, I have only to prove *its possibility*. This is already sufficiently established. But if I should prove that a house, i.e., a physical fact, *may* exist, it does not at all mean that it exists really. If I prove that a man *may* own the house it is no proof that he owns it.

Our relations to an idea and to a house are quite different. It is possible by a certain effort to destroy a house — to burn, to wreck it. The house will cease to exist. But suppose you attempt to destroy, by an effort, an idea. The more you try to contest, argue, refute, ridicule, the more the idea is likely to spread, grow, strengthen. And contrariwise, silence, oblivion, *non-action*, "non-resistance" will exterminate, or in any case will weaken the idea. Silence, oblivion, will not wreck a house, will not hurt a stone. It is clear that the existence of a house and that of an idea are quite different existences.

Of such *different existences* we know very many. A book exists, and also *the contents of a book*. Notes exist, and so does *the music that the notes combine to make*. A coin exists, and so does *the purchasing value of a coin*. A *word* exists, and the *energy* which it contains.

We discern on the one hand, a whole series of *physical facts*, and on the other hand, a series of *metaphysical facts*.

As facts of the first kind exist, so also do facts of the second kind exist, but differently.

From the usual positivist point of view it will seem naïve in the highest degree to speak of *the purchasing value of a coin* separately from the coin; of *the energy of a word* separately from the word; of the *contents of a book* separately from the book, and so on. We all know that these are only "what people say," that in reality *purchasing value, energy of a word*, and *contents of a book* do not exist, that by these conceptions we only denote a series of phenomena in some way linked with coin, word, book, but in substance quite separate from them.

But is it so?

We decided to accept nothing as given, consequently we shall not *negate* anything as given.

We see in things, in addition to what is external, something internal. We know that this internal element in things constitutes a continuous part of things, usually their *principal substance*. And quite naturally we ask ourselves, *where* is this internal element, and *what* does it represent in and by itself. We see that it is not embraced within our space. We begin to conceive of the idea of a "higher space" possessing more dimensions than ours. Our space then appears to be somehow a part of higher space, i.e., we begin to believe that we know, feel, and measure only part of space, that part which is measurable in terms of length, width and height.

As was said before, we usually regard space as a form of the universe, or as a form of the matter of the universe. To make this clear it is possible to say that a "cube" is the form of the matter in a cube; a "sphere" is the form of the matter in a sphere; "space" — an infinite sphere — is the form of the entire matter of the universe.

H. P. Blavatsky, in *The Secret Doctrine,* has this to say about space:

> The superficial absurdity of assuming that Space itself is measurable in any direction is of little consequence. The familiar phrase (the fourth dimension of space) can only be an abbreviation of the fuller form — the *"Fourth dimension of Matter in Space."*. . . The progress of evolution may be destined to introduce us to new characteristics of matter. . . ." *

But the formula defining "space" as "the form of matter in the universe" suffers from this deficiency, that there is introduced in it the concept of "matter," i.e., *the unknown.*

I have already spoken of that "dead-end siding," $x = y$, $y = x$, to which all attempts at the physical definition of matter inevitably lead.

Psychological definitions lead to the same thing.

In a well-known book, *The Psychology of the Soul,* A. I. Herzen says:

> We call matter everything which directly or indirectly offers resistance to motion, directly or indirectly produced by us, manifesting a remarkable analogy with our *passive* states.
>
> And we call force (motion) that which directly or indirectly communicates movement to us or to other bodies, thus manifesting the greatest similitude to our *active* states.

Consequently, "matter" and "motion" are something like projections of our active and passive states. It is clear that it is possible to define the passive state only in terms of the active, and the active in terms of the passive — again two unknowns, defining one another.

E. Douglas Fawcett, in an article entitled *Idealism and the Problem of Nature* in *the Quest* (April, 1910), discusses matter from this point of view.

* "The Secret Doctrine," The Theosophical Publishing Society. Third Edition, p. 271, vol. I.

Matter (like force) does not give us any trouble. We know all about it, for the very good reason that *we invented it*. By "matter" we think of sensuous objects. It is mental change of concrete but too complicated facts, which are difficult to deal with.

Strictly speaking, matter exists only as a concept. Truth to tell, the character of matter, even when treated only as a conception, is so unobvious that the majority of persons are unable to tell us exactly what they mean by it.

An important fact is here brought to light: *matter* and *force* are just *logical concepts*, i.e., only *words* accepted for the designation of a lengthy series of complicated facts. It is difficult for us, educated almost exclusively along physical lines, to understand this clearly, but in substance it may be stated as follows: Who has seen *matter* and *force*, and when? We see things, see phenomena. *Matter*, independently of the substance from which a given thing is made, or of which it consists, we have never seen and never shall see; but *the given substance* is not quite *matter*, this is *wood*, or *iron* or *stone*. Similarly, we shall never see *force* separately from *motion*. What does this mean? It means that *"matter"* and *"force"* are just such abstract conceptions as "value" or "labor," as "the purchasing value of a coin" or the "contents" of a book; it means that matter is "such stuff as dreams are made of." And because we can never touch this "stuff" and can see it only in dreams, so we can never touch physical matter, nor see, nor hear, nor photograph it, *separately from the object*. We cognize things and phenomena which are bad or good, but we never cognize *"matter"* and *"force"* separately from *things* and *phenomena*.

Matter is as much an abstract conception as are truth, good and evil.

It is as impossible to put matter or any part of matter into a chemical retort or crucible as it is impossible to sell *"Egyptian darkness"* in vials. However as it is said that "Egyptian darkness" is sold as a black powder in Athos, or elsewhere, therefore perhaps somewhere, by some one, even matter has been seen.*

In order to discuss questions of this order a certain preparation is necessary, or a high degree of intuition; but unfortunately it is customary to consider fundamental questions of cosmogony very lightly.

A man easily admits his incompetency in music, dancing, or higher

---

* This is irony which the English speaking may easily fail to understand. Some unscrupulous monks of the monastery of Athos, famous throughout Greece and Russia, made a practice, it is said, of selling "Egyptian darkness" in little vials, thus making capital out of the credulity and piety of the illiterate Russian pilgrims who were wont to visit this monastery in great numbers. *Transl.*

How Study Space?

mathematics, but he always maintains the privilege of *having an opinion* and being a judge of questions relating to "first principles."

It is difficult to discuss with such men.

For how will you answer a man who looks at you in perplexity, knocks on the table with his fingers and says, *"This is matter. I know it; feel!* How can *it* be an abstract conception?" To answer this is as difficult as to answer the man who says: "I *see* that the sun rises and sets!"

Returning to the consideration of space, we shall under no circumstances introduce unknown quantities in the definition of it. We shall define it only in terms of those two *data* which we decided to accept at the very beginning.

The world and consciousness are the facts which we decided to recognize as existing.

By the world we mean the combination of all the causes of our sensations in general.

By the material world we mean the combination of causes of *a definite series of sensations:* those of sight, hearing, touch, smell, taste, sensations of weight, and so on.

Space is either a property of the world or a property of our knowledge of the world.

Three-dimensional space is either a property of the *material world* or a property of *our* receptivity of the material world.

Our inquiry is confined to the problem: how shall we approach the study of space?

CHAPTER III

IF we consider the very great difference between the point and the line, between the line and the surface — surface and solid, i.e., the difference between the laws to which line and plane, plane and surface, etc., are subjected, and the difference of phenomena possible in point, in line, in surface, we shall indeed come to understand how much of the new and inconceivable the fourth dimension holds for us.

As in the point it is impossible to imagine the line and the laws of the line; as in the line it is impossible to imagine the surface and the laws of the surface; as in the surface it is impossible to imagine the solid and the laws of the solid; so in our space it is impossible to imagine the body having more than three dimensions, and impossible to understand the laws of the existence of such a body.

But studying the mutual relations between the point, the line, the surface, the solid, we begin to learn something about the fourth dimension, i.e., of four-dimensional space. We begin to learn *what it can be* in comparison with our three-dimensional space, *and what it cannot be.*

The last we learn first of all. And it is especially important, because it saves us from many deeply inculcated illusions, which are very detrimental to right knowledge.

We learn *what cannot be* in four-dimensional space, and this permits us to set forth *what can be there.*

In his book, *The Fourth Dimension*, Hinton makes an interesting statement concerning the method by which we may approach the problem of higher dimensions. He says:

Relations within Space

Our space itself bears within it relations through which we can establish relations to other (higher) spaces.

For within space are given the conception of point and line, line and plane, which really involve the relation of space to a higher space.

Let us consider these relations within our space, and see what conclusions we can derive from their investigation.

We know that our geometry regards the line as a tracing of the movement of a point; the surface as a tracing of the movement of a line; and the solid as a tracing of the movement of a surface. On these premises we put to ourselves this question: Is it not possible to regard the "four-dimensional body" as a tracing of the movement of a three-dimensional body?

But what is this movement, and in what direction?

The *point*, moving in space, and leaving the tracing of its movement, a line, moves in a direction not contained in it, because in a point there is no direction whatsoever.

The *line*, moving in space, and leaving the tracing of its movement, the surface, moves in a direction not contained in it because, moving in a direction contained in it, a line will continue to be a line.

The *surface*, moving in space, and leaving a tracing of its movement, the solid, moves also in a direction not contained in it. If it should move otherwise, it would remain always the surface. In order to leave a tracing of itself as a "solid," or three-dimensional figure, it must *set off from itself*, move in a direction which in itself it has not.

In analogy with all this, the solid, in order to leave as the tracing of its movement the four-dimensional figure (hypersolid), shall move in a direction not confined in it; or in other words it shall come out of itself, *set off from itself*, move in a direction which is not present in it. Later on it will be shown in what manner we shall understand this.

But for the present we can say that the direction of the movement in the fourth dimension lies *out of all those directions which are possible in a three-dimensional figure*.

We consider the line as an infinite number of points; the surface as an infinite number of lines; the solid as an infinite number of surfaces.

In analogy with this it is possible to consider that it is necessary to regard a four-dimensional body as an infinite number of three-dimensional bodies, and four-dimensional space as an infinite number of three-dimensional spaces.

Moreover, we know that the line is limited by points, that the surface is limited by lines, that the solid is limited by surfaces.

It is possible that a four-dimensional body is limited by *three-dimensional bodies*.

Or it is possible to say that the line is the distance between two points; the surface the distance between two lines; the solid — between two surfaces.

Or again, that the line separates two points or several points from one another (for a straight line is the shortest distance between two points); that the surface separates two or several lines from each other; that the solid separates several surfaces one from another; as *the cube* separates six flat surfaces one from another — its faces.

The line binds several separate points into a certain whole (the straight, the curved, the broken line); the surface binds several lines into a certain whole (the quadrilateral, the triangle); the solid binds several surfaces into a certain whole (the cube, the pyramid).

It is possible that four-dimensional space is the distance between a group of solids, separating these solids, yet at the same time binding them into some to us inconceivable whole, even though they seem to be separate from one another.

Moreover, we regard the point as *a section* of a line; the line as a section of a surface; the surface as a section of a solid.

By analogy, it is possible to regard the solid (the cube, sphere, pyramid) as *a section* of a four-dimensional body, and our entire three-dimensional space as a section of a four-dimensional space.

If every three-dimensional body is the section of a four-dimensional one, then every point of a three-dimensional body is the section of a four-dimensional line. It is possible to regard an "atom" of a physical body, *not as something material*, but as an intersection of a four-dimensional line by the plane of our consciousness.

The view of a three-dimensional body as the section of a four-dimensional one leads to the thought that many (for us) separate bodies may be *the sections of parts* of one four-dimensional body.

A simple example will clarify this thought. If we imagine a horizontal plane, intersecting the top of a tree, and parallel to the surface of the earth, then *upon this plane* the sections of branches will seem separate, and not bound to one another. Yet in our space, from our standpoint, these are sections of branches of *one* tree, comprising together one top, nourished from one root, casting one shadow.

Or here is another interesting example expressing the same idea, given

Plane Projections of Solids

by Mr. Leadbeater, the theosophical writer, in one of his books. If we touch the surface of a table with our finger tips, then upon the surface will be just five circles, and from this plane presentment it is impossible to construe any idea of the hand, and of the man to whom this hand belongs. Upon the table's surface will be five *separate* circles. How from them is it possible to imagine a man, with all the richness of his physical and spiritual life? It is impossible. Our relation to the four-dimensional world will be analogous to the relation of that consciousness which sees five circles upon the table to *a man*. We see just "finger tips" — to us the fourth dimension is inconceivable.

We know that it is possible to *represent* a three-dimensional body upon a plane, that it is possible to draw a cube, a polyhedron or a sphere. This will not be a real cube or a real sphere, but the projection of a cube or of a sphere on a plane. We may conceive of the three-dimensional bodies of our space somewhat in the nature of *images* in our space of to us incomprehensible four-dimensional bodies.

CHAPTER IV

We have established by a comparison of the relation of lower dimensional figures to higher dimensional ones that it is possible to regard a
four-dimensional body as the tracing of the motion of a three-dimensional body upon the dimension not contained in it; i.e., that the direction of the motion upon the fourth dimension lies outside of all the
directions which are possible in three-dimensional space.

But in what direction is it?

In order to answer this question it will be necessary to discover
whether we do not know some motion not confined in three-dimensional space.

We know that every motion in space is accompanied by that which
we call *motion in time*. Moreover, we know that everything existing,
even if not moving in space, moves eternally in time.

And equally in all cases, whether speaking of motion or absence of
motion, we have in mind an idea of what was before, what now becomes,
and what will follow after. In other words, we have in mind the idea of
time. The idea of motion of any kind, also the idea of absence of motion,
is indissolubly bound up with the idea of time. Any motion or absence
of motion proceeds in time and cannot proceed out of time. Consequently, before speaking of what motion is, we must answer the question, what is time?

What is Time?

Time is the most formidable and difficult problem which confronts humanity.

Kant regards time as he does space: as a subjective form of our receptivity; i.e., he says that we *create time* ourselves, as a function of our receptive apparatus, for convenience in perceiving the outside world. Reality is continuous and constant, but in order to make possible the perception of it, we must dissever it into separate moments; imagine it as an infinite series of separate moments out of which there exists for us only one. In other words, we perceive reality as if through a narrow slit, and what we *are seeing* through this slit we call the present; what we did see and now do not see — the past; and what we do not quite see but are expecting — the future.

Regarding each phenomenon as an *effect* of another, or others, and this in its turn as a cause of a third; that is, regarding all phenomena in functional interdependence one upon another, by this very act we are contemplating them in time, because we picture to ourselves quite clearly and precisely first a cause, then an effect; first an action, then its function; and cannot contemplate them otherwise. Thus we may say that the idea of time is bound up with the idea of causation and functional interdependence. Without time, causation cannot exist, just as without time, motion or the absence of motion cannot exist.

But our perception concerning our "being in time" is entangled and misty up to improbability.

First of all let us analyze our relation toward the past, present and future. *Usually we think that the past already does not exist.* It has passed, disappeared, altered, transformed itself into something else. The future also does not exist — it does not exist *as yet*. It has not arrived, has not formed. By the present we mean the moment of transition of the future into the past, i.e., *the moment of transition of a phenomenon from one non-existence into another non-existence.* For that moment only does the phenomenon exist for us in reality; before, it existed in potentiality, afterward it will exist in remembrance. But this short moment is after all only a fiction: it has no measurement. We have a full right to say that the present does not exist. We can never catch it. That which we did catch *is always the past!*

If we are to stop at that we must admit that the world does not exist, or exists only in some phantasmagoria of illusions, flashing and disappearing.

Usually we take no account of this, and do not reflect that our customary view of time leads to utter absurdity.

33

Let us imagine a stupid traveller going from one city to another and half way between these two cities. A stupid traveller thinks that the city from which he has departed last week does not exist *now*: only the memory of it is left; the walls are ruined, the towers fallen, the inhabitants have either died or gone away. Also, that city at which he is destined to arrive in several days does not exist now either, but is being hurriedly built for his arrival, and on the day of that arrival will be ready, populated, and set in order, and on the day after his departure will be destroyed just as was the first one.

We are thinking of things in time exactly in this way — everything passes away, nothing returns! The spring has passed, it does not exist *still*. The autumn has not come, it does not exist *as yet*.

But what does exist?

The present.

But *the present* is not a seizable moment, it is continuously transitory into the past.

So, strictly speaking, neither the past, nor the present, nor the future exists for us. *Nothing exists!* And yet we are living, feeling, thinking — and something surrounds us. Consequently, in our usual attitude toward time there exists some mistake. This error we shall endeavor to detect.

We accepted at the very beginning that *something* exists. We called that something the world. How then can the world exist if it is not existing in the past, in the present and in the future?

That conception of the world which we deduced from our usual view of time makes the world appear like a continuously gushing out igneous fountain of fireworks, each spark of which flashes for a moment and disappears, *never* to appear any more. Flashes are going on continuously, following one after another, there are an infinite number of sparks, and everything together produces the impression of a flame, *though it does not exist in reality*.

The autumn has not yet come. *It will be, but it does not exist now.* And we give no thought to how that can *appear* which *is not*.

We are moving upon a plane, and recognize as really existing only the small circle lighted by our consciousness. Everything out of this circle, which we do not see, we negate; we do not like to admit that it exists. We are moving upon the plane in one direction. This direction we consider as eternal and infinite. But the direction *at right angles* to it, those lines which we are intersecting, we do not like to recognize as eternal and infinite. We imagine them as going into non-existence at once, as soon as we have passed them, and that the lines before us have not as yet risen out of non-existence. If, presupposing that we are moving upon a sphere, upon its equator or one of its parallels, then it will appear that we recognize as really existing *only one* meridian: those which are behind us have disappeared and those ahead of us have not appeared as yet.

We are going forward like a blind man, who feels paving stones and lanterns and walls of houses with his stick and *believes* in the real existence of only that which he touches *now*, which he feels *now*. That which has passed has disappeared and will never return! That which has not as yet been does not exist. The blind man remembers the route which he has traversed; he expects that ahead the way will continue, but he sees neither forward nor backward *because he does not see anything;* because his instrument of knowledge — the stick — has a definite, and not very great length, and beyond the reach of his stick non-existence begins.

Wundt, in one of his books, called attention to the fact that our vaunted five organs of sense are in reality just *feelers* by which we feel the world around us. We live groping about. *We never see anything.* We are always just feeling everything. With the help of the microscope and the telescope, the telegraph and the telephone, we are extending our feelers a little, so to speak, but we are not beginning *to see.* To say that we *are seeing* would be possible only in case we could know the past and the future. But we do not see, and because of this we can never assure ourselves of that which we cannot *feel.*

This is the reason why we count as really existing only that circle which our feelers grasp at a given moment. Beyond that — darkness and non-existence.

But have we any right *to think* in this way?

Let us imagine a consciousness that is not bound by the conditions of sensuous receptivity. Such a consciousness can rise above the plane upon which we are moving; it can see far beyond the limits of the circle enlightened by our usual consciousness; it can see that not only does the line upon which we are moving exist, but also all lines perpendicular to it which we are intersecting, which we have ever intersected, and which we shall intersect. After rising above the plane this consciousness can *see* the plane, can convince itself that it is really a plane, and not a single line. Then it can see the past and the future, lying together and existing simultaneously.

That consciousness which is not bound by the conditions of sensuous receptivity can outrun the stupid traveller, ascend the mountain to see in the distance the town to which he is going, and be convinced that this town is not being built anew for his arrival, but exists quite independently of the stupid traveller. And that consciousness can look off and see on the horizon the towers of that city where that traveller had been, and be convinced that those towers have not fallen, that the city continues to stay and live just as it stayed and lived before the traveller's advent.

It can rise above the plane of time and see the spring behind and the autumn ahead, see simultaneously the budding flowers and ripening fruits. It can make *the blind man* recover his sight and see the road along which he passed and that which still lies before him.

The past and the future cannot *not exist*, because if they do not exist then neither does the present exist. Unquestionably they exist *somewhere* together, but we do not see them.

The present, compared with the past and the future, is the most unreal of all unrealities.

We are forced to admit that the past, the present and the future do not differ in anything, one from another; there exists just *one present* — *the Eternal Now* of Hindu philosophy. But we do not perceive this, because in every given moment we experience just a little bit of that present, and this alone we count as existent, denying a real existence to everything else.

If we admit this, then our view of everything with which we are surrounded will change very considerably.

Usually we regard time as *an abstraction*, made by us *during the observation of really existing motion*. That is, we think that observing motion, or changes of relations between things and comparing the relations which existed before, which exist now, and which may exist in the future, that we are deducing the idea of time. We shall see later on how far this view is correct.

Thus the idea of time is composed of the conception of the past, of the present, and of the future.

Our conceptions of the past and present, though not very clear, are yet very much alike. As to *the future* there exists a great variety of views.

It is necessary for us to analyze *the theories of the future* as they exist in the mind of contemporary man.

There are in existence two theories — that of the foreordained future, and that of the free future.

Foreordination is established in this way: we say that every future event is the result of those which happened before, and is created such as it will be and not otherwise as a consequence of a definite direction of forces which are contained in preceding events. This means, in other words, that future events are wholly contained in preceding ones, and if we could know the force and direction of all events which have happened up to the present moment, i.e., if we knew all the past, by this we could know *all* the future. And sometimes, knowing the *present moment* thoroughly, in all its details, we may really *foretell* the future. If the prophecy is not fulfilled, we say that we *did not know all that had been*, and we discover in the past some *cause* which had escaped our observation.

The idea of the free future is founded upon the possibility of voluntary action and *accidental* new combinations of causes. The future is regarded as quite indefinite, or defined only in part, because in every given moment new forces, new events and new phenomena are born which lie in a potential state, not causeless, but so incommensurable with causes — as the firing of a city from one spark — that it is impossible to detect or measure them.

This theory affirms that one and the same action can have different results; one and the same cause, different effects; and it introduces the hypothesis of quite arbitrary volitional actions on the part of a man, bringing about profound changes in the subsequent events of his own life and the lives of others.

Supporters of the foreordination theory contend on the contrary that volitional, involuntary actions depend also upon causes, making them necessary and unavoidable at a given moment; that there is nothing accidental, and that there cannot be; that we call accidental only those things the causes of which we do not see by reason of our limitations; and that different effects of causes seemingly the same occur because the causes are different in reality and only seem similar for the reason that we do not understand them well enough nor see them sufficiently clearly.

The dispute between the theory of the foreordained future and that of the free future is an infinite dispute. Neither of these theories can say anything decisive. This is so because both theories are too literal, too inflexible, too material, and one repudiates the other: both say, "either this or the other." In the one case there results a complete cold predestination: *that which will be, will be, nothing can be changed* — that which will befall tomorrow was predestined tens of thousands of years ago. There results in the other case a life upon some sort of needle-point called *the present*, which is surrounded on all sides by an abyss of nonexistence, *a journey in a country which does not as yet exist*, a life in a world which is born and dies every moment, in which *nothing ever returns*. And both these opposite views are equally untrue, because the truth, in the given case, as in so many others, is contained in a union of two opposite understandings in one.

In every given moment all the future of the world is predestined and is existing, but is predestined conditionally, i.e., it will be such or another future according to the direction of events at a given moment, unless there enters *a new fact*, and a new fact can enter only from the side of *consciousness* and the will resulting from it. It is necessary to understand this, and to master it.

Besides this we are hindered from a right conception of the relation of the present toward the future by our misunderstanding of the relation of the present to the past. The difference of opinion exists only concerning *the future*; concerning the past all agree that it has past, that it does not exist now — *and that it was such as it has been*. In this last lies the key to the understanding of the incorrectness of our views of the future. As a matter of fact, in reality our relation both to the past and to the future is far more complicated than it seems to us. In the past, behind us, lies not only that which really happened, *but that which could have been*. In the same way, in the future lies not only that which will be, *but everything that may be*.

The past and the future are equally undetermined, equally exist in all their possibilities, and equally exist simultaneously with the present.

By time we mean *the distance* separating events in the order of their succession and binding them in different wholes. This distance lies in a direction not contained in *three-dimensional space*, therefore it will be *the new dimension of space*.

This new dimension satisfies all possible requirements of the fourth dimension on the ground of the preceding reasoning.

It is incommensurable with *the dimensions of three-dimensional space*, as *a year* is incommensurable with *St. Petersburg*. It is perpendicular to all directions of three-dimensional space and is not parallel to any of them.

As a deduction from all the preceding we may say that *time* (as it is usually understood) includes in itself *two ideas*: that of a certain to us unknown space (the fourth dimension), and that of a motion upon this space. Our constant mistake consists in the fact that in time we never see two ideas, but see always only one. Usually we see in *time* the idea of motion, but cannot say from whence, where, whither, nor upon what space. Attempts have been made heretofore to unite the idea of the fourth dimension with the idea of time. But in those theories which have attempted to combine the idea of time with the idea of the fourth dimension appeared always the idea of some spatial element as existing in time, and along with it was admitted *motion upon that space*. Those who were constructing these theories evidently did not understand that leaving out the possibility of motion they were advancing the demand for a *new* time, because motion cannot proceed out of time. And as a result time goes ahead of us, like our shadow, receding according as we approach it. All our perceptions of motion have become confused. If we imagine the new dimension of space and *the possibility* of motion upon this new dimension, time will still elude us, and declare that it is unexplained, exactly as it was unexplained before.

It is necessary to admit that by one term, *time*, we designate really two ideas — "a certain space" and "motion upon that space." This motion does not exist in reality, and it seems to us as existing only because *we do not see* the spatiality of time. That is, the sensation of motion in time (and motion out of time does not exist) arises in us because we are looking at the world as if through a narrow slit, and are seeing the *lines of intersection* of the time-plane with our three-dimensional space only.

Therefore it is necessary to declare how profoundly incorrect is our usual theory that the idea of time is deduced by us from the observation of motion, and is really nothing more than the idea of that succession which is observed by us in motion.

It is necessary to recognize quite the reverse: that the idea of motion is deduced by us out of an incomplete sensation of time, or of the time-sense, i.e., out of a sense or sensation of the fourth dimension, but out of an *incomplete* sensation. This incomplete sensation of time (of the fourth dimension) — the sensation through the slit — gives us the sensation of motion, that is, creates an illusion of motion which does not exist in reality, but instead of which there exists in reality only the extension upon a direction inconceivable to us.

One other aspect of the question has very great significance. The fourth dimension is bound up with the ideas of "time" and "motion." But up to this point we shall not be able to understand *the fourth dimension* unless we shall understand the fifth dimension.

Attempting to look at time as at an object, Kant says that it has one dimension: i.e., he imagines time as a line extending from the infinite future into the infinite past. Of one point of this line we are conscious — always only one point. And this point has no dimension because that which in the usual sense we call the present, is the recent past, and sometimes also the near future.

This would be true in relation to our *illusory* perception of time. But in reality *eternity* is not the infinite dimension of time, but the one *perpendicular to time*; because, if eternity exists, then every moment is eternal. The line of time extends in that order of succession of phenomena which are in causal interdependence — first the cause, then the effect: before, now, after. *The line of eternity* extends perpendicularly to that line.

It is impossible to understand the idea of time without conceiving in imagination the idea of eternity; it is likewise impossble to understand space if we have no idea of time.

From the standpoint of eternity, *time* does not differ in anything from the other lines and dimensions of space — length, breadth, and height. This means that just as in space exist the things that we do not see, or speaking differently, not alone that which we see, so in time "events" exist before our consciousness has touched them, and they still exist after our consciousness has left them behind.

Consequently, *extension in time* is extension into unknown space, and therefore time is *the fourth dimension of space*.

It is necessary that we should regard time *as a spatial conception* considered with relation to our two data — the world and consciousness (psychic life).

The idea of time arises through the knowledge of the world by means of sensuous receptivity. It has been previously explained that because of the properties of our sensuous receptivity we see the world as through a narrow slit.

Out of this the following questions arise:

1. What accounts for the existence in the world of illusionary motion? That is, why do we not see, through this slit, *the same thing?* Why, behind the slit, do changes proceed creating the illusion of motion: that is, how and in what manner does the focus of our receptivity run over the world of phenomena? In addition to all this it is necessary to remember that through the same slit through which we see the world we observe ourselves and see in ourselves changes similar to the changes in the rest of things.

2. Why can we not extend that slit?

It is necessary to answer these questions.

First of all it is important to note that within the limits of our usual observation our receptivity is always conditioned in the same way and cannot escape these conditions. In other words, it is chained, as it were, to some plane above which it cannot rise. These *conditions*, or that *plane* we call, in the inner world, consciousness or level of consciousness; in the outer world we call them *matter* or the density of matter. (The word density is used in this connection not in the sense of a solid, liquid or gaseous state, but in the sense of the physical, the astral and the mental plane — accepting temporarily the terminology employed in contemporary theosophical literature.) Our usual psychic life proceeds upon some definite plane (of consciousness or matter) and never rises above it. If our receptivity could rise above this plane it would undoubtedly perceive *simultaneously*, below itself, a far greater number of events than it usually sees while on a plane. Just as a man, ascending a mountain, or going up in a balloon, begins to see *simultaneously* and *at once* many things which it is impossible to see simultaneously and at once from below — the movement of two trains toward one another between which a collision will occur; the approach of an enemy detachment to a sleeping camp; two cities divided by a ridge, etc. — so consciousness rising above the plane in which it usually functions, must see simultaneously the events divided for ordinary consciousness by *periods of time*. These will be the events which ordinary consciousness *never* sees together, as: *cause* and *effect*; the work and the payment; the crime and the punishment; the movement of trains toward one another and their collision; the approach of the enemy and the battle; the sunrise and the sunset; the morning and the evening; the day and the night; spring, autumn, summer and winter; the birth and the death of a man.

The angle of vision will enlarge during such an ascent, the *moment* will expand.

If we imagine a receptivity which is on a level higher than *our consciousness*, possessing a broader angle of view, then this receptivity will be able to grasp, as something simultaneous, i.e., *as a moment*, all that is happening for us during a certain length of time — minutes, hours, a day, a month. Within the limits of its moment such a receptivity will not be in a position to discriminate between *before, now, after*; all this will be for it *now*. Now will expand.

But in order for this to *happen* it would be necessary for us to liberate ourselves from matter, because matter is nothing more than the conditions of space and time in which we dwell. Thence arises the question: can consciousness leave the conditions of a given material existence without itself undergoing fundamental changes, or without disappearing altogether, as men of positivistic views would affirm?

This is a debatable question, and later I shall give examples and proofs, speaking on behalf of the idea that our consciousness can leave the conditions of a given materiality. For the present I wish to establish *what must proceed* during this leaving.

There would ensue *the expansion of the moment*, i.e., all that we are apprehending *in time* would become something like a single moment, in which the past, the present, and the future would be seen at once. This shows the relativity of motion, as depending for us upon the limitation of the moment, which includes only a very small part of the moments of life perceived by us.

We have a perfect right to say, not that "*time*" is deduced from "*motion*," but that motion is sensed because of the *time-sense*. We have that sense, therefore we sense motion. The time-sense is the sensation of changing moments. If we did not have this time-sense we could not feel motion. The "time-sense" is itself, in substance, *the limit* or *the surface* of our "space-sense." Where the "space-sense" ends, there the "time-sense" begins. It has been made clear that "time" is identical in its properties with "space," i.e., it has all the signs of *space extension*. However, we do not feel it as spatial extension, but we feel it as time, that is, as something specific, inexpressible — in other words, uninterruptedly bound up with "motion." This inability to sense time spatially has its origin in the fact that the time-sense is a *misty space-sense*; by means of our time-sense we feel obscurely the new characteristics of space, which extend out from the sphere of three dimensions.

But what is the time-sense and why does there arise the illusion of motion?

To answer this question at all satisfactorily is possible only by studying the forms and levels of psychic life.

"I" is a complicated quantity, and within it goes on a continuous motion. About the nature of this motion we shall speak later, but this very motion inside of us creates the illusion of motion around us, motion in the material world.

The noted mathematician Riemann understood that when higher dimensions of space are in question, *time, by some means, translates itself into space,* and he regarded the MATERIAL ATOM as *the entrance of the fourth dimension into three-dimensional space.*

In one of his books Hinton writes very interestingly about "surface tensions."

The relationship of a surface to a solid or of a solid to a higher solid is one which we often find in nature.

A surface is nothing more nor less than the relation between two things. Two bodies touch each other. The surface is the relationship of one to the other.

If our space is in the same co-relation with higher space as is the surface to our space, then it may be that our space is really the surface, that is, the place of contact, of two higher-dimensional spaces.

It is a fact worthy of notice that in the surface of a fluid different laws obtain from those which hold throughout the mass. There is a whole series of facts which are grouped together under the name of surface tensions, which are of great importance in physics, and by which the behavior of the surfaces of liquids is governed.

And it may well be that the laws of our universe are the surface tensions of a higher universe.

If the surface be regarded as a medium lying between bodies, then indeed it will have no weight, but be a powerful means of transmitting vibrations. Moreover, it would be unlike any other substance, and it would be impossible to get rid of it. However perfect a vacuum be made, there would be in this vacuum just as much of this unknown medium (i.e., of that surface) as there was before.

Matter would pass freely through this medium . . . vibrations of this medium would tear asunder portions of matter. And involuntarily the conclusion would be drawn that this medium was unlike any ordinary matter. . . . These would be very different properties to reconcile in one and the same substance.

Now is there anything in our experience which corresponds to this medium? . . .

Do we suppose the existence of any medium through which matter freely moves, which yet by its vibrations destroys the combinations of matter — some medium which is present in every vacuum however perfect, which penetrates all bodies, is weightless, and yet can never be laid hold of.

The "substance" which possesses all these qualities is called the "ether."

The properties of the ether are a perpetual object of investigation in science. . . . But taking into consideration the ideas expressed before it would be interesting to look at the world supposing that we are not in it but on the ether; where the "ether" is the surface of contact of two bodies of higher dimensions.*

Hinton here expresses an unusually interesting thought, and brings the idea of the "ether" nearer to the idea of time. The materialistic, or even the energetic understanding of contemporary physics of the ether is perfectly fruitless — a dead-end siding. For Hinton the ether is not a substance but only a "surface," the "boundary" of *something*. But of what? Again not that of a *substance*, but the boundary, the surface, the limit of *one form* of *receptivity* and the beginning of another. . . .

In one sentence the walls and fences of the materialistic dead-end siding are broken down and before our thought open wide horizons of regions unexplored.

* Hinton, "A New Era of Thought," pp. 52, 56, 57.

CHAPTER V

FOUR-DIMENSIONAL space, if we try to imagine it to ourselves, will be the infinite repetition of our space, of our infinite three-dimensional sphere, as a line is the infinite repetition of a point.

Many things that have been said before will become much clearer to us when we dwell on the fact that the fourth dimension must be sought for *in time*.

It will become clear what is meant by the fact that it is possible to regard a four-dimensional body as the tracing of the movement in space of a three-dimensional body in a direction not confined within that space. Now the direction not confined in three-dimensional space in which any three-dimensional body moves — this is the direction of time. Any three-dimensional body, *existing,* is at the same time moving in time and leaves as a tracing of its movement the temporal, or four-dimensional body. We never see or feel this body, because of the limitations of our receptive apparatus, but we see the *section* of it only, which section we call the three-dimensional body. Therefore we are in error in thinking that the three-dimensional body is in itself something real. It is the *projection* of the four-dimensional body — its picture — the image of it *on our plane.*

The four-dimensional body is the infinite number of three-dimensional bodies. That is, the four-dimensional body is the infinite number of *moments of existence* of the three-dimensional one — its states and positions. The three-dimensional body which we see appears as a single figure — one of a series of pictures on a cinematographic film as it were.

Four-dimensional space (time) is really the distance between the forms, states, and positions of one and the same body (and different bodies, i.e., those seeming different to us). It separates those states, forms, and positions each from the other, and it binds them also into some to us incomprehensible whole. This incomprehensible whole can be formed in time out of one physical body — and out of *different* bodies.

It is easier for us to imagine *the temporal whole* as related to *one* physical body.

If we consider the physical body of a man, we shall find in it besides its "matter" *something*, it is true, changing, but undoubtedly *one and the same* from birth until death.

This something is the *Linga-Sharîra* of Hindu philosophy, i.e., *the form on which our physical body is moulded.* (H. P. Blavatsky: *The Secret Doctrine*.) Eastern philosophy regards the physical body as something *impermanent* which is in a condition of perpetual interchange with its surroundings. The particles come and go. *After one second* the body is already not absolutely the same as it was one second before. Today it is in a considerable degree not that which it was yesterday. After seven years it is *a quite different body*. But despite all this, *something* always persists from birth to death, changing its aspect a little, but remaining the same. This is the *Linga-Sharîra*.

The *Linga-Sharîra* is the form, *the image*: it changes, but remains the same. That image of a man which we are able to represent to ourselves is not the *Linga-Sharîra*. But if we try to represent to ourselves mentally the image of a man from birth to death, with all the particularities and traits of childhood, manhood and senility, as if extended in time, then it will be the *Linga-Sharîra*.

Form pertains to all *things*. We say that everything consists of *matter and form*. Under the category of "matter," as already stated, the cause of a lengthy series of mixed sensations is predicated, but matter without form is not comprehensible to us; we cannot even *think* of matter without form. But we can think and imagine form without matter.

The *thing*, i.e., the union of form and matter, is never *constant*; it always changes in the course of time. This idea afforded Newton the possibility of building his theory of *fluents* and *fluxions*.

Newton came to the conclusion that *constant quantities* do not exist in nature. Variables do exist — *flowing, fluents* only. The velocities with which different fluents change were called by Newton *fluxions*.

From the standpoint of this theory all things known to us — men, plants, animals, planets — are fluents, and they differ by the magnitude of their fluxions. But the *thing*, changing continuously in time, sometimes very much, and quickly, as in the case of a living body for example, still remains *one and the same*. The body of a man in youth, and the body of a man in senility — these are one and he same, though we know that in the old body there is not one atom left that was in the young one. The matter changes, but *something* remains one under all changes, this something is the *Linga-Sharîra*. Newton's theory is valid for the three-dimensional world existing in time. In this world there is nothing constant. All is variable because every consecutive moment the thing is already not that which it was before. We never see the *Linga-Sharîra*, we see always its parts, and they appear to us variable. But if we observe more attentively we shall see that it is an illusion. Things of three dimensions are unreal and variable. They cannot be real because they do not exist in reality, just as the *imaginary sections* of a solid do not exist. Four-dimensional bodies alone are real.

In one of the lectures contained in the book, A *Pluralistic Universe*, Prof. James calls attention to Prof. Bergson's remark that science studies always only the *t* of the *universe*, i.e., not the universe in its entirety, but the *moment*, the "temporal section" of the universe.

The properties of four-dimensional space will become clearer to us if we compare in detail three-dimensional space with the surface, and discover the differences existing between them.

Hinton, in his book, A *New Era of Thought*, examines these differences very attentively. He represents to himself, on a plane, two equal rectangular triangles, cut out of paper, the right angles of which are placed in opposite directions. These triangles will be equal, but *for some reason* quite different. The right angle of one is directed to the right, that of the other to the left. If anyone wants to make them quite similar, it is possible to do so only with the help of three-dimensional space. That is, it is necessary to take one triangle, turn it over, and put it back on the plane. Then they will be two equal, and *exactly similar* triangles. But in order to effect this, it was necessary to take one triangle from the plane into three-dimensional space, and turn it over in that space. If the triangle is left on the plane, then it will never be possible to make it identical with the other, keeping the same relation of angles of the one to those of the other. If the triangle is merely rotated in the plane this similarity will never be established. In our world there are figures quite analogous to these two triangles.

We know certain shapes which are equal the one to the other, which are exactly similar, and yet which we cannot make fit into the same portion of space, either practically or by imagination.

If we look at our two hands we see this clearly, though the two hands represent a complex case of a symmetrical similarity. Now there is one way in which the right hand and the left hand may practically be brought into likeness. If we take the right hand glove and the left hand glove, they will not fit any more than the right hand will coincide with the left hand; but if we turn one glove inside out, then it will fit. Now suppose the same thing done with the solid hand as is done with the glove when it is turned inside out, we must suppose it, so to speak, pulled through itself. . . . If such an operation were possible, the right hand would be turned into an exact model of the left hand.*

But such an operation would be possible in the higher dimensional space only, just as the overturning of the triangle is possible only in a space relatively higher than the plane. Even granting the existence of four-dimensional space, it is possible that the turning of the hand inside out and the pulling of it through itself is a practical impossibility on account of causes independent of geometrical conditions. But this does not diminish its value as an example. Things like the turning of the hand inside out are possible theoretically in four-dimensional space because in this space different, and even distant points of our space *and time* touch, or have the possibility of contact. All points of a sheet of paper lying on a table are separated one from another, but by taking the sheet from the table it is possible to fold it in such a way as to bring together any given points. If on one corner is written *St. Petersburg*, and on another *Madras*, nothing prevents the putting together of these corners. And if on the third corner is written the year 1812, and on the fourth 1912, these corners can touch each other too. If on one corner the year is written in red ink, and the ink has not yet dried, then the figures may imprint themselves on the other corner. And if afterwards the sheet is straightened out and laid on the table, it will be perfectly incomprehensible, to a man who has not followed the operation, how the figure from one corner could transfer itself to another corner. For such a man the possibility of the contact of remote points of the sheet will be incomprehensible, and it will remain incomprehensible so long as he thinks of the sheet in two-dimensional space only. The moment he imagines the sheet in three-dimensional space this possibility will become real and obvious to him.

In considering the relation of the fourth dimension to the three

* C. H. Hinton, "A New Era of Thought," p. 44.

known to us, we must conclude that our geometry is obviously insufficient for the investigation of higher space.

As before stated, a four-dimensional body is as incommensurable with a three-dimensional one as *a year* is incommensurable with *St. Petersburg*.

It is quite clear why this is so. The four-dimensional body consists of an infinitely great number of three-dimensional bodies; accordingly, there cannot be a common measure for them. The three-dimensional body, in comparison with the four-dimensional one, is *equivalent to the point* in comparison with the line.

And just as the point is incommensurable with the line, so is the line incommensurable with the surface; as the surface is incommensurable with the solid body, so is the three-dimensional body incommensurable with the four-dimensional one.

It is clear also why the geometry of three dimensions is insufficient for the definition of *the position* of the region of the fourth dimension in relation to three-dimensional space.

Just as in the geometry of one dimension, that is, upon the line, it is impossible to define *the position* of the surface, the side of which constitutes the given line; just as in the geometry of two dimensions, i.e., upon the surface, it is impossible to define the position of the solid, the side of which constitutes the given surface, so in the geometry of three dimensions, in three-dimensional space, it is impossible to define a four-dimensional space. Briefly speaking, as planimetry is insufficient for the investigation of the problems of stereometry, so is stereometry insufficient for four-dimensional space.

As a conclusion from all of the above we may repeat that every point of our space is the section of a line in higher space, or as B. Riemann expressed it: the material atom is the entrance of the fourth dimension into three-dimensional space.

For a nearer approach to the problem of higher dimensions and of higher space it is necessary first of all to understand the constitution and properties of the higher dimensional region in comparison with the region of three dimensions. Then only will appear the possibility of a more exact investigation of this region, and a classification of the laws governing it.

What is it that it is necessary to understand?

It seems to me that first of all it is necessary to understand that we

Tertium Organum

are considering not *two* regions spatially different, and not two regions of which one (again spatially, "geometrically") constitutes a part of the other, but two methods of receptivity of one and the same *unique* world of a space which is unique.

Furthermore it is necessary to understand that all objects known to us exist not only in those categories in which they are perceived by us, but in an infinite number of others in which we do not and cannot sense them. And we must learn first *to think* things in other categories, and then so far as we are able, to imagine them therein. Only after doing this can we possibly develop the faculty to apprehend them in higher space — and to sense "higher" space itself.

Or perhaps the first necessity is the direct perception of everything in the outside world which does not fit into the frame of three dimensions, which exist independently of the categories of time and space — everything that for this reason we are accustomed to consider as nonexistent. If *variability* is an indication of the three-dimensional world, then let us search for *the constant* and thereby approach to an understanding of the four-dimensional world.

We have become accustomed to count as really existing only that which is measurable in terms of length, breadth and height; but as has been shown it is necessary to expand the limits of the *really existing*. Mensurability is too rough an indication of existence, because mensurability itself is too conditioned a conception. We may say that for any approach to the exact investigation of the higher dimensional region the certainty obtained by the immediate sensation is probably indispensable; that much that is *immeasurable* exists just as really as, and even more really than, much that is measurable.

CHAPTER VI

A SERIES of analogies and comparisons are used for the definition of that which can be, and that which cannot be, in the region of the higher dimension.

We imagine "worlds" of one, and of two dimensions, and out of the relations of lower-dimensional worlds to higher ones we deduce possible relations of our world to one of four dimensions; just as out of the relations of points to lines, of lines to surfaces, and of surfaces to solids we deduce the relations of our solids to four-dimensional ones.

Let us try to investigate everything that this method of analogy can yield.

Let us imagine *a world of one dimension*.

It will be a line. Upon this line let us imagine living beings. Upon this line, which represents the universe for them, they will be able to move forward and backward only, and these beings will be as the points, or segments of a line. Nothing will exist for them outside their line — and they will not be aware of the line upon which they are living and moving. For there will exist only two points, ahead and behind, or maybe just one point ahead. Noticing the change in states of these points, the one-dimensional being will call these changes *phenomena*. If we suppose the line upon which the one-dimensional being lives to be passing through the different objects of our world, then of all these objects the one-dimensional being will perceive one point only; if different bodies intersect his line, the one-dimensional being will sense them only as the appearance, the more or less prolonged existence, and the disappearance of a point. This appearance, existence, and disappearance of a point will

51

constitute *a phenomenon*. Phenomena, according to the character and properties of passing objects and the velocity and properties of their motions, for the one-dimensional being will be constant or variable, long or short timed, periodical or unperiodical. But the one-dimensional being will be absolutely unable to understand or explain the constancy or variability, the duration or brevity, the periodicity or unperiodicity of the phenomena of his world, and will regard these simply as properties of such phenomena. The solids intersecting his line may be different, but for the one-dimensional being all phenomena will be absolutely *identical* — just the appearance or the disappearance of a point — and phenomena will differ only in duration and in greater or less periodicity.

Such strange monotony and similarity of the diverse and heterogeneous phenomena of our world will be the characteristic peculiarity of the one-dimensional world.

Moreover, if we assume that the one-dimensional being possesses memory, it is clear that recalling all the points seen by him as phenomena, he will refer them to time. The point which *was*: this is the phenomenon already non-existent, and the point which may appear tomorrow: this is the phenomenon which does not exist *as yet*. All of our space except one line will be in the category of time, i.e., something wherefrom phenomena come and into which they disappear. And the one-dimensional being will declare that the idea of time arises for him out of the observation of motion, that is to say, out of the appearance and disappearance of points. These will be considered as temporal phenomena, beginning at that moment when they become visible, and ending — *ceasing to exist* — at that moment when they become invisible. The one-dimensional being will not be in a position to imagine that the phenomenon goes on existing somewhere, though invisibly to him; or he will imagine it as existing somewhere on his line, far ahead of him.

We can imagine this one-dimensional being more vividly. Let us take an atom hovering in space, or simply a particle of dust, carried along by the air, and let us imagine that this atom or particle of dust possesses a consciousness, i.e., separates himself from the outside world, and is conscious only of that which lies in the line of his motion, and with which he himself comes in contact. He will then be a one-dimensional being in the full sense of the word. He can fly and move in all directions, but it will always seem to him that he is moving upon a single line; outside of this line will be for him only a great *Nothingness* — the whole universe will appear to him as one line. He will feel none of the turns and angles of his line, for to feel an angle it is necessary to be conscious of that which

The One-Dimension World

lies to right or left, above or below. In all other respects such a being will be absolutely identical with the before-described imaginary being living upon the imaginary line. Everything that he comes in contact with, that is, everything that he is conscious of, will seem to him to be emerging from time, i.e., from nothing, vanishing into time, i.e., into nothing. This *nothing* will be all our world. All our world except one line will be called *time* and will be counted as *actually* non-existent.

Let us next consider the two-dimensional world, and the being living on a plane. The universe of this being will be one great plane. Let us imagine beings on this plane having the shape of points, lines, and flat geometrical figures. The objects and "solids" of that world will have the shape of flat geometrical figures too.

In what manner will a being living on such a plane universe cognize his world?

First of all we can affirm that he will not feel the plane upon which he lives. He will not do so because he will feel the objects, i.e., figures which are on this plane. He will feel the lines which limit them, and for this reason he will not feel his plane, for in that case he would not be in a position to discern the lines. The lines will differ from the plane in that they produce sensations; therefore they exist. The plane does not produce sensations; therefore it does not exist. Moving on the plane, the two-dimensional being, feeling no sensations, will declare that nothing now exists. After having encountered some figure, having sensed its lines, he will say that something appeared. But gradually, by a process of reasoning, the two-dimensional being will come to the conclusion that the figures he encounters exist *on something*, or *in something*. Thereupon he may name such a plane (he will not know, indeed, that it is a plane) the "ether." Accordingly he will declare that the "ether" fills all space, but differs in its qualities from "matter." By "matter" he will mean lines. Having come to this conclusion the two-dimensional being will regard all processes as happening in his "ether," i.e., in his space. He will not be in a position to imagine anything outside of this ether, that is, out of his plane. If anything, proceeding out of his plane, comes in contact with his consciousness, then he will either deny it, or regard it as something subjective, the creation of his own imagination; or else he will believe that it is proceeding right on the plane, *in the ether*, as are all other phenomena.

Sensing lines only, the plane being will not sense them as we do.

First of all, he will see no angle. It is extremely easy for us to verify this by experiment. If we will hold before our eyes two matches, inclined one to the other in a horizontal plane, then we shall see one line. To see the angle we shall have *to look from above*. The two-dimensional being cannot look from above and therefore cannot see the angle. But measuring the distance between the lines of different "solids" of his world, the two-dimensional being will come continually in contact with the angle, and he will regard it as a strange property of the line, which is sometimes manifest and sometimes is not. That is, he will refer the angle to time; he will regard it as a temporary, evanescent phenomenon, a change in the state of a "solid," or as *motion*. It is difficult for us to understand this. It is difficult to imagine how the angle can be regarded as motion. But it must be absolutely so, and cannot be otherwise. If we try to represent to ourselves how the plane being studies the square, then certainly we shall find that for the plane being the square will be *a moving body*. Let us imagine that the plane being is opposite one of the angles of the square. He does not see the angle — before him is a line, but a line possessing very curious properties. Approaching this line, the two-dimensional being observes that a strange thing is happening to the line. One point remains in the same position, and other points *are withdrawing back* from both sides. We repeat, that the two-dimensional being has no idea of an angle. *Apparently* the line remains the same as it was, yet something is happening to it, without a doubt. The plane being will say that the line is moving, but so rapidly as to be imperceptible to sight. If the plane being goes away from the angle and follows along a side of the square, then the side will become immobile. When he comes to the angle, he will notice *the motion* again. After going around the square several times, he will establish the fact of regular, periodical motions of the line. Quite probably in the mind of the plane being the square will assume the form of a body possessing the property of periodical motions, invisible to the eye, but producing definite physical effects (molecular motion) — or it will remain there as a perception of periodical *moments* of rest and motion in one complex line, and still more probably it will seem to be a *rotating body*.

Quite possibly the plane being will regard the angle as his own subjective perception, and will doubt whether any objective reality corresponds to this subjective perception. Nevertheless he will reflect that if there is *action*, yielding to measurement, so must there be the cause of it, consisting in the change of the state of the line, i.e., in motion.

The lines visible to the plane being he may call *matter*, and the angles

The Two-Dimension World

— *motion*. That is, he may call the broken line with an angle, *moving* matter. And truly to him such a line by reason of its properties will be quite analogous to matter in motion.

If a cube were to rest upon the plane upon which the plane being lives, then this cube will not exist for the two-dimensional being, but only the square face of the cube in contact with the plane will exist for him — as a line, with periodical motions. Correspondingly, all other solids lying outside of his plane, in contact with it, or passing through it, will not exist for the plane being. The planes of contact or cross-sections of these bodies will alone be sensed. But if these planes or sections move or change, then the two-dimensional being will think, indeed, that the *cause* of the change or motion is in the bodies themselves, i.e., right there on his plane.

As has been said, the two-dimensional being will regard the straight lines only as immobile matter; irregular lines and curves will seem to him as moving. So far as *really moving* lines are concerned, that is, lines limiting the cross-sections or planes of contact passing through or moving along the plane, these will be for the two-dimensional being something inconceivable and *incommensurable*. It will be as though there were in them the presence of something independent, depending upon itself only, *animated*. This effect will proceed from two causes: He can measure the immobile angles and curves, the properties of which the two-dimensional being calls motion, for the reason that they are immobile; moving figures, on the contrary, he cannot measure, because the changes in them will be out of his control. These changes will depend upon the properties *of the whole body* and its motion, and of that whole body the two-dimensional being will know only one side or section. Not perceiving the existence of this body, and contemplating the motion pertaining to the sides and sections *he probably will regard them as living beings*. He will affirm that there is something in them which differentiates them from other bodies: vital energy, or even soul. That something will be regarded as inconceivable, and really will be inconceivable to the two-dimensional being, because to him it is the result of an incomprehensible motion of inconceivable solids.

If we imagine an immobile circle upon the plane, then for the two-dimensional being it will appear as a moving line with some very strange and to him inconceivable motions.

The two-dimensional being will never see that motion. Perhaps he will call such motion *molecular motion*, i.e., the movement of minutest invisible particles of "matter."

Moreover, a circle rotating around an axis passing through its centre, for the two-dimensional being will differ in some inconceivable way from the immobile circle. *Both will appear to be moving, but moving differently*.

For the two-dimensional being a circle or a square, rotating around its centre, on account of its double motion will be an inexplicable and incommensurable phenomenon, like *a phenomenon of life* for a modern physicist.

Therefore, for a two-dimensional being, a straight line will be immobile matter; a broken or a curved line — matter in motion; and a moving line — *living* matter.

The centre of a circle or a square will be inaccessible to the plane being, just as the centre of a sphere or of a cube made of solid matter is inaccessible to us — and for the two-dimensional being even the idea of a centre will be incomprehensible, since he possesses no idea of a centre.

Having no idea of phenomena proceeding outside of the plane — that is, out of his "space" — the plane being will think of all phenomena as proceeding on his plane as has been stated. And all phenomena which he regards as proceeding on his plane, he will consider as being in causal interdependence *one with another*: that is, he will think that one phenomenon is the effect of another *which has happened right there*, and the cause of a third which will happen right on the same plane.

If a multi-colored cube passes through the plane, the plane being will perceive the entire cube and its motion as a change in color of lines lying in the plane. Thus, if a blue line replaces a red one, then the plane being will regard the red line as *a past event*. He will not be in a position to realize the idea that the red line is still existing somewhere. He will say that the line is single, but that it *becomes blue* as a consequence of certain causes of a physical character. If the cube moves backward so that the red line appears again after the blue one, then for the two-dimensional being this will constitute *a new phenomenon*. He will say that the line became red again.

For the being living on a plane, everything above and below (if the plane be horizontal), and on the right or left (if the plane be vertical) will be existing in time, in the past and in the future: that which in reality is located outside of the plane will be regarded as non-existent, either as that which is already past, i.e., as something which has disappeared, ceased to be, will never return; or as in the future, i.e., as not existent, not manifested, as a thing in potentiality.

Plane Phenomena

Let us imagine that a wheel with the spokes painted different colors is rotating through the plane upon which the plane being lives. To such a being all the motion of the wheel will appear as a variation of the color of the line of intersection of the wheel and the plane. The plane being will call this variation of the color of the line a phenomenon, and observing these phenomena he will notice in them a certain succession. He will know that the black line is followed by the white one, the white by the blue, the blue by the red, and so on. If simultaneously with the appearance of the white line some other phenomenon occurs — say the ringing of a bell — the two-dimensional being will say that the white line is the cause of that ringing. The change of the color of the lines, in the opinion of the two-dimensional being, will depend on causes lying right in his plane. Any pre-supposition of the possibility of the existence of causes lying *outside of the plane* he will characterize as fantastic and entirely unscientific. It will seem so to him because he will never be in a position to represent the wheel to himself, i.e., the parts of the wheel on both sides of the plane. After a rough study of the color of the lines, and knowing the order of their sequence, the plane being, perceiving one of them, say the blue one, will think that the black and the white ones have already passed, i.e., disappeared, ceased to exist, *gone into the past*; and that those lines which have not as yet appeared — the yellow, the green, and so on, and the *new* white and black ones still to come — do not yet exist, but lie in the future.

Therefore, though not conceiving the form of his universe, and regarding it as infinite in all directions, the plane being will nevertheless involuntarily think of the past as situated somewhere at one side *of all*, and of the future as somewhere at the other side of this totality. In such manner will the plane being conceive of *the idea of time*. We see that this idea arises because the two-dimensional being senses only two out of three dimensions of space; the third dimension he senses only after its effects become manifest upon the plane, and therefore he regards it as something different from the first two dimensions of space, calling it *time*.

Now let us imagine that through the plane upon which the two-dimensional being lives, *two wheels* with multi-colored spokes are rotating and are rotating in opposite directions. The spokes of one wheel come from above and go below; the spokes of the other come from below and go above.

The plane being will never notice it.

He will never notice that where for one line (which he sees) there lies the past, for another line there lies the future. This thought will never even come into his head, because he will conceive of the past and the future very confusedly, regarding them as concepts, not as actual facts. But at the same time he will be firmly convinced that the past goes in *one direction*, and the future in another. Therefore it will seem to him a wild absurdity that on one side something past and *something future* can lie together, and on another side — and also beside these two — something future and *something past*. To the plane being the idea that some phenomena come whence others go, and vice versa, will seem equally absurd. He will tenaciously think that the future is that wherefrom everything comes, and the past is that whereto everything goes *and wherefrom nothing returns*. He will be totally unable to understand that events may arise from the past just as they do from the future.

Thus we see that the plane being will regard the changes of color of the lines lying on the plane very naïvely. The appearance of *different* spokes he will regard as the change of color of *one and the same line*, and the repeated appearance of the same colored spoke he will regard every time as a *new* appearance of a given color.

But nevertheless, having noticed periodicity in the change of the color of the lines upon the surface, having remembered the order of their appearance, and having learned to define the "time" of the appearance of certain spokes in relation to some other more constant phenomenon, the plane being will be in a position to foretell the change of the line from one color to another. Thereupon he will say that he has *studied* this phenomenon, that he can apply to it "the mathematical method" — can "calculate" it.

If we ourselves enter the world of plane beings, then its inhabitants will sense the lines limiting the sections of our bodies. These sections will be for them *living beings;* they will not know from whence they appear, why they alter, or whither they disappear in such a *miraculous manner*. So also, the sections of all our inanimate but moving objects will seem independent living beings.

If the consciousness of a plane being should suspect our existence, and should come into some sort of communion with our consciousness, then to him we would appear as higher, omniscient, possibly omnipotent, but above all incomprehensible beings *of a quite inconceivable category*.

Two-Dimensional Psychology

We could see his world *just as it is,* and not as it seems to him. We could see the past and the future; could foretell, direct, and even create events.

We could know the very substance of things — could know what "matter" (the straight line) is, what "motion" (the broken line, the curve, the angle) is. We could see an *angle,* and we could see a *centre.* All this would give us an enormous advantage over the two-dimensional being.

In all the phenomena of the world of the two-dimensional being we could see considerably more than he sees — or could see quite other things than he.

And we could tell him very much that was new, amazing, and unexpected about the phenomena of his world, provided indeed that he could hear us and *understand us.*

First of all we could tell him that what he regards as phenomena — angles and curves, for instance — are *properties* of higher figures; that other "phenomena" of his world are not phenomena, but only "parts" or "sections" of phenomena; that what he calls "solids" are only sections of solids — and many things besides.

We would be able to tell him that on both sides of his plane (i.e., of his space or ether) lies infinite space (which the plane being calls time); and that in this space lie the causes of all his phenomena, and the phenomena themselves, the past as well as the future ones; moreover, we might add that "phenomena" themselves are not something happening and then ceasing to be, but combinations of properties of higher solids.

But we should experience considerable difficulty in explaining anything to the plane being; and it would be very difficult for him to understand us. First of all it would be difficult because he would not have the *concepts* corresponding to our concepts. He would lack "necessary words."

For instance, "section" — this would be for him a quite new and inconceivable word; then "angle" — again an inconceivable word; "centre" — still more inconceivable; the *third* perpendicular — something incomprehensible, lying outside of his geometry.

The fallacy of his conception of time would be the most difficult thing for the plane being to understand. He could never understand that *that which has passed* and *that which is to be* are existing simultaneously on the lines perpendicular to his plane. And he could never conceive the idea that the past is identical with the future, because phenomena come from both sides and go in both directions.

59

But the most difficult thing for the plane being would be to conceive the idea that "time" includes in itself *two ideas*: the idea of space, and the idea of motion upon this space.

We have shown that what the two-dimensional being living on the plane calls motion has for us a quite different aspect.

In his book *The Fourth Dimension,* under the heading "The First Chapter in the History of Four-space," Hinton writes:

Parmenides, and the Asiatic thinkers with whom he is in close affinity, propound a theory of existence which is in close accord with a conception of a possible relation between a higher and lower dimensional space. . . . It is one which in all ages has had a strong attraction for pure intellect, and is the natural mode of thought for those who refrain from projecting their own volition into nature under the guise of causality.

According to Parmenides of the school of Elea the all is one, unmoving and unchanging. The permanent amid the transient — that foothold for thought, that solid ground for feeling, on the discovery of which depends all our life — is no phantom; it is the image amidst deception of true being, the eternal, the unmoved, the one. Thus says Parmenides.

But how is it possible to explain the shifting scene, these mutations of things?

"Illusion," answers Parmenides. Distinguishing between truth and error, he tells of the true doctrine of the one — the false opinion of a changing world. He is no less memorable for the manner of his advocacy than for the cause he advocates.

Can the mind conceive a more delightful intellectual picture than that of Parmenides pointing to the one, the true, the unchanging, and yet on the other hand ready to discuss all manner of false opinion! . . .

In support of the true opinion he proceeded by the negative way of showing the self-contradictions in the ideas of change and motion. . . . To express his doctrine in the ponderous modern way we must make the statement that motion is phenomenal, not real.

Let us represent his doctrine.

Imagine a sheet of still water into which a slanting stick is being lowered with a motion vertically downward. Let 1, 2, 3 (Fig. 1) be three consecutive positions of the stick. A, B, C will be three connective positions of the meeting of the stick with the surface of the water. As the stick passes down, the meeting will move from A on to B and C.

Suppose now all the water to be removed except a film. At the meeting of the film and the stick there will be an interruption of the film. If we suppose the film to have a property, like that of a soap bubble, of closing up round any penetrating object, then as the stick goes vertically downward the interruption of the film will move on. If we pass a spiral through the film the intersection will give a point moving in a circle (shown by the dotted lines in Fig. 2).

For the plane being such a point, moving in a circle in its plane, would probably constitute a cosmical phenomenon, something like the motion of a planet in its orbit.

Suppose now the spiral to be still and the film to move vertically upward, the whole spiral will be represented in the film in the consecutive positions of the point of intersection.

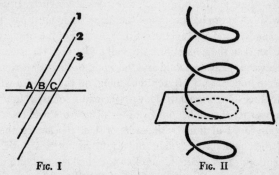

FIG. I   FIG. II

If instead of one spiral we take a complicated construction consisting of spirals, inclined and straight lines, broken and curved lines, and if the film move vertically upward we shall have *an entire universe* of moving points the movements of which will appear to the plane being as original.

The plane being will explain these movements as depending one upon another, and indeed he will never happen to think that these movements are fictitious and are dependent upon the spirals and other lines lying outside his space.*

Returning to the plane being and his perception of the world, and analyzing his relations to the three-dimensional world, we see that for the two-dimensional or plane being it will be very difficult to understand all the *complexity* of the phenomena of our world, as it appears to us. He (the plane being) is accustomed to perceive the world as being too simple.

Taking into consideration the sections of figures instead of the figures themselves, the plane being will compare them in relation to their length and their greater or lesser curvature, i.e., their *for him* more or less rapid motion.

The differences between the objects of our world, as they exist *for us* he would not understand. The functions of the objects of our world

* C. H. Hinton, "The Fourth Dimension," pp. 23, 24 and 25.

would be completely mysterious to his mind — incomprehensible, "supernatural."

Let us imagine that a coin, and a candle the diameter of which is equal to that of the coin, are on the plane upon which the two-dimensional being lives. To the plane being they will seem two equal circles, i.e., two moving, and *absolutely* identical lines; he will never discover any difference between them. The functions of the coin and of the candle in our world — these are for him absolutely a *terra incognita*. If we try to imagine what an enormous evolution the plane being must pass through in order to understand the function of the coin and of the candle and the difference between these functions, we shall understand the nature of the division between the plane world and the world of three dimensions, and the complete impossibility of even imagining, on the plane, anything at all like the three-dimensional world, with its manifoldness of function.

The properties of the phenomena of the plane world will be extremely monotonous; they will differ by the order of their appearance, their duration, and their periodicity. Solids, and the things of this world will be flat and uniform, *like shadows*, i.e., like the shadows of quite different solids, which seem to us uniform. Even if the plane being could come in contact with our consciousness, he would never be in a position to understand all the manifoldness and richness of the phenomena of our world and the variety of function of the things of that world.

Plane beings would not be in a position to master our most ordinary concepts.

It would be extremely difficult for them to understand that phenomena, *identical for them*, are in reality different; and on the other hand, that phenomena quite separate for them are in reality parts of one great phenomenon, and even of one object or one being.

This last will be one of the most difficult things for the plane being to understand. If we imagine our plane to be inhabiting a horizonal plane, intersecting the top of a tree, and parallel to the surface of the earth, then for such a being each of the various sections of the branches will appear as a *quite separate* phenomenon or object. The idea of the tree and its branches will never occur to him.

Generally speaking, the understanding of the most fundamental and simple things of our world will be infinitely long and difficult to the plane being. He would have to entirely reconstruct his concepts of space and time. This would be the first step. Unless it is taken, nothing is accomplished. Until the plane being shall imagine all our universe as existing in time, i.e., until he refers to time everything lying on both sides of his

The Plane Being is Incommunicado

plane, he will never understand anything. In order to begin to understand "the third dimension" the inhabitant of the plane must conceive of his time concepts *spatially*, that is, translate his time into space.

To achieve even the spark of a true understanding of our world he will have to reconstruct completely all his ideas — *to revaluate all values*, to revise all concepts, to dissever the uniting concepts, to unite those which are dissevered; and, what is most important, to create an infinite number of new ones.

If we put down the five fingers of one hand on the plane of the two-dimensional being they will be for him five separate *phenomena*.

Let us try to imagine what an enormous mental evolution he would have to undergo in order to understand that these five separate phenomena on his plane are the finger-tips of the hand of a large, active and intelligent being — man.

To make out, step by step, how the plane being would attain to an understanding of our world, lying in the region of the to him mysterious *third dimension* — i.e., partly in the past, partly in the future — would be interesting in the highest degree. First of all, in order to understand the world of three dimensions, he must *cease to be* two-dimensional — he must become three-dimensional himself, or in other words he must feel an interest in the life of three-dimensional space. After having felt the interest of this life, he will by so doing transcend his plane, and will never be in a position thereafter to return to it. Entering more and more within the circle of ideas and concepts which were entirely incomprehensible to him before, he will have already become, not two-dimensional, but three-dimensional. But all along the plane being *will have been* essentially three-dimensional, that is, he *will have had* the third dimension, without his being conscious of it himself. To *become* three-dimensional he must *be* three-dimensional. Then as the end of ends he can address himself to the self-liberation from the *illusion* of the two-dimensionality of himself and the world, and to the apprehension of the three-dimensional world.

CHAPTER VII

Now that we have studied those "relations which our space itself bears within it" we shall return to the questions: *But what in reality do the dimensions of space represent — and why are there three of them?*

The fact that it is impossible to define *three-dimensionality* mathematically must appear most strange.

We are little conscious of this, and it seems to us a paradox, because we speak of the *dimensions* of space, but it remains a fact that mathematics *does not sense* the dimensions of space.

The question arises, how can such a fine instrument of analysis as mathematics not feel dimensions, if they represent some real properties of space?

Speaking of mathematics, it is necessary to recognize first of all, as a fundamental premise, that *correspondent to each mathematical expression is always the relation of some realities.*

If there is no such a thing, if it be not true — then there is no mathematics. This is its principal substance, its principal contents. To express the correlations of magnitudes is the problem of mathematics. But these correlations must be between something. Instead of algebraical a, b and c it must be possible to substitute some reality. This is the ABC of all mathematics; a, b and c are credit bills; they can be good ones only if behind them there is a real *something,* and they can be counterfeited if behind them there is no reality whatever.

"Dimensions" play here a very strange rôle. If we designate them by the algebraic symbols a, b and c, they have the character of counterfeit credit bills. For this a, b and c it is impossible to substitute any real magnitudes which are capable of expressing the correlations of dimensions.

Dimensions Not Mathematical

Usually dimensions are represented by powers: the first, the second, the third; that is, if a line is called a, then a square, the sides of which are equal to this line, is called a^2, and a cube, the face of which is equal to this square, is called a^3.

This among other things gave Hinton the foundation on which he constructed his theory of *tesseracts*, four-dimensional solids — a^4. But this is pure fantasy. First of all, because the representation of "dimensions" by powers is entirely conditional. It is possible to represent all powers on a line. For example, take the segment of a line equal to five millimetres; then a segment equal to twenty-five millimetres will be the square of it, i.e., a^2 and a segment of one hundred and twenty-five millimetres will be the cube — a^3.

How shall we understand that mathematics does not feel dimensions — that it is impossible to express mathematically the difference between dimensions?

It is possible to understand and explain it by one thing only — namely, that *this difference does not exist*.

We really know that all three dimensions are in substance identical, that it is possible to regard each of the three dimensions either as following the sequence, *the first, the second, the third*, or the other way about. This alone proves that dimensions are not mathematical magnitudes. All the real properties of a thing can be expressed mathematically as quantities, i.e., numbers, showing the relation of these properties to other properties.

But in the matter of dimensions it is as if mathematics sees more than we do, or farther than we do, *through* some boundaries which arrest us but not it — and sees that no realities whatever correspond to our concepts of dimensions.

If the three dimensions *really* corresponded to three powers, then we should have the right to say that only these three powers refer to geometry, and that all the other higher powers, beginning with the fourth, lie beyond geometry.

But even this is denied us. The representation of dimensions by powers is perfectly arbitrary.

More accurately, geometry, from the standpoint of mathematics, is an artificial system for the solving of problems based *on conditional data*, deduced, probably, from the properties of our psyche.

The system of investigation of "higher space" Hinton calls *metageometry*, and with metageometry he connects the names of Lobachevsky, Gauss, and other investigators of non-Euclidian geometry.

Tertium Organum

We shall now consider in what relation the questions touched upon by us stand to the theories of these scientists.

Hinton deduces his ideas from Kant and Lobachevsky.

Others, on the contrary, place Kant's ideas in opposition to those of Lobachevsky. Thus Roberto Bonola, in *Non-Euclidian Geometry*, declares that Lobachevsky's conception of space is contrary to that of Kant. He says:

> The Kantian doctrine considered space as a subjective intuition, a necessary presupposition of every experience. Lobachevsky's doctrine was rather allied to sensualism and the current empiricism, and compelled geometry to take its place again among the experienced sciences.*

Which of these views is true, and in what relation do Lobachevsky's ideas stand to our problem? The correct answer to this question is: in no relation. Non-Euclidian geometry is not *metageometry*, and non-Euclidian geometry stands in the same relation to metageometry as Euclidian geometry itself.

The results of non-Euclidian geometry, which have submitted the fundamental axioms of Euclid to a revaluation, and which have found the most complete expression in the works of Bolyai, Gauss, and Lobachevsky, are embraced in the formula:

The axioms of a given geometry express the properties of a given space.

Thus geometry on the plane accepts all three Euclidian axioms, i.e.:

1. A straight line is the shortest distance between two points.
2. Any figure may be transferred into another position without changing its properties.
3. Parallel lines do not meet.

(This last axiom is formulated differently by Euclid.)

In geometry on a sphere, or on a concave surface the first two axioms alone are true, because the meridians which are separated at the equator meet at the poles.

In geometry on the surface of irregular curvatures only the first axiom is true — the second, regarding the transference of figures, is impossible because the figure taken in one part of an irregular surface can change when transferred into another place. Also, the sum of the angles of a triangle can be either more or less than two right angles.

* Roberto Bonola, "Non-Euclidean Geometry," The Open Court Publishing Co., Chicago, 1912, pp. 92, 93.

Metageometry

Therefore, *axioms* express the difference of properties of various kinds of surfaces.

A geometrical axiom is a law of given surface.

But what is a surface?

Lobachevsky's merit consists in that he found it necessary to revise the fundamental concepts of geometry. But he never went so far as to revalue these concepts from Kant's standpoint. At the same time he is in no sense contradictory to Kant. A *surface* in the mind of Lobachevsky, as a geometrician, was only a means for the generalization of certain properties on which this or that geometrical system was constructed, or the generalization of the properties of certain given lines. About the reality or the unreality of a surface, he probably never thought.

Thus on the one hand, Bonola, who ascribed to Lobachevsky views opposite to Kant, and their nearness to "sensualism" and "current empiricism," is quite wrong, while on the other hand, it is not impossible to conceive that Hinton entirely subjectively ascribes to Gauss and Lobachevsky their inauguration of a new era *in philosophy*.

Non-Euclidian geometry, including that of Lobachevsky, has no relation to *metageometry* whatever.

Lobachevsky does not go outside of the three-dimensional sphere.

Metageometry regards the three-dimensional sphere as *a section* of higher space. Among mathematicians, Riemann, who understood the relation of time to space, was nearest of all to this idea.

The point, of three-dimensional space, is a section of a metageometrical line. It is impossible to generalize on any surface whatever the lines considered in metageometry. Perhaps this last is the most important for the definition of the difference between geometries (Euclidian and non-Euclidian and metageometry). It is impossible to regard metageometrical lines as distances between points in our space, and it is impossible to represent them as forming any figures in our space.

The consideration of the possible properties of lines lying out of our space, the relation of these lines and their angles to the lines, angles, surfaces and solids of our geometry, forms the subject of *metageometry*.

The investigators of non-Euclidian geometry could not bring themselves to reject the consideration of surfaces. There is something almost tragic in this. See what surfaces Beltrami invented in his investigations of non-Euclidian geometry — one of his surfaces *resembles the surface of a ventilator*, another, the inner surface of a funnel. But he could not decide to reject the surface, to cast it aside once and for all, to imagine *that the line can be independent of the surface*, i.e., a series of lines which are parallel or nearly parallel cannot be generalized on any surface, or even in three-dimensional space.

And because of this, both he and many other geometers, developing non-Euclidian geometry, could not transcend the three-dimensional world.

Mechanics recognizes *the line in time,* i.e., such a line as it is impossible by any means to imagine upon the surface, or as the distance between two points of space. This line is taken into consideration in the calculations pertaining to machines. But geometry never touched this line, and dealt *always* with its sections only.

Now it is possible to return to the question: *what is space?* and to discover if the answer to this question has been found.

The answer would be the exact definition and explanation of the *three-dimensionality* of space as a property of the world.

But this is not the answer. The *three-dimensionality* of space as an objective phenomenon remains just as enigmatical and inconceivable as before. In relation to three-dimensionality it is necessary:

Either to accept it as *a thing given,* and to add this to the two data which we established in the beginning.

Or to recognize the fallacy of all objective methods of reasoning, and return to another method, outlined in the beginning of the book.

Then, on the basis of the two fundamental data, *the world* and *consciousness,* it is necessary to establish whether three-dimensional space is a *property of the world,* or *a property of our knowledge of the world.*

Beginning with Kant, who affirms that space is a *property of the receptivity of the world by our consciousness,* I intentionally deviated far from this idea and regarded space as *a property of the world.*

Along with Hinton, I postulated that our space itself bears within it the relations which permit us to establish its relations to higher space, and on the foundation of this postulate I built a whole series of analogies which somewhat clarified for us the problems of space and time and their mutual co-relations, but which, as was said, did not explain anything concerning the principal question of *the causes of the three-dimensionality of space.*

The method of analogies is, generally speaking, a rather tormenting thing. With it, you walk in a vicious circle. It helps you to elucidate certain things, and the relations of certain things, but in substance it never gives a direct answer to anything. After many and long attempts to ana-

The Direct Approach

lyze complex problems by the aid of the method of analogies, you feel the uselessness of all your efforts; you feel that you are walking alongside of a wall. Thereupon you begin to experience simply a hatred and aversion for analogies, and you find it necessary to search in the direct way which leads where you need to go.

The problem of higher dimensions has usually been analyzed by the method of analogies, and only very lately has science begun to elaborate that direct method which will be shown later on.

If we desire to go straight, without deviating, we shall keep strictly up to the fundamental propositions of Kant. But if we formulate Hinton's above-mentioned thought from the point of view of these propositions, it will be as follows: *We bear within ourselves the conditions of our space, and therefore within ourselves we shall find the conditions which will permit us to establish correlations between our space and higher space.*

In other words, we shall find the conditions of the three-dimensionality of the world in our psyche, in our receptive apparatus — *and shall find exactly there the conditions of the possibility of the higher dimensional world.*

Propounding the problem in this way, we put ourselves upon the direct path, and we shall receive an answer to our question, what is space and its three-dimensionality?

How may we approach the solution of this problem?

Plainly, by studying our consciousness and its properties.

We shall free ourselves from all analogies, and shall enter upon the correct and direct path toward the solution of the fundamental question about the objectivity or subjectivity of space, if we shall decide to study the psychical forms by which we perceive the world, and to discover if there does not exist a correspondence between them and the three-dimensionality of the world — that is, if the three-dimensional extension of space, with its properties, does not result from properties of the psyche which are known to us.

CHAPTER VIII

In order exactly to define the relation of our psyche to the external world, and to determine what, in our receptivity of the world, belongs to it, and what belongs to ourselves, let us turn to elementary psychology and examine the mechanism of our receptive apparatus.

The fundamental unit of our receptivity is *a sensation*. This sensation is an elementary change in the state of our psyche, produced, *as it seems to us,* either by some change in the state of the external world in relation to our consciousness, or by a change in the state of our psyche in relation to the external world. Such is the teaching of physics and psycho-physics. Into the consideration of the correctness or incorrectness of the construction of these sciences I shall not enter. Suffice it to define a sensation as an *elementary* change in the state of the psyche — as the element, that is, as the fundamental unit of this change. Feeling the sensation we assume that it appears, so to speak, as the reflection of some change in the external world.

The sensations felt by us leave a certain trace in our memory. The accumulating memories of sensations begin to blend in consciousness into groups, and according to their similitude tend to associate, to sum up, to be opposed; the sensations which are usually felt in close connection with one another will arise in memory in the same connection. Gradually, out of the memories of sensations, *perceptions* are compounded. Perceptions — these are so to speak the group memories of sensations. During the compounding of perceptions, sensations are polarizing in two

70

Sensation and Perception

clearly defined directions. The first direction of this grouping will be *according to the character of sensations.* (The sensations of a yellow color will combine with the sensations of a yellow color; sensations of a sour taste with those of a sour taste.) The second direction will be *according to the time of the reception of sensations.* When various sensations, constituting a single group, and compounding *one* perception, enter simultaneously, then the memory of this definite group of sensations is ascribed to a common cause. This "common cause" is projected into the outside world as the object, and it is assumed that the given perception itself reflects the real properties of this object. Such group remembrance constitutes *perception,* the perception, for example, of a tree — *that tree.* Into this group enter the green color of the leaves, their smell, their shadows, their rustle in the wind, etc. All these things taken together form as it were a focus of rays coming out of the psyche, gradually concentrated upon the outside object and coinciding with it either well or ill.

In the further complication of the psychic life, the memories of perception proceed as with the memories of sensations. Mingling together, the memories of perceptions, or the "images of perceptions," combine in various ways: they sum up, they stand opposed, they form groups, and in the end give rise to concepts.

Thus out of various sensations, experienced (in groups) at different times, a child gets the perception of a tree (that tree), and afterwards, out of the images of perceptions of different trees there emerges *the concept of a tree,* i.e., not "that tree," but trees in general.

The formation of perceptions leads to the formation of *words,* and the appearance of *speech.*

The beginning of speech may appear on the lowest level of psychic life, during the period of living by sensations, and it will become more complex during the period of living by perceptions; but unless there be concepts it will not be *speech* in the true meaning of the word.

On the lower levels of psychic life certain sensations can be expressed by certain sounds. Therefore it is possible to express common impressions of horror, anger, pleasure. These sounds may serve as signals of danger, as commands, demands, threats, etc., but it is impossible to say much by means of them.

In the further development of speech, if words or sounds express *perceptions,* as in the case of children, this means that the given sound or the given word designates only that object to which it refers. For each new *similar* object must exist another *new* sound, or a new word. If the speaker designates *different* objects by one and the same sound or word, it means that in his opinion the objects are the same, or *that knowingly* he is calling different objects by the same name. In either case it will be difficult to understand him, and such speech cannot serve as an example of clear speech. For instance, if a child call a tree by a certain sound or word, having in view *that tree* only, and not knowing other trees at all, then any new tree which he may see he will call by a new word, or else he will take it for the same tree. The speech in which "words" correspond to perceptions is as it were made up of proper nouns. There are no appellative nouns; and not only substantives, but verbs, adjectives and adverbs have the character of "proper nouns" — that is, they apply to a *given* action, to a *given* quality, or to a given property.

The appearance of words of *a common meaning* in human speech signifies the appearance of concepts in consciousness.

Speech consists of words, each word expressing a concept. Concept and word are in substance one and the same thing; only the first (the concept) represents, so to speak, the inner side, and the second (the word) the outer side. Or, as says Dr. R. M. Bucke (the author of the book *Cosmic Consciousness*, about which I shall have much to say later on), "A word (i.e., concept) is the *algebraical* sign of a thing."

It has been noticed thousands of times that the brain of a thinking man does not exceed in size the brain of a non-thinking wild man in anything like the proportion in which the mind of the thinker exceeds the mind of the savage. The reason is that the brain of a Herbert Spencer has very little more work to do than has the brain of a native Australian, for this reason, that Spencer does all his characteristic mental work by signs or counters which stand for concepts, while the savage does all or nearly all his by means of cumbersome recepts. The savage is in a position comparable to that of the astronomer who makes his calculations by arithmetic, while Spencer is in the position of one who make them by algebra. The first will fill many great sheets of paper with figures and go through immense labor; the other will make the same calculations on an envelope and with comparatively little mental work.*

In our speech words express concepts or ideas. By ideas are meant broader concepts, not representing the group sign of similar perceptions, but embracing various groups of perceptions, or even *groups of concepts*. Therefore an idea is a complex or an abstract concept.

In addition to the simple sensations of these sense organs (color,

* R. M. Bucke, "Cosmic Consciousness," p. 12.

Concepts

sound, touch, smell and taste), in addition to the simple emotions of pleasure, pain, joy, anger, surprise, wonder, curiosity and many others, there is passing through our consciousness a series of complex sensations and higher (complex) emotions (moral, esthetic, religious). The content of emotional feelings, even the simplest — to say nothing of the complex — can never be wholly confined to concepts or ideas, and therefore can never be correctly or exactly expressed in words. Words can only allude to it, point to it. The interpretation of emotional feelings and *emotional understanding* is the problem of *art*. In combinations of words, in their meaning, their rhythm, their music — the combination of meaning, rhythm and music; in sounds, colors, lines, forms — men are creating a new world, and are attempting therein to express and transmit that which they feel, but which they are unable to express and transmit simply in words, i.e., in concepts. The emotional tones of life, i.e., of "feelings," are best transmitted by music, but it cannot express concepts, i.e., thought. Poetry endeavors to express both music and thought together. The combination of feeling and thought of high tension leads to a higher form of psychic life. Thus in art we have already the first experiments in *a language of the future*. Art anticipates a psychic evolution and divines its future forms.

At the present time an average man, taken as a norm, has attained to three units of psychic life: *sensation, perception,* and *conception*. Furthermore, observation reveals the fact that some people at certain times acquire a new, fourth unit of psychic life, which different authors and different schools name differently, but in which an element of knowledge or ideas is always united with an emotional element.

If Kant's ideas are correct, if space with its characteristics is a property of our consciousness, and not of the external world, then the three-dimensionalities of the world must in this or some other manner depend upon the constitution of our psychic apparatus.

It is possible to put the question concretely in the following manner: What bearing upon the three-dimensional extension of the world has the fact that in our psychical apparatus we discover the categories above described — sensations, perceptions and concepts?

We possess *such* a psychical apparatus and the world is *three-dimensional*. How is it possible to establish the fact that the three-dimensionality of the world depends upon *such* a constitution of our psychical apparatus?

This could be proven or disproven *undeniably* only with the aid of experiments.

If we could *change our psychic apparatus* and should then discover that *the world around us was changing*, this would constitute for us the proof of the dependence of the properties of space upon the properties of our consciousness.

For example if we could make the above-mentioned higher form of psychic life (which appears now accidentally as it were and depends upon insufficiently studied conditions) just as definite, exact, and *subject to our will* as is the concept; and if the number of characteristics of space increased, i.e., if space became four-dimensional instead of being three-dimensional, this would affirm our presupposition, and would prove Kant's contention that space with its properties is a *form of our sensuous receptivity*.

Or if we could diminish the number of units of our psychic life, and deprive ourselves or someone else of *conceptions*, leaving the psyche to act by perceptions and sensations only; and if by so doing the number of characteristics of the space surrounding us diminished; i.e., if for the person subjected to the test the world became two-dimensional instead of three-dimensional, and indeed one-dimensional as a result of a still greater limitation of the psychic apparatus, by depriving the person of perceptions — this would affirm our presupposition, and Kant's idea could be considered proven.

That is to say, Kant's idea would be proven *experimentally* if we could be convinced that for the being possessing sensations only, the world is one-dimensional; for the being possessing sensations and perceptions the world is two-dimensional; and for the being possessing, in addition to concepts and ideas, the higher forms of knowledge the world is four-dimensional.

Or, more exactly, Kant's thesis in regard to the subjectivity of space-perception could be regarded as proven (a) if for the being possessing sensations only, our entire world with all its variety of forms should seem *a single line*; if the universe of this being should possess but one dimension, i.e., should this being be *one-dimensional* in the properties of its receptivity; and (b) if for the being possessing, in addition to the faculty of feeling sensations, the faculty of forming perceptions, the world should have a two-dimensional extension; if all our world with its blue sky, clouds, green trees, mountains and precipices, should seem to him one plane; if the universe of this being should have only two dimensions, i.e., if this being were two-dimensional in the properties of its receptivity.

More briefly, Kant's thesis would be proven could we be made to

What is "Instinct"?

see that for the conscious being the number of characteristics of the world changes in accordance with the changes of its psychic apparatus.

To perform such an experiment, effecting the *diminution* of psychic characteristics is not possible under ordinary conditions — we cannot arbitrarily limit our own, or anyone else's psychic apparatus.

Experiments with *the augmentation* of psychic characteristics have been made and are recorded, but in consequence of many diverse causes they are insufficiently convincing. The chief reason for this is that the augmentation of psychic faculties yields, first of all, so much of *newness* in the psychic realm that this *newness* obscures *the changes* proceeding simultaneously in the previous perception of the world; one feels the new, but is not capable of defining the difference *exactly*.

The entire body of teachings of religio-philosophic movements have as their avowed or hidden purpose, *the expansion of consciousness.* This also is the aim of *mysticism* of every age and of every faith, the aim of occultism, and of the Oriental *yoga*. But the question of the expansion of consciousness demands special study; the final chapters of this book will be dedicated to it.

For the present, in proof of the above stated propositions with regard to the change of the world in relation to psychic changes, it is sufficient to consider the assumption concerning the possibility of a smaller number of psychic characteristics.

If experiments in this direction are impossible, perhaps observation may furnish what we seek.

Let us put the question: Are there not beings in the world *standing toward us in the necessary relation*, whose psyche is of a lower grade than ours?

Such psychically inferior beings undoubtedly exist. These are animals.

Of the difference between the psychical nature of an animal and of a man we know very little: the usual "conversational" psychology deals with it not at all. Usually we deny altogether that animals have minds, or else we ascribe to them our own psychology, but "limited" — though *how* and *in what* we do not know. Again, we say that animals do not possess reason, but are governed by instinct. As to what exactly we mean by *instinct* we do not ourselves know. I am speaking not alone of popular, but so-called "scientific" psychology.

Let us try to discover what instinct is, and learn something about animal psychology. First of all let us analyze the *actions* of animals, and see wherein they differ from ours. If these actions are instinctive, what inference is to be drawn from the fact?

75

What are those actions in general, and how do they differ?

In the actions of living beings within the limits of our usual observations we discriminate between those which are reflex, instinctive, rational and automatic.

Reflex actions are simply *responses by motion*, reactions upon external irritations, taking place always in the same way, regardless of their utility or futility, expediency, or inexpediency in any given case. Their origin and laws are due to the simple *irritability* of a cell.

What is the irritability of a cell, and what are these laws?

The irritability of a cell is defined as its faculty to respond to external irritation by a motion. Experiments with the simplest mono-cellular organisms have shown that this *irritability* acts according to definite laws. The cell responds by a motion to outside irritation. The force of the responsive motion increases as the force of the irritation is intensified, but in no definite proportionality. In order to provoke the responsive movement the irritation must be of a sufficient intensity. Each experienced irritation leaves *a certain trace* in the cell, making it more receptive to the new irritations. In this we see that the cell responds to the *repetitive* irritation of an *equal force* by a more forceful motion than the first one. And if the irritations be repeated further the cell will respond to them by more and more forceful motions, up to a certain limit. Having reached this limit the cell experiences *fatigue*, and responds to the same irritation by more and more feeble reactions. It is as if the cell becomes accustomed to the irritation. It becomes for the cell part of *a constant environment*, and it ceases to react, because it is reacting generally only to *changes* in conditions which are constant. If from the very beginning the irritation is so weak that it fails to provoke the responsive motion, it nevertheless leaves in the cell a certain *invisible* trace. This can be inferred from the fact that by repeating these weak irritations, the cell finally begins to react to them.

Thus *in the law of irritability* we observe, as it were, the beginnings of memory, fatigue, and habit. The cell produces the illusion, if not of a conscious and reasoning being, at any rate of a remembering being, habit-forming, and susceptible to fatigue. If we can be thus deceived by a cell, how much more liable are we to be deceived by the greater complexity of animal life.

But let us return to the analysis of *actions*. By the reflex actions of an organism are meant actions in which either an entire organism or its separate parts acts *as a cell*, i.e., within the limits of the law of variability. We observe such actions both in men and in animals. A man shudders all over from unexpected cold, or from a touch. His eyelids wink at the swift approach or touch of some object. The freely-hanging foot of a person in a sitting position moves forward if the leg be struck on the tendon below the knee. These movements proceed independently of consciousness, they may even proceed counter to consciousness. Usually consciousness registers them as accomplished facts. Moreover these movements are not at all governed by expediency. The foot moves forward in answer to the blow on the tendon even though a knife or a fire be in front of it.

By instinctive actions are meant actions governed by expediency, but made without conscious *selection* or without conscious *aim*.

They appear with the appearance of a sensuous tincture to sensations, i.e., from that moment when the sensation begins to be associated with a sense of pleasure or pain.

As a matter of fact, before the dawn of human intellect, throughout the entire animal kingdom "actions" were governed by the tendency to receive or to retain pleasure, or to escape pain.

We may declare with entire assurance that instinct is a *pleasure-pain* which, like the positive and negative poles of an electro-magnet, repels and attracts the animal in this or that direction, compelling it to perform whole series of complex actions, sometimes expedient to such a degree that they appear to be sensible, and not only sensible, but founded upon foresight of the future, almost upon some clairvoyance, like the migration of birds, the building of nests for the young which have not as yet appeared, the finding of the way south in the autumn, and north in the spring, etc.

But all these actions are explained in reality by a single instinct, i.e., by the subservience to *pleasure-pain*.

During periods in which millenniums may be regarded as days, by selection among all animals the types have been perfected, living along the lines of this subservience. This subservience is expedient, that is, the results of it lead to the *desired* goal. Why this is so is clear. Had the sense of pleasure arisen from that which is detrimental, the given species could not live, and would quickly die out. Instinct is the guide of its life, but only as long as instinct is expedient solely; just as soon as it ceases to be expedient it becomes the guide of death, and the species soon dies out. Normally "pleasure-pain" is pleasant or unpleasant not *for* the usefulness or the harm which may result, but because of it. Those influences which proved to be beneficial for a given species during the vegetative life, with the transition to the more active and complex animal life begin to be sensed as *pleasant,* the detrimental influences as unpleasant. As regards two different species, one and the same influence — say a certain temperature — may be useful and pleasant for one, and for another detrimental and unpleasant. It is clear, therefore, that the subservience to "pleasure-pain" must be governed by expediency. The pleasant is pleasant because it is *beneficial,* the unpleasant is unpleasant because it is *harmful.*

Next after instinctive actions follow those actions which are rational and automatic.

By rational action is meant such an action as is known to the acting subject *before its execution;* such an action as the acting subject can *name, define, explain,* can show its cause and purpose *before its execution.*

Automatic actions are actions which have been rational for a given subject, but because of frequent repetitions they have become habitual and are performed unconsciously. The acquired automatic actions of trained animals were previously rational not in the animal, but in the trainer. Such actions often appear as rational but this is a complete illusion. The animal remembers the sequence of actions, and therefore its actions appear to be considered and expedient. They really were considered, *but not by it.* Automatic actions are often confounded with instinctive ones — in reality they resemble instinctive ones, but there is an enormous difference between them. Automatic actions are developed by the subject during its own life, and for a long time before they become automatic it must be conscious of them. Instinctive actions, on the other hand, are developed during the life-periods of the *species,* and the aptitude for them is transmitted in a definite manner by heredity. *It is possible* to call automatic actions instinctive actions worked out for itself by a given subject. *It is impossible,* however, to call instinctive actions automatic actions worked out by a given species, because they never were rational in different individuals of a given species, but were compounded out of a series of complex reflexes.

REFLEXES, INSTINCTIVE AND "RATIONAL" ACTIONS, ALL MAY BE RE-GARDED AS REFLECTED, i.e., AS NOT SELF-ORIGINATED. BOTH THESE AND OTHERS, AND STILL A THIRD CLASS, COME NOT FROM MAN HIMSELF, BUT FROM THE OUTSIDE WORLD. MAN IS THE TRANSMITTING OR TRANSFORM-ING STATION FOR CERTAIN FORCES: ALL OF HIS ACTIONS IN THESE THREE CATEGORIES ARE CREATED AND DETERMINED BY HIS IMPRESSIONS OF THE OUTSIDE WORLD. MAN IN THESE THREE SPECIES OF ACTION IS, IN SUB-

The Animal Psyche

STANCE, AN AUTOMATON, UNCONSCIOUS OR CONSCIOUS OF HIS ACTIONS.
NOTHING COMES FROM HIM HIMSELF.

With the exception of sensations of the outer world, only the higher category of actions, i.e., *conscious actions* * appears to depend on something else. But the aptitude for such actions is seldom met with — only in some few persons whom it is possible to describe as MEN OF A HIGHER TYPE.

Having established the differences between various kinds of actions, let us return to the question propounded before: *In what manner does the psyche of an animal differ from that of a human being?* Out of the four categories of actions the two lower ones are accessible to animals. The category of "conscious" actions is inaccessible to animals. This is proven first of all by the fact that animals have not the power of speech as we have it.

As has been shown before, the possession of speech is indissolubly bound up with the possession of concepts. Therefore we may say that animals do not possess concepts.

Is this true, and is it possible to possess the instinctive mind without possessing concepts?

All that we know about the instinctive mind teaches us that it acts possessing sensations and perceptions only, and that in the lower grades it possesses sensation only. The being which does its thinking by means of perceptions possesses the instinctive mind which gives it the possibility of exercising that *choice* between the perceptions presented to it which produces the impression of judging and reasoning. In reality the animal does not reason its actions, but lives by its emotions, subject to that emotion which happens to be strongest. *Although indeed,* in the life of the animal, acute moments sometimes occur when it is confronted with the necessity of *choosing* among a certain series of perceptions. At such moments its actions may seem to be quite reasoned out. For example, the animal, being put in a situation of danger, acts often very cautiously and wisely, but in reality its actions are directed not by thoughts but principally by emotional memory and motor perceptions. It has been previously shown that emotions are expedient, and that the subjection to them in a normal being must be expedient. Any perception of an animal, any recollected image, is bound up with some emotional sensation or emotional remembrance — there are no non-emotional, cold

---

* Generally speaking, we do not observe these actions, because we confuse them with "rational" actions; the principal cause of this confusion is that we call "rational" actions conscious — which they are not.

thoughts in the animal soul, or even if there are, these are inactive, and incapable of becoming the springs of action.

Thus all actions of animals, sometimes highly complex, expedient, and apparently reasoned, we can explain without attributing to them concepts, judgments, and the power of reasoning. Indeed, we must recognize that animals have no *concepts,* and the proof of this is that they have no speech.

If we take two *men* of different nationalities, different races, each ignorant of the language of the other, and put them together, they will find a way to communicate at once.

One perhaps draws a circle with his finger, the other draws another circle beside it. By these means they have already established that they can understand one another. If a thick wall were put between them it would not hamper them in the least — one of them knocks three times, and the other knocks three times in response.

The communication is established. The idea of communicating with the inhabitants of other planets is founded upon the idea of light signals. It is proposed to make on the earth an enormous lighted circle or a square to attract the attention of the inhabitants of Mars and to be answered by them by means of the same signal. We live side by side with animals and yet cannot establish such communication. Evidently the distance between us and them is greater, and the difference deeper, than between *men* divided by the ignorance of language, stone walls, and enormous distances.

Another proof of the absence of concepts in the animal is its inability to use a lever, i.e., its incapacity to come independently to an understanding of the principle of the action of the lever. The usual objection that an animal cannot operate a lever because its organs (paws et cetera) are not adapted to such actions does not hold for the reason that almost any animal can be *taught* to operate a lever. This shows that the difficulty is not in the organs. The animal simply cannot of itself come to a comprehension of the idea of a lever.

The invention of the lever immediately divided primitive man from the animal, and it was inextricably bound up with the appearance of concepts. The psychic side of the understanding of the action of a lever consists in the construction of a correct syllogism. Without constructing the syllogism correctly it is impossible to understand the action of a lever. Having no concepts it is impossible to construct the syllogism. The syllogism in the psychic sphere is literally the same thing as the lever in the physical sphere.

The Aristotelian *Organon*

His mastery of the lever differentiates man as strongly from the animal as does speech. If some learned Martians were looking at the earth, and should study it objectively from afar by means of a telescope, not hearing speech, nor entering into the subjective world of the inhabitants of the earth, nor coming in contact with them, they would divide the beings living on the earth into two groups: those acquainted with the action of the lever, and those unacquainted with such action.

The psychology of animals is in general very misty to us. The infinite number of observations made concerning all animals, from elephants to spiders, and the infinite number of anecdotes about the mind, spirit, and moral qualities of animals change nothing of all that. We represent animals to ourselves either as living automatons or as stupid men.

We too much confine ourselves within the circle of our own psychology. We fail to imagine any other, and think involuntarily that the only possible sort of soul is such as we ourselves possess. But it is this illusion which prevents us from understanding life. If we could participate in the psychic life of an animal, understand *how* it perceives, thinks and acts, we would find much of unusual interest. For example, could we represent to ourselves, and re-create mentally, *the logic* of an animal, it would greatly help us to understand our own logic and the laws of our own thinking. Before all else we would come to understand the conditionality and relativity of our own logical construction and with it the conditionality of our entire conception of the world.

An animal would have a peculiar logic. It indeed would not be logic in the true meaning of the word, because logic presupposes the existence of *logos*, i.e., of a word or concept.

Our usual logic, by which we live, without which "the shoemaker will not sew the boot," is deduced from the simple scheme formulated by Aristotle in those writings which were edited by his pupils under the common name of *Organon*, i.e., the "Instrument" (of thought). This scheme consists in the following:

A *is* A.
A *is not* Not-A.
Everything is either A *or* Not-A.

The logic embraced in this scheme — the logic of Aristotle — is quite sufficient *for observation*. But for *experiment* it is insufficient, because the experiment proceeds *in time*, and in the formulæ of Aristotle time is not taken into consideration. This was observed at the very dawn of the establishment of our experimental science — observed by Roger Bacon, and formulated several centuries later by his famous namesake, Francis Bacon, Lord Verulam, in the treatise *Novum Organum* — the "New Instrument" (of thought). Briefly, the formulation of Bacon may be reduced to the following:

> *That which was A, will be* A.
> *That which was Not-A, will be Not-A.*
> *Everything was and will be, either* A *or Not-A.*

Upon these formulæ, acknowledged or unacknowledged, all our scientific experience is built, and upon them, too, is shoe-making founded, because if a shoemaker could not be sure that the leather bought yesterday would be leather tomorrow, in all probability he would not venture to make a pair of shoes, but would find some other more profitable employment.

The formulæ of logic, such as those both of Aristotle and of Bacon, are themselves deduced from the observation of facts, and do not and cannot include anything except the contents of these facts. They are not the laws of *reasoning*, but the laws of the outer world as it is perceived by us, or the laws of our relation to the outer world.

Could we represent to ourselves the "logic" of an animal we should understand its relation to the outer world. Our cardinal error concerning the psychology of animals consists in the fact that we ascribe to them our own logic. We assume that *logic is one*, that our logic is something absolute, existing outside and independent of us, while as a matter of fact, logic but formulates the laws of the relations of our psyche to the outside world, or the laws which our psyche discovers in the outside world. Another psyche will discover other laws.

The logic of animals will differ from ours, first of all, from the fact that it will not be *general*. It will exist separately for each case, for each perception. Common properties, class properties, and the generic and specific signs of *categories* will not exist for animals. Each object will exist in and by itself, and all its properties will be the specific properties of it alone.

This house and *that house* are entirely different objects for an animal, because one is *its* house and the other is a strange house. Generally speaking, we recognize objects by the signs of their similarity; the animal

Animal Logic

must recognize them by the signs of their difference. It remembers each object by that sign which had for it the greatest emotional meaning. In such a manner, i.e., by their emotional tones, perceptions are stored in the memory of an animal. It is clear that such perceptions are much more difficult to store up in the memory, and therefore the memory of an animal is more burdened than ours, although in the amount of knowledge and in the quantity of that which is preserved in the memory, it stands far below us.

After seeing an object once, we refer it to a certain class, genus and species, place it under this or that concept, and fix it in the mind by means of some "word," i.e., algebraical symbol; then by another, defining it, and so on.

The animal has no concepts: it has not that mental algebra by the help of which we think. It must know always *a given object*, and must remember it with all its signs and peculiarities. No forgotten sign will return. For us, on the other hand, the principal signs are contained in the concept with which we have correlated that object, and we can find it in our memory by means of the sign for it.

From this it is clear that the memory of an animal is more burdened than ours, and *this* is the principal hindering cause to the mental evolution of an animal. Its mind is *too busy*. It *has no time* to develop. The mental development of a child may be arrested by making it memorize a series of words or a series of figures. The animal is in just such a position. Herein lies the explanation of the strange fact that an animal is *wiser when it is young*.

In man the flower of intellectual force blooms at a mature age, often even in senility; in the animal, quite the reverse is true. It is *receptive* only while it is young. At maturity its development stops, and in old age it undoubtedly degenerates.

The logic of animals, were we to attempt to express it by means of formulæ similar to those employed by Aristotle and Bacon would be as follows:

The formula A *is* A, the animal will understand. It will say (as it were) *I am I*, etc.; but the formula, A *is not* Not-A, it will be incapable of understanding. *Not Not-A* is indeed *the concept*.

The animal will reason thus:

> *This is this.*
> *That is that.*
> *This is not that.*

Tertium Organum

This man is this man.
That man is that man.
This man is not that man.

I shall be obliged to return to the logic of animals later on; for the present it is only necessary to establish the fact that the psychology of animals is peculiar, and differs in a fundamental way from our own. And not only is it peculiar, but it is decidedly *manifold*.

Among the animals known to us, even among domestic animals, the psychological differences are so great as to differentiate them into entirely separate planes. We ignore this, and place them all under a single rubric — *"animals."*

A goose, having entangled its foot in a piece of watermelon rind, drags it along by the web and thus cannot get it out, but it never thinks of raising its foot. This indicates that its mind is so vague that it does not know its own body, scarcely distinguishing between it and other objects. This would happen neither with a dog nor with a cat. They know their bodies very well. But in relation to outside objects the dog and cat differ widely. I have observed a dog, a "very intelligent" setter. When the little rug on which he slept got folded and was uncomfortable to sleep on, he understood that the nuisance was *outside of him*, that it was in the rug, and in a certain definite position of the rug. Therefore he caught the rug in his teeth, turned it and pushed it here and there, the while growling, sighing, and moaning until some one came to his aid, for he was never able to rectify the difficulty.

With the cat such a question could not even appear. The cat knows her body very well, but everything outside of herself she takes as her due, as given. To *correct* the outside world, to accommodate it to her own comfort, never comes into the cat's head. Perhaps this is because she lives more in another world, in the world of dreams and fantasies, than in this. Accordingly, if there were something wrong with her bed the cat would turn herself about repeatedly until she could lie down comfortably, or she would go and lie in another place.

The monkey would spread the rug very easily indeed.

Here we have *four* beings, all quite different; and this is only one example: it would be possible to collect others by the hundred. And meanwhile there is for us just one "animal." We mix together many things that are entirely different; our "divisions" are often incorrect, and this hinders us when it comes to the examination of ourselves. To declare that manifest differences determine the "evolutionary grade," that animals of one type are "higher" or "lower" than those of another, would be entirely false. The dog and the monkey by their *intellect*, their aptness to imitate, and by reason of the dog's fidelity to man, are as it were higher than the cat, but the cat is infinitely superior to them in intuition, esthetic sense, independence, and force of will. The dog and the monkey manifest themselves *in toto:* all that they have is seen. The cat, on the other hand, is not without reason regarded as a magical and occult animal. In her there is much hidden of which she herself does not know. If one speaks in terms of evolution, it is more correct to say that the cat and the dog are animals of different evolutions, just as in all probability, not one, but several evolutions are simultaneously going forward in humanity.

The recognition of several independent and from one standpoint equivalent evolutions, developing entirely different properties, would lead us out of a labyrinth of endless contradictions in our understanding of *man* and would show us the path to the only real and important evolution for us — the evolution into superman.

CHAPTER IX

W E have established the enormous difference existing between the psychology of a man and of an animal. This difference undoubtedly profoundly affects the receptivity of the outer world by the animal. But *how* and *in what?* This is exactly what we do not know, and what we shall try to discover.

To this end we shall return to *our* receptivity of the world, investigate *in detail* the nature of that receptivity, and then imagine how the animal, with its more limited psychic equipment, receives its impression of the world.

Let us note first of all that we receive the most incorrect impressions of the world as regards its outer form and aspect. We know that the world consists of solids, but we see and touch *only surfaces.* We never see and touch *a solid.* The solid — this is indeed *a concept,* composed of a series of perceptions, the result of reasoning and experience. For immediate sensation, surfaces alone exist. Sensations of gravity, mass, volume, which we mentally associate with the "solid," are in reality associated with the sensations of surfaces. We only *know* that the sensation comes from the solid, but the solid itself we never sense. Perhaps it would be possible to call the complex sensation of surfaces: weight, mass, density, resistance, "the sensation of a solid," but rather do we combine *mentally* all these sensations into one, and call that composite sensation a solid. We sense directly only surfaces; the weight and resistance of the solid, as such, we never *separately* sense.

But we *know* that the world does not consist of surfaces: we know that we see the world incorrectly, and that we *never* see it *as it is,* not alone in the philosophical meaning of the expression, but in the most simple *geometrical* meaning. We have never seen *a cube, a sphere*, etc., but only their surfaces. Knowing this, we mentally correct that which we see. Behind the surfaces we *think* the solid. But we can never even *represent* the solid to ourselves. We cannot imagine the cube or the sphere seen, not in perceptive, but simultaneously from all sides.

It is clear that the world does not exist in perspective; nevertheless we cannot see it otherwise. We see everything only in perspective; that is, in the very act of receptivity the world is distorted in our eye, and we know that it is distorted. We know that it is not such as it appears, and mentally we are continuously *correcting* that which the eye sees, substituting the real content for those symbols of things which sight reveals.

Our sight is a complex faculty. It consists of visual sensations *plus* the memory of sensations of touch. The child tries to feel with its finger-tips everything that it sees — the nose of its nurse, the moon, the reflection of sun rays from the mirror on the wall. Only gradually does it learn to discern the near and the distant *by means of sight alone*. But we know that even in mature age we are easily subject to optical illusions.

We see distant objects as flat, even more incorrectly, because relief is after all a symbol revealing a certain property of objects. A man at a long distance is pictured to us in silhouette. This happens because we never feel anything at a long distance, and the eye has not been taught to discern the difference in surfaces which at short distances are felt by the finger-tips.*

* In this connection, there have been some interesting observations made upon the blind who are just beginning to see.

In the magazine *Slepetz* (The Blind, 1912) there is a description from direct observation of how those born blind *learn to see after the operation* which restored their sight.

This is how a seventeen-year-old youth, who recovered his sight after the removal of a cataract, describes his impressions. On the third day after the operation he was asked what he saw. He answered that he saw an enormous field of light and misty objects moving upon it. These objects he did not discern. Only after four days did he begin to discern them, and after an interval of two weeks, when his eyes were accustomed to the light, he started to use his sight practically, for the discernment of objects. He was shown all the colors of the spectrum and he learned to distinguish them very soon, except yellow and green, which he confused for a long time. The cube, sphere and pyramid, when placed before him seemed to him like the square, the flat disc, and the triangle. When the flat disc was put alongside the sphere he distinguished no difference between them. When asked what impression both kinds of figures produced on him just at first, he said that he noticed at once the difference between the cube and the sphere, and understood that they were not drawings, but was unable to deduce from them their relation to the square and to the circle, until he felt in his finger tips the desire to touch these objects. When he was allowed to take the cube,

We can never see, even in the minute, any part of the outer world as it is, that is, *as we know it*. We can never see the desk or the wardrobe *all at once, from all sides and inside*. Our eye distorts the outside world in a certain way, in order that, looking about, we may be able to define the position of objects relatively to ourselves. But to look at the world from any other standpoint than our own is impossible for us, nor can we ever see it correctly, without distortion by our sight.

Relief and perspective — these constitute the distortions of the object by our eye. They are optical illusions, delusions of sight. The cube in perspective is but a conventional sign of the three-dimensional cube, and all that we see is the conditional image of that conditionally real three-dimensional world with which our geometry deals, and not that world itself. On the basis of what we see we surmise that it exists in reality. We know that what we see is incorrect, and we think of the world as other than it appears. If we had no doubt about the correctness of our sight, if we knew that the world were such as it appears, then obviously we should think of the world in the manner in which we see it. In reality we are constantly engaged in making corrections.

It is clear that the ability to make corrections in that which the eye sees demands, undoubtedly, the possession of the concept, because the corrections are made by a process of reasoning, which is impossible without concepts. Deprived of the faculty to make corrections in that which the eye sees we should have a different outlook on the world, i.e., much of *that which* is we should see incorrectly; we should not see much of *that which is*, but we should see *much of that which does not exist in reality at all*. First of all, we should see an enormous number of *non-existent motions*. Every motion of ours in our direct sensation of it, is bound up with the motion of everything around us. We *know* that this motion is an illusory one, but we *see* it as real. Objects turn in front of us, run past us, overtake one another. If we are riding slowly past houses, these turn slowly, if we are riding fast they turn quickly; also, trees grow up before us unexpectedly, run away and disappear.

---

sphere and pyramid in his hands he at once identified these solids by the sense of touch, and wondered very much that he was unable to recognize them by sight. He lacked the perception of space, perspective. All objects seemed flat to him: though he knew that the nose protrudes, and that the eyes are located in cavities, the human face seemed flat to him. He was delighted with his recovered vision, but in the beginning it fatigued him to exercise it: the impressions oppressed and exhausted him. For this reason, though possessing perfect sight, he sometimes turned to the sense of touch as to repose.

How Animals See the World

This *seeming* animation of objects, coupled with dreams, has always inspired, and still inspires the fairy tale.

The "motions" of objects, to a person in motion, are very complex indeed. Observe how strangely the field of wheat behaves just beyond the window of the car in which you are riding. It runs to the very window, stops, turns slowly around itself and runs away. The trees of the forest run apparently at different speeds, overtaking one another. The entire landscape is one of illusory motion. Behold also the sun, which even up to the present time "rises" and "sets" in all languages — this "motion" having been in the past so passionately defended!

This is all seeming, and though we know that these motions are illusory, we see them nevertheless, and sometimes we are deluded. To how many more illusions should we be subject had we not the power of mentally analyzing their determining causes, but were obliged to believe that everything exists as it appears!

I see it; therefore this exists.

This affirmation is the principal source of all illusions. To be true, it is necessary to say:

I see it; therefore this does not exist — or at least, *I see it; therefore this is not so.*

Although we *can* say the last, the animal cannot, for to its apprehension things are as they appear. It must believe what it sees.

How does the world appear to the animal?

The world appears to it as a series of complicated moving surfaces. The animal lives *in a world of two dimensions.* Its universe has for it the properties and appearance of *a surface*. And upon this surface transpire an enormous number of different movements of a most fantastic character.

Why should the world appear to the animal as a surface?

First of all, because it appears as a surface *to us.*

But we *know* that the world is not a surface, and the animal cannot know it. It accepts everything just as it appears. It is powerless to correct the testimony of its eyes — or it cannot do so to the extent that we do.

We are able to measure in three mutually independent directions: the nature of our mind permits us to do this. The animal can measure simultaneously in two directions only — it can never measure in three directions at once. This is due to the fact that, not possessing concepts, it is unable to retain in the mind the idea of the first two directions, for measuring the third.

Let me explain this more exactly.

Suppose we imagine that we are measuring *the cube.*

In order to measure the cube in three directions, it is necessary while measuring in one direction, to keep in mind two others — *to remember.* But it is possible to keep them in mind as concepts only, that is, associating them with different concepts — pasting upon them different labels. So, pasting upon the first two directions the labels of *length* and *breadth,* it is possible to measure the *height.* It is impossible otherwise. As *perceptions,* the first two measurements of the cube are completely identical, and assuredly will mingle into one in the mind. The animal, without the aid of concepts, cannot paste upon the first two measurements the labels of length and breadth. Therefore, at the moment when it begins to measure the height of the cube, the first two measurements will be confused in one. The animal, attempting to measure the cube by means of perceptions only without the aid of concepts, will be like a cat I once observed. Her kittens — five or six in number — she dragged asunder into different rooms, and could not then collect them together. She seized one, put it beside another, ran for a third and brought it to the first two, but then she seized the first and carried it away to another room, putting it beside the fourth; after that she ran back, seized the second and dragged it to the room containing the fifth, and so on. For a whole hour the cat had no rest with her kittens, she suffered severely, and could accomplish nothing. It is clear that she lacked the concepts which would enable her to remember how many kittens she had altogether.

It is in the highest degree important to understand the relation of the animal consciousness to the measuring of bodies.

The great point is that the animal sees surfaces only. (We may say this with complete assurance, because we ourselves see surfaces only.) Thus seeing only surfaces the animal can *imagine* but two dimensions. The third dimension, in contradistinction to the other two, can only be *thought;* that is, this dimension must be a concept; but animals do not possess concepts. The third dimension like the others appears as a perception. Therefore, at the moment of its appearance, the first two will inevitably mingle into one. The animal is capable of perceiving the difference between two dimensions: the difference between *three* it cannot perceive. This difference must be *known* beforehand, and to know it concepts are necessary.

Identical perceptions mix into one for the animal, just as we ourselves confuse two simultaneous, similar phenomena proceeding from the same point. For the animal it will be *one phenomenon,* just as for us all similar, simultaneous phenomena proceeding from a single point will be one phenomenon.

Therefore the animal will see the world as a surface, and will measure this surface in two directions only.

But how is it possible to explain the fact that the animal, inhabiting a two-dimensional world, or rather, perceiving itself as in a two-dimensional world, is perfectly oriented in our three-dimensional world? How explain the fact that the bird flies up and down, sideways and straight ahead — in all three directions; that the horse jumps over ditches and barriers; that the dog and cat appear to understand the properties of depth and height simultaneously with those of length and breadth?

In order to explain these things it is necessary to return to the fundamental principles of animal psychology. It has been previously shown that many properties of objects remembered by us *as general* properties of genus, class, species, are remembered by animals as individual properties of objects. To orientate in this enormous reserve of individual properties preserved in the memory, animals are assisted by the emotional tone which is linked up in them with each perception and each remembered sensation.

For example, an animal knows two roads as two entirely separate phenomena having nothing in common; that is, one road consists of a series of definite perceptions colored by definite emotional tones; the other phenomenon — the other road — consists of another series of definite perceptions colored with other tones. We say that this, that, and the other are roads. One leads to one place, a second to another. For an animal the two roads have *nothing in common.* But it remembers in their proper sequence all the emotional tones which are linked with the first road and with the second one, and it therefore remembers both roads with their turns, ditches, fences, etc.

Thus *the remembering* of definite properties of observed objects helps the animal to *find* itself in the world of phenomena. But as a rule before *new* phenomena an animal is much more helpless than a man.

An animal sees two dimensions; the third dimension it senses constantly, but does not see. It senses the third dimension as something *transient,* just as we sense *time.*

The surfaces which an animal sees possess for it many strange properties; first of all, *numerous and various motions.*

As has been said already, all those illusory motions which *seem* to us real, but which we *know* to be illusory, are entirely real to the animal:

the turning about of the houses as we ride past, the growth of a tree out of some corner, the passing of the moon between clouds, etc., etc.

But in addition to all this, many motions must exist for the animal of which we have no suspicion. The fact is that innumerable objects quite immobile for us — properly *all objects* — must seem to the animal to be *in motion;* AND THE THIRD DIMENSION OF SOLIDS WILL APPEAR TO IT IN THESE MOTIONS; i.e., THE THIRD DIMENSION OF SOLIDS WILL APPEAR TO IT AS A MOTION.

Let us try to imagine how the animal perceives the objects of the outer world.

Suppose it is confronted with a *large disc, and simultaneously with a large sphere* of the same diameter.

Standing directly opposite them at a certain distance, the animal will see two circles. Beginning to walk around them, it will observe that the sphere remains a circle, while the disc gradually narrows, transforming itself into a narrow strip. On moving farther around, the strip begins to expand and gradually transforms itself into a circle. The sphere will not change during this circumambulation. But when the animal approaches toward it certain strange phenomena ensue.

Let us try to understand how the animal will perceive the surface of the sphere as contrasted with the surface of the disc.

One thing is sure: it will perceive the spherical surface *differently from us.* We perceive convexity or sphericity as *a common property* of many surfaces. The animal, on the contrary, because of the very properties of its psychic apparatus, will perceive that sphericality as an individual property of a given sphere. Now how will this sphericality as an individual property of a given sphere appear to it?

We may declare with complete assurance that the sphericality will appear to the animal as a movement on the surface which it sees.

During the approach of the animal toward the sphere something like the following must happen: the surface which the animal sees starts to move quickly; its center spreads out, and all of the other points run away from the center with a velocity proportional to their distance from the center (or the square of their distance from the center).

It is in this way that the animal senses the spherical surface — *much as we sense sound.*

At a certain distance from the sphere the animal perceives it as a plane. Approaching or touching some point on the sphere it sees that all other points have changed with relation to this particular point, they have all altered their position on the plane — have moved to one side, as it were. Touching another point, it sees that all the rest have moved in similar fashion.

This property of the sphere will appear as its *motion*, its "vibration." The sphere will actually resemble a vibrating, oscillating surface, in the same way that *each angle* of an immobile object will appear to the animal as *a motion*.

The animal can see an angle of a three-dimensional object only while moving past it, and during the time it takes, the object will seem to the animal to have turned — a new side has appeared, and the side first seen has disappeared or moved away. The *angle* will be perceived as rotation, as the motion of the object, i.e., as something transient, temporal, as a change of state in the object. Remembering the angles which it has seen before — seen as the motion of bodies — the animal will consider that they have ceased, have ended, have disappeared — that they are *in the past*.

Of course the animal cannot *reason* in this way, but it acts as though it had thus reasoned.

Could the animal think about these phenomena which have not yet entered into its life (i.e., angles and curved surfaces) it would undoubtedly imagine them *in time only:* it could not prefigure for them any real existence at the present moment *when they have not yet appeared*. And were it able to express an opinion on this subject, it would say that angles exist *in potentiality*, that they *will be*, but that for the present *they do not exist*.

The angle of a house past which a horse runs every day is *a phenomenon, repeating under certain circumstances*, but nevertheless *a phenomenon proceeding in time*, and not a spatial and constant property of the house.

For the animal the angle will be a temporal phenomenon and not a spatial one, as it is for us.

Thus we see that the animal will perceive the properties of our third dimension as motions, and will refer these properties to *time*, i.e., to the past or future, or to the present — the moment of the transition of the future into the past.

This circumstance is in the highest degree important, for therein lies the key to our own receptivity of the world; we shall therefore examine into it more in detail.

Tertium Organum

Up to the present time we have taken into consideration only the higher animals: the dog, the cat, the horse. Let us now try the lower: let us take the snail. We know nothing about its inner life, but undoubtedly its receptivity resembles ours scarcely at all. In all probability the snail possesses some obscure sensations of its environment. Probably it feels heat, cold, light, darkness, hunger — and it instinctively (i.e., urged by pleasure-pain guidance) strives to reach the uneaten edge of the leaf on which it rests, and instinctively avoids the dead leaf. Its movements are guided by *pleasure-pain:* it constantly strives toward the one, and away from the other. It *always moves upon a single line,* from the unpleasant to the pleasant, and in all probability except for this line it is not conscious of anything and does not sense anything. This line is its entire world. All sensations, *entering* from the outside, the snail senses upon this line of its motion, and these come to it *out of time* — from the potential they become the present. For the snail our entire universe exists in the future and in the past — i.e., *in time.* In space only one line exists; all the rest is time. It is more than probable that the snail is not conscious of its movements. Making efforts with its entire body it moves forward to the fresh edge of the leaf, but it seems as if the leaf were coming to it, appearing at that moment, coming out of time as *the morning* comes to us.

The snail is a one-dimensional being.

The higher animals — the dog, cat, the horse — are two-dimensional beings. To the higher animal all space appears as a surface, as a *plane.* Everything out of this plane lives for it in time.

Thus we see that the higher animal — the two-dimensional being compared with the one-dimensional — extracts or *captures from time one more dimension.*

The world of a snail has one dimension; our second and third dimensions are for it in time.

The world of a dog is two-dimensional; our third dimension is for it in time.

An animal can remember all "phenomena" which it has observed, i.e., all properties of three-dimensional solids with which it has come in contact, but it cannot know that the (for it) recurring phenomenon is a constant property of the three-dimensional solid — an angle, curvature, or convexity.

Such is the psychology of the receptivity of the world by a two-dimensional being.

For such a being *a new sun* will rise every day. Yesterday's sun is gone, and will not appear again; tomorrow's does not as yet exist.

Animal Perception of Motion

Rostand did not understand the psychology of *"Chantecler."* The cock could not think that he woke up the sun by his crowing. To him the sun does not go to sleep, it goes into the past, disappears, suffers annihilation, *ceases to be.* If it comes on the morrow it will be a new sun, just as for us with every new year comes *a new spring.* In order *to be* the sun shall not wake up, but *arise,* be born. The cock (if it could think without losing its characteristic psychology) could not believe in the appearance today of the same sun which was *yesterday.* This is purely human reasoning.

For the animal *a new sun* rises every morning, just as for us *a new morning comes* with every day and *a new spring* with every year.

The animal is not in a position to understand that the sun is the same yesterday and today, EXACTLY IN THE SAME WAY THAT WE PROBABLY CANNOT UNDERSTAND THAT THE MORNING IS THE SAME AND THE SPRING IS THE SAME.

The motion of objects which is not illusory, even for us, but a real motion, like that of a revolving wheel, a passing carriage, and so on, will differ for the animal very much from that motion which it sees in all objects which are for us immobile — i.e., from that motion in which the third dimension of solids is as it were revealed to it. The first mentioned motion (real for us) will seem to the animal arbitrary, *alive.*

And these two kinds of motion will be incommensurable for it.

The animal will be in a position to measure an angle or a convex surface, though not understanding their true nature, and though regarding them as motion. But true motion, i.e., that which is true motion to us, it will never be in a position to measure, because for this it is necessary to possess our *concept of time,* and to measure all motions with reference to some one more constant motion, i.e., to compare all motions with some *one.* Without concepts the animal is powerless to do this. Therefore the (for us) real motions of objects will be incommensurable for it, and being incommensurable, will be incommensurable with other motions which are real and measurable for it, but which are illusory for us — motions which in reality represent the third dimension of solids.

This last conclusion is inevitable. If the animal apprehends and measures *as motion* that which is not motion, clearly it cannot measure by one and the same standard that which is motion and that which is not motion.

But this does not mean that it cannot know the character of motions going on in the world and cannot conform itself to them. On the contrary, we see that the animal orientates itself perfectly among the motions of the objects of our three-dimensional world. Here comes into play the aid of instinct, i.e., the ability, developed by millenniums of selection, to act expediently without consciousness of purpose. Moreover, the animal discerns perfectly the motions going on around it.

But discerning two kinds of phenomena, *two kinds of motion*, the animal will explain one of them by means of some incomprehensible inner property of objects, i.e., in all probability it will regard this motion as the result of the *animation* of objects, and the moving objects as *animated beings*.

The kitten plays with the ball or with its tail because ball and tail *are running away from it*.

The bear will fight with the beam which threatens to throw him off the tree, because in the swinging beam he senses something alive and hostile.

The horse is frightened by the bush because the bush unexpectedly turned and waved a branch.

In the last case the bush need not even have moved at all, for the horse was running, and it seemed therefore as though the bush moved, and consequently that it was animated. In all probability all movement is thus animated for the animal. Why does the dog bark so desperately at the passing carriage? This is not entirely clear to us for we do not realize that to the eyes of the dog the carriage is turning, twisting, grimacing all over. It is alive in every part — the wheels, the top, the mud-guards, seats, passengers — all these are moving, turning.

Now let us draw certain conclusions from all of the foregoing.

We have established the fact that man possesses sensations, perceptions and concepts; that the higher animals possess sensations and perceptions, and the lower animals sensations only. The conclusion that animals have no concepts we deduced from the fact that they have no speech. Next we have established that having no concepts, animals cannot comprehend the third dimension, but see the world as a surface; i.e., they have no means — no instrument — for the correction of their incorrect sensations of the world. Furthermore, we have found that seeing the world as a surface, animals see upon this surface many motions which for us are non-existent. That is, all those properties of solids which we regard as the properties of three-dimensionality, animals represent to themselves *as motions*. Thus the angle and the spherical surface appear to them as the movements of a plane. After that we came to the conclusion that

Space Depends on the Space-sense

everything which we regard as *constant* in the region of the third dimension, animals regard as *transient* things which happen to objects — temporal phenomena.

Thus in all its relations to the world the animal is quite analogous to the imagined, unreal two-dimensional being living upon a plane. All our world appears to the animal as the plane through which phenomena are passing, moving upon time, or in time.

And so we may say that we have established the following: that under certain limitations of the psychic apparatus for receiving the outer world, for the subject possessing this apparatus, the entire aspect and all properties of the world will suffer change. And two subjects, living side by side, but possessing different psychic apparatus, will inhabit different worlds — the properties of the extension of the world will be different for them. And we observed the conditions, not invented for the purpose, not concocted in imagination, but really existing in nature; that is, the psychic conditions governing the lives of animals, under which the world appears as a plane or as a line.

That is to say, we have established that the three-dimensional extension of the world depends upon the properties of our psychic apparatus.

Or, that the three-dimensionality of the world is not its property, but a property of *our* receptivity of the world.

In other words, the three-dimensionality of the world is a property of its reflection in our consciousness.

If all this is so, then it is obvious that we have really proved the dependence of space upon the *space-sense*. And if we have proved the existence of a space-sense *lower in comparison with ours*, by this we have proved the possibility of a space-sense *higher in comparison with ours*.

And we shall grant that if in us there develops the *fourth unit* of reasoning as different from the concept as the concept is different from perception, so simultaneously with it will appear for us in the surrounding world a fourth characteristic which we may designate geometrically as the fourth direction or the fourth perpendicular, because in this characteristic will be included the properties of objects perpendicular to all properties known to us, and not parallel to any of them. In other words, we shall see, or we shall feel ourselves in a space not of three, but of four dimensions; and in the objects surrounding us, and in our own bodies, will appear *common properties* of the fourth dimension which we did not notice before, or which we regarded as individual properties of objects (or their motion), just as animals regard the extension of objects in the third dimension as their motion.

And when we shall see or feel ourselves in the world of four dimensions we shall see that the world of three dimensions does not really exist and has never existed: that it was the creation of our own fantasy, a phantom host, an optical illusion, a delusion — anything one pleases excepting only reality.

And all this is not an "hypothesis," not a supposition, but exact *fact*, just such a fact as the existence of infinity. For positivism to insure its existence it was necessary to annihilate infinity somehow, or at least to call it an "hypothesis" which may or may not be true. Infinity however is not an hypothesis, but a fact, and such a fact is the multi-dimensionality of space and all that it implies, namely, the unreality of everything three-dimensional.

CHAPTER X

Now from the basis of those conclusions already made, let us seek to define how we may discover the real four-dimensional world obscured from us by the illusory three-dimensional world. "See" it we may by two methods: either by sensing it directly, by developing the "space-sense" and other higher faculties, which will be discussed later; or by understanding it mentally by a perception of its possible properties through the exercise of the reason.

By abstract reasoning, we have already come to the conclusion that the fourth dimension of space *must* lie in time, i.e., that time is the fourth dimension of space. We have already discovered psychological proofs of this thesis. Comparing the receptivity of the world by living beings of different grades of consciousness — snail, dog and man — we have seen how different for them are the properties of one *and the same world*; namely, those properties which are expressed for us in the concepts of time and space. We have seen that time and space are sensed by each in a different manner: that what for the lower being (the snail) is *time,* for the being standing one degree higher (the dog) becomes *space,* and that the *time* of this being becomes space to a being standing still higher — man.

This is a confirmation of the supposition previously expressed, that our idea of time is complex in its nature, and that in it are properly included *two ideas* — that of a certain space and that of motion upon this space. Or to put the matter more exactly, the contact with a certain space of which we are not clearly conscious calls forth in us the sensation of motion upon that space; and all this taken together, i.e., the unclear consciousness of a certain space and the sensation of motion upon that space, we call time.

This last confirms the conception that the idea of time has not arisen from the observation of motion existing in nature, but that the very sensation and idea of motion has arisen from a "time-sense" existing in ourselves, which is *an imperfect sense of space*: the fringe, or limit of our space-sense.

The snail feels the line as space, i.e., as something constant. It feels the rest of the world as time, i.e., as something eternally moving. The horse feels the plane as space. It feels the rest of the world as time.

We feel *an infinite sphere* as space; the rest of the world, that which *was* yesterday and that which will be tomorrow, we feel as time.

In other words, every being feels as space that which is grasped by his space-sense: the rest he refers to time; i.e., *the imperfectly felt* is referred to time. Or it is possible to formulate the matter thus: every being feels as space that which, by the aid of his space-sense he is able to *represent to himself* in form, outside of himself; and that which he is not able thus to represent he feels as time, i.e., eternally moving, impermanent, so unstable that it is impossible to imagine it in terms of form.

THE SENSE OF SPACE (SPACE-SENSE) IS THE POWER OF REPRESENTATION BY MEANS OF FORM.

The "infinite sphere" by which we represent the universe to ourselves is constantly and continuously changing: in every consecutive moment *it is not that* which it was before. A constant change of pictures, images, relations, is going on therein. It is for us as it were the screen of a cinematograph upon which the swiftly running images of pictures appear and disappear.

But where are the pictures themselves? Where is the light throwing the image upon the screen? Whence do the pictures come, and whither do they go?

If the "infinite sphere" is the screen of the cinematograph so our consciousness is *the light*, penetrating through our psyche: i.e., through the stores of our impressions (pictures) it (the light) throws upon the screen their images which we call *life*.

But where do the impressions come from to us?

From the same screen.

And herein dwells the most incomprehensible mystery of life as we see it. We are creating it and we are receiving everything from it.

We Must Study the Consciousness

Imagine a man sitting in the ordinary moving-picture theatre. Imagine that he knows nothing of the construction of the cinematograph, nothing of the existence of the lantern *behind his back*, nor of the small transparent picture on the moving film. Let us imagine that he wants to *study* the cinematograph, and begins to study that which proceeds on the screen, to make notes, to take pictures, to observe the order, to calculate, to construct hypotheses, and so forth.

At what will he arrive?

Evidently at nothing at all, unless he will turn his back to the screen, and will begin to study *the cause of the appearance of the pictures upon the screen*. The cause is confined in the lantern (i.e., in consciousness), and in the moving films of pictures (in the psyche). These it is necessary to study, desiring to understand the "cinematograph."

Positive philosophy studies only the screen and the pictures passing upon it. For this reason the eternal enigma remains for it: wherefrom are the pictures coming and where are they going, and *why* are they coming and going instead of remaining eternally the same?

But it is necessary to study the cinematograph beginning with *the source of light*, i.e., with *consciousness*, then to pass on to *the pictures* on the moving film, and only after that to study *the projected image*.

We have established that the animal (the horse, the cat, the dog) must perceive the immobile angles and curves of the third dimension as motion, i.e., as temporal phenomena.

The question arises: do not *we* perceive as motion, i.e., as temporal phenomena, the immobile angles and curves of the fourth dimension? We ordinarily say that our sensations are the moments of the apprehension of certain changes proceeding outside of us; such are sound, light, etc., all "vibrations of the ether." But what are these "changes"? Perhaps in reality there are no changes at all. Perhaps the immobile sides and angles of certain *things* which exist outside of us — of certain things which we know nothing about — only appear to us as motions, i.e., as changes.

It may be that our consciousness, not being able to embrace these things *with the aid of the organs of sense*, and *to represent them to itself in their entirety, just as they are*, and grasping only the separate moments of its contact with them, is constructing the illusion of motion, and conceives that something is moving outside of it (of consciousness), i.e., that the "things" are themselves moving.

If such is the case, then "motion" must be in reality something only "derived," arising in our intellect during its contact with things which it does not grasp in their totality. Let us imagine that we are approaching an unknown city, and that it is slowly "growing up" before us as we approach. It appears to us as if it is really growing up, i.e., as though it did not exist before. There *disappeared* the river, which was visible for so long a time; there *appeared* the bell-tower, which was invisible before.

Such, exactly, is our relation to time, which is a continual coming — arising, as it were, from *nothing* and going into naught.

Every thing lies for us in time, and only *the section of the thing* lies in space. Transferring our consciousness from the section of the thing to those parts of it which lie in time, we receive the illusion of motion *on the part of the thing itself*.

It is possible to formulate the matter thus: the sensation of motion is the consciousness of the transition from space to time, i.e., from a clear space-sense to one that is unclear. With this in mind it is not difficult to realize that we are receiving as sensations, and projecting into the outside world as phenomena, *the immobile angles and curves of the fourth dimension*.

On this account is it not necessary and possible to recognize that the world is immobile and constant, and that it seems to us to be moving and evolving simply because we are looking at it through the narrow slit of our sensuous receptivity?

We are returning again to the question: what is the world and what is consciousness? But now the question concerning the relation of our consciousness to the world is beginning to be formulated for us.

If the world is a *Great Something*, possessing the consciousness of itself, so we are rays of that consciousness which are conscious of themselves, but unconscious of the whole.

If there be no motion, if it be an illusion, then we must search further — whence could this illusion have arisen?

The phenomena of life — biological phenomena — much resemble the transition through our space of certain four-dimensional *circles*, the circles being extremely complicated, every one consisting of a great number of interlaced lines.

The life of a man or of any other living being suggests a complicated circle. It begins always at one point (birth) and ends always at one point (death). We have complete justification for supposing that it is *one and the same point.* The circles are large and small, but they begin and end similarly, and they end at the same point where they began, i.e., at the point of non-existence, from the physico-biological standpoint, or of some existence other than the psychological one.

What is the biological phenomenon, the phenomenon of life? Our science does not answer this question. This is the enigma. In the living organism, in the living cell, in the living protoplasm there is *something* indefinable, differentiating living matter from dead matter. We recognize this *something* only by its functions. The chief of these functions is *the power of self-reproduction* — absent in the dead organism, the dead cell, dead matter.

The living organism multiplies infinitely, incorporating and assimilating dead matter into itself. This ability to reproduce itself and to absorb dead matters with its mechanical laws is the inexplicable function of "life," showing that life is not simply a complex of mechanical forces, as the positivist philosophy attempts to prove.

This thesis, that life is not a complex of mechanical forces, is corroborated also by the *incommensurability* of the phenomena of mechanical motion with the phenomena of life. Life phenomena cannot be expressed in terms of mechanical energy, calories of heat or units of horse power; nor can the phenomena of life be artificially created by the physico-chemical method.

If we shall regard every separate life as a circle of the fourth dimension, this will make clear to us why every circle is inevitably escaping from our space. This happens because the circle inevitably ends in the same point at which it began, and the "life" of the separate being, beginning with birth, must end in death, which is the return to the point of departure. But during its transit through our space, the circle puts forth from itself certain lines, which, uniting with others, yield new circles.

In reality of course all this proceeds quite otherwise: nothing is born and nothing dies; it only so represents itself to us, because we see but the sections of things. In reality, the *circle of life* is only the section of *something*, and that *something* undoubtedly exists before birth, i.e., before the appearance of the circle in our space, and continues to exist after death, i.e., after the disappearance of the circle from the field of our vision.

To our observation *the phenomena of life* are similar to *the phenomena of motion* as these appear to the two-dimensional being; and therefore it may be that this is "the motion in the fourth dimension."

We have seen that the two-dimensional being is bound to regard the properties of the three-dimensionality of solids as motions, and the real motions of solids, going on in the higher space as *the phenomena of life*.

In other words, that motion which *remains* a motion in the higher space appears to the lower being as a phenomenon of life, and that which *disappears* in the higher space, transforming itself into *the property* of an immobile solid, appears to the lower being as mechanical motion.

The phenomena of "life" and the phenomena of "motion" are just as incommensurable for us as are the two kinds of motion in its world for the two-dimensional being; one of these motions being real and the other illusory.

Hinton says of this incommensurability: "There is something in life not included in our conception of mechanical movement. Is this something a four-dimensional movement?

"If we look at it from the broadest point of view there is something striking in the fact that where life comes in there arises an entirely different set of phenomena from those of the inorganic world." *

Upon this basis it is justifiable to assume that those phenomena which we call *the phenomena of life* are movements in higher space. Those phenomena which we call mechanical motion become in turn *the phenomena of life* in a space lower relatively to ours, and in one higher, simply the properties of immobile solids. This means that if we consider three kinds of existence — the two-dimensional, ours, and the higher dimensional — then it will appear that the "motion" which is observed by the two-dimensional being in two-dimensional space, is *for us* a property of immobile solids; "life" as it is apprehended in two-dimensional space, is "motion" as we observe it in our space. Moreover, motions in three-dimensional space, i.e., all our mechanical motions and the manifestations of physico-chemical forces — light, sound, heat, etc., — are only our sensations of some to us incomprehensible properties of four-dimensional solids; and our "phenomena of life" are the motions of solids of higher space which appear to us as the birth, growth, and life of living beings. But if we presuppose a space not of four, but of five dimensions, then in it the "phenomena of life" would probably appear as the properties of *immobile solids* — genus, species, families, peoples, races, and so forth — and motions would seem, perhaps, only *the phenomena of thought*.

* "The Fourth Dimension," p. 77.

Time is Conditional

We know that the phenomena of motion or the manifestations of energy are involved with the expenditure of time, and we see how, with the gradual transcendence of the lower space by the higher, motion disappears, being converted into the properties of immobile solids; i.e., the expenditure of time disappears — and the necessity for time. To the two-dimensional being *time* is necessary for the understanding of the most simple phenomena — an angle, a hill, a ditch. For us time is not necessary for the understanding of such phenomena, but is necessary for the explanation of the phenomena of motion and physical phenomena. In a space still higher, our phenomena of motion and physical phenomena would probably be regarded independently of time, as properties of immobile solids; and biological phenomena — birth, growth, reproduction, death — would be regarded as phenomena of motion.

Thus we see how the idea of time recedes with the expansion of consciousness.

We see its complete conditionality.

We see that by time are designated the characteristics of a space relatively higher than a given space — i.e., the characteristics of the perceptions of a consciousness relatively higher than a given consciousness.

For the one-dimensional being all the indices of two-, three-, four-dimensional space and beyond, lie in time — all this is time. For the two-dimensional being time embraces within itself the indices of three-dimensional space, four-dimensional space, and all spaces beyond. For man, i.e., the three-dimensional being, time contains the indices of four-dimensional space and all spaces beyond.

Therefore, according to the degree of expansion and elevation of the consciousness and the forms of its receptivity the indices of space are augmented and the indices of time are diminished.

In other words, the growth of the space-sense is proceeding at the expense of the time-sense. Or one may say that the time-sense is an imperfect space-sense (i.e., an imperfect power of representation which, being perfected, translates itself into the space-sense, i.e., into the power of representation in forms).

If, taking as a foundation the principles elucidated here, we attempt to represent to ourselves the universe very abstractedly, it is clear that this will be quite other than the universe which we are accustomed to imagine to ourselves. *Everything* will exist in it *always*.

This will be the universe of the *Eternal Now* of Hindu philosophy — a universe in which will be neither *before* nor *after*, in which will be just one present, *known or unknown*.

Tertium Organum

Hinton feels that with the expansion of *the space-sense* our vision of the world will change completely, and he tells about this in his book, *A New Era of Thought*. (p. 66.)

The conception which we shall form of the universe will undoubtedly be as different from our present one, as the Copernican view differs from the more pleasant view of a wide, immovable earth beneath a vast vault. Indeed, any conception of our place in the universe will be more agreeable than the thought of being on a spinning ball, kicked into space without any means of communication with any other inhabitants of the universe.

But what does the world of many dimensions represent in itself — what are these solids of many dimensions the lines and boundaries of which we perceive as motion?

A great power of imagination is necessary to transcend the limits of *our* perceptions and to visualize mentally the world in other categories even for a moment.

Let us imagine some object, say *a book*, outside of time and space. What will this last mean? Were we to take the book out of time and space it would mean that *all books* which have existed, exist now, and will exist, *exist together*, i.e., occupy one and the same place and exist simultaneously, forming as it were *one book* which includes within itself the properties, characteristics and peculiarities of all books possible in the world. When we say simply, *a book*, we have in mind *something* possessing the common characteristic of all books — this is *a concept*. But that *book* about which we are talking now, possesses not only these common characteristics but the individual characteristics of all separate books.

Let us take other things — a table, a house, a tree, a man. Let us imagine them out of time and space. The mind will have to open its doors to *objects* each possessing such an enormous, such an infinite number of signs and characteristics that to comprehend them by means of the reason is absolutely impossible. And if one wants to comprehend them by one's reason one will certainly be forced to dismember these objects somehow, to take them at first in some one sense, from one side, in one section of their being. What is "man" out of space and time? He is all humanity, man as the "species" — *Homo Sapiens*, but at the same time possessing the characteristics, peculiarities and individual earmarks of *all* separate men. This is you, and I, and Julius Caesar and the conspirators who killed him, and the newsboy I pass every day — all kings, all slaves, all saints, all sinners — all taken together, *fused* into one indivisible being

The Eternal Recurrence

of *a man*, like a great living tree in which are bark, wood, and dry twigs; green leaves, flowers and fruit. Is it possible to conceive of and understand such a being by our reason?

The idea of such a "great being" inspired the artist or artists who created *the Sphinx*.

But what is motion? Why do we feel it if it does not exist? About this last, Mabel Collins, a theosophical writer of the first period of modern theosophy, writes very beautifully in her poetical *Story of the Year*.

. . . The entire true meaning of the earthly life consists only in the mutual contact between personalities and in the efforts of growth. Those things which are called events and circumstances and which are regarded as the real contents of life — are in reality only the conditions which make these contacts and this growth possible.

In these words there sounds already quite a new understanding of *the real*. And truly the illusion of motion cannot arise out of nothing. When we are travelling by train, and the trees are running, overtaking one another, we know that this motion is an illusory one, that the trees are immobile, and that the illusion of their motion is created by our own.

As in these particular cases, so also in general as regards all *motion* in the material world, the foundation of which the "positivists" consider to be motion in the finest particles of matter, we, recognizing this motion as an illusory one, will ask: Is not an illusion of this motion created by some motion inside our consciousness?

So it will be.

And having established this, we shall endeavor to define what kind of motion is going on inside our consciousness, i.e., what is moving relatively to what?

H. P. Blavatsky, in her first book, *Isis Unveiled*, touched upon the same question concerning the relation of *life* to *time* and *motion*. She writes:

As our planet revolves every year around the sun and at the same time turns once in every twenty-four hours upon its own axis, thus traversing minor cycles within a larger one, so is the work of the smaller cyclic periods accomplished and recommenced

The revolution of the physical world, according to the ancient doctrine, is attended by a like revolution in the world of intellect — the spiritual evolution of the world proceeding in cycles, like the physical one.

Tertium Organum

Thus we see in history a regular alternation of ebb and flow in the tide of human progress. The great kingdoms and empires of the world, after reaching the culmination of their greatness, descend again in accordance with the same law by which they ascended; till, having reached the lowest point, humanity reasserts itself and mounts up once more, the height of its attainment being, by this law of ascending progression by cycles, somewhat higher than the point from which it had before descended.

The division of the history of mankind into Golden, Silver, Copper and Iron Ages, is not a fiction. We see the same thing in the literature of peoples. An age of great inspiration and unconscious productiveness is invariably followed by an age of criticism and consciousness. The one affords material for the analyzing and critical intellect of the other.

Thus all those great characters who tower like giants in the history of mankind, like Buddha-Siddârtha, and Jesus, in the realm of spiritual, and Alexander the Macedonian and Napoleon the Great, in the realm of physical conquests, were but reflexed images of human types which had existed ten thousand years before, in the preceding decimillennium, reproduced by the mysterious powers controlling the destinies of our world. There is no prominent character in all the annals of sacred or profane history whose prototype we cannot find in the half-fictitious and half-real traditions of bygone religions and mythologies. As the star, glimmering at an immeasurable distance above our heads, in the boundless immensity of the sky, reflects itself in the smooth waters of a lake, so does the imagery of men of the antediluvian ages reflect itself in the periods we can embrace in an historical retrospect.

As above, so below. That which has been will return again. As in heaven, so on earth.

Anything that can be said about the understanding of temporal relations is inevitably extremely vague. This is because our language is absolutely inadequate to the *spatial expression of temporal relations*. We lack the necessary words for it, we have no verbal forms, strictly speaking, for the expression of these relations which are new to us, and some other quite new forms — *not verbal* — are indispensable. The language for the transmission of the new temporal relations must be a language without verbs. *New parts of speech* are necessary, an infinite number of new words. At present, in our human language we can speak about "time" by hints only. Its true essence is *inexpressible* for us.

We should never forget about this inexpressibility. *This is the sign of the truth*, the sign of reality. That which can be expressed, cannot be true.

All systems dealing with the relation of the human soul to time — all ideas of *post-mortem existence, the theory of reincarnation, that of the transmigration of souls, of karma* — are symbols, trying to transmit relations which cannot be expressed *directly* because of the poverty and the weakness of our language. They should not be understood literally any more than it is possible to understand the symbols and allegories of art literally. It is necessary to search for their *hidden meanings*, that which cannot be expressed in words.

The literal understanding of these symbolical forms in certain lines of contemporary literature, and the union with them of ideas of "evolution" and "morals" taken in the most narrow, dualistic meaning, completely disfigures the inner content of these forms, and deprives them of their value and meaning.

CHAPTER XI

SPEAKING generally with regard to the problems propounded in the foregoing chapters — those of time, space, and the higher dimensions — it is impossible not to dwell once more upon the relation of science to these problems. To many persons the relation of "exact science" to these questions which undoubtedly constitute the most important problem now engaging human thought appears highly enigmatical.

If it is important why does not science deal with it? And why, on the contrary, does science repeat the old, contradictory affirmations, pretending not to know or not to notice an entire series of theories and hypotheses advanced?

Science should *be the investigation of the unknown*. Why, therefore, is it not anxious to investigate *this unknown*, which has been in process of revelation for a long time — which soon will cease to be the unknown?

It is possible to answer this question only by acknowledging that unfortunately official, academic science is doing but a small part of what it should be doing in regard to the investigation of the new and unknown. For the most part, it is only teaching that which has already become the commonplace of the independent thinker; or still worse, has already become antiquated and rejected as valueless.

So it is the more pleasant to remark that even in science may sometimes be discerned an aspiration toward the search of new horizons of thought; or, to put it differently, not always and not in all the academic routine, with its obligatory repetition of an endless number of commonplaces, has the love of knowledge and the power of independent thinking been crowded out.

Although timidly and tentatively, science, through its boldest representatives, in the last few decades has after all been touching upon the

A Scientist's Credo

The demand for stability in the household and the brevity of the personal experience in comparison with the evolution of the earth lead men to faith, and create in them an image of the durability of the surrounding order of things not for the present only, but for the future. The pioneers of natural science do not enjoy such a serene point of view, and to this circumstance the natural sciences are indebted for their continuous development. I venture to lift the brilliant and familiar veil and throw open the sanctuaries of scientific thought, now poised upon the summit of two contrasted contemplations of the world.

The steersman of science shall be ceaselessly vigilant, despite the felicity of his voyage; above him shall invariably shine the stars by which he finds his way upon the ocean of the unknown.

At the time in which we are living now the constellations in the skies of our science have changed, and a new star has flashed out, having no equal to itself in brightness.

Persistent scientific investigation has expanded the volume of the knowable to dimensions which could scarcely be imagined only a short time — fifteen or twenty years — ago. Number remains, as before, the lawmaker of nature, but, being capable of representation, it has escaped from that mode of contemplating the world which regarded as possible its representation by mechanical models.

This augmentation of knowledge gives a sufficient number of images for the construction of the world, but they destroy its architecture as that is known to us, and create as it were a new order, extending far, in its free lines, beyond the limits not only of the old visible world, but even beyond the fundamental forms of our thinking.

I have now to lead you to the summits from which open the perspectives that are re-forming the very basis of our understanding of the world.

The ascent to them amid the ruins of classical physics is attended with no small difficulty, and I ask in advance your indulgence and shall exercise all my efforts to simplify and shorten our path as far as possible.

Prof. Oumoff proceeds to picture the evolution of form "from the atom to the electron," from materialistic and mechanistic ideas about the universe to the electro-magnetic theory.

The axioms of mechanics are only fragments, and their application may be compared to the judgment concerning the contents of an entire chapter by means of a single sentence.

Therefore it is not strange that the attempt of the mechanistic explanation of the properties of the electro-magnetic ether by the aid of axioms in which these properties were either denied or one-sidedly predetermined was doomed to failure. . . .

The mechanistic contemplation of the world appeared as one-sided. . . . In the image of the world, unity was not in evidence. The electro-magnetic world could not remain as something quite alien, unrelated to matter. The material mode of contemplating the world, with its fixed formulæ, had no sufficient flexibility to bring about unification through it and its principles. There remained only one way out — to sacrifice one of the worlds — the material, the mechanistic, or the electro-magnetic. It was necessary to find sufficient foundation for decision on the one side or on the other. These were not slow to appear.

The consequent development of physics is a process against matter, which ended with its expulsion. But along with this negative activity has gone the creative work of the reformation of electro-magnetic symbolics; it was forced to became adequate to express the properties of the material world: its atomic structure, inertia, radiation and absorption of energy, electro-magnetic phenomena. . . .

. . . On the horizon of scientific thought was arising the electronic theory of matter.

Through electrical corpuscles was opening the connection between matter and vacuum. . . .

. . . The idea of a special substratum filling the vacuum — ether — became superfluous.

. . . Light and heat are born by the motion of electrons. They are the suns of microcosms.

. . . The universe consists of positive and negative corpuscles, bound by electro-magnetic fields.

Matter disappeared; its variety was replaced by a system of mutually related electric corpuscles and instead of the accustomed material world one deeply different — the electro-magnetic world — is envisaging itself to us. . . .

But the recognition of the electro-magnetic world did not annihilate many unsolved problems and difficulties, and the necessity for a generalizing system was felt.

In our difficult ascent we have reached the point [according to Prof. Oumoff] at which the road divides. One stretches horizontally to that plane which has been pictured, another goes to the high summit which is already visible, and the grade is not steep.

Let us look about us at the point which we have reached. It is very dangerous; not one theory only has suffered wreck there. It is the more dangerous that its subtlety is covered by the mask of simplicity. Its basis is the experimental attempts which gave a negative answer to the researches of careful and skilled experimenters.

Prof. Oumoff shows the contradictions which were the outcome of certain experiments. The necessity to explain these contradictions served as the incentive to the discovery of the unifying principle: this was the *principle of relativity*.

The deductions of Lorentz, which were made in 1909, and which in gen-

Relativity

eral had in view electro-optical phenomena only, gave the impetus to the promulgation by Albert Einstein of a new principle and to its remarkable generalization by the recently deceased Hermann Minkowsky.

We are approaching the summit of modern physics. It is occupied by the principle of relativity, the expression of which is so simple that it is difficult to discern its all-important significance. It asserts that the laws of phenomena in the system of bodies for the observer who is connected with it, will be the same, whether this system is at rest, or is moving uniformly and rectilinearly.

Hence it follows that the observer cannot detect by the aid of the phenomena which are proceeding in the system of bodies with which he is connected, whether this system has a uniform translational motion or not.

Thus we cannot detect from any phenomena proceeding on the earth, its translational motion in space.

The principle of relativity includes the observing intellect within itself, which is a circumstance of extraordinary significance. The intellect is connected with a complex physical instrument — the nervous system. This principle therefore gives directions concerning things proceeding in moving bodies, not only in relation to physical and chemical phenomena, but also in relation to the phenomena of life and therefore to the quests of man. It is remarkable as an example of a thesis, founded upon strictly scientific experiments, in a purely physical region, which erects a bridge between two worlds usually regarded as quite distinct.

Prof. Oumoff gives examples of the explanation of complex phenomena by the aid of the principle of relativity.

He shows further how the most enigmatical problems of life are explained from the standpoint of the electro-magnetic theory and the principle of relativity, and he comes at last to that which is the most interesting to us.

*Time is involved in all spatial measurements.** We cannot define the geometrical form of a solid moving in relation to us; we are always defining its kinematical form. Therefore our spatial measurements are in reality proceeding not in a three-dimensional manifold, i.e., having three dimensions, of height, length and width, like this hall; but in a four-dimensional manifold: the first three dimensions we can represent by the divisions of a tape-measure upon which are marked feet, yards, or some other measure of length; the fourth dimension we will represent by the film of a cinematograph upon which each point corresponds to a new phase of the world's phenomena. The distances between the points of this film are measured by a clock going indifferently with this or that velocity. One observer will measure the distance between two points by a year — another by a hundred years. The transition from one point to another of this film corresponds to our concept of the flow of time. This fourth dimension we will call, therefore, time. The film of a cinematograph can replace the reel of any tape-measure, and contrariwise. The ingenious*

* Italicized by me. P. Ouspensky.

mathematician, Minkowsky, who died too young, proved that all these four dimensions are equivalent. How shall we comprehend this? Persons who arrive in St. Petersburg from Moscow have passed through Tver. They are not at this station (Tver) any longer, but nevertheless it continues to exist. In the same manner, that moment of time corresponding to some event which has already passed — the beginning of life on earth, for example — has not disappeared, it exists still. It is not outlived by the universe, but only by the earth. The place of this event is defined by a certain point in the four-dimensional universe and this point existed, is existing, and will exist; now through it, through this station passed by the earth, passes another wanderer. Time does not flow, any more than space flows. It is we who are flowing, wanderers in a four-dimensional universe. Time is just the same measurement of space as is length, breadth and height. Having changed them in the expression of some law of nature we are returning to the identical law.

These new concepts are embodied by Minkowsky in an elegant mathematical theory; we shall not enter the magnificent temple erected by his genius, from which proceeds this voice:

"In nature all is given: for her the past and future do not exist; she is the eternal present; she has no limits, either of space or of time. Changes are proceeding in individuals and correspond to their displacements upon worldways in a four-dimensional eternal and limitless manifold. These concepts in the region of philosophical thought will produce a revolution considerably greater than that caused by the displacement of the earth from the centre of the universe by Copernicus." From the times of Newton to those of natural science, more brilliant perspectives have never opened up. Is not the power of natural science proclaimed in the transition from the undoubted experimental fact — the impossibility of the absolute motion of the earth — to a problem of the soul! A contemporary philosopher exclaimed in his confusion, "beyond truth and falsehood."

When the cult of a new God is born his word is not perfectly understood; the true meaning only becomes clear after the lapse of time. I think that this is true also as regards the principle of relativity. The elimination of anthropomorphism from scientific conceptions was of enormous service to science. On the same path stands the principle of relativity showing the dependence of our observations on general conditions of phenomena.

The electro-magnetic theory of the world (and the principle of relativity) explains only those phenomena the place of which is defined by that part of the universe which is occupied by matter; the rest of it, which presents itself to our senses as a vacuum remains as yet beyond the reach of science. But at the shores of the material world is changelessly dashing the surf of new energy from that deep ocean empty for our senses, but not for our reason.

Is not this dualism of matter and vacuum the anthropomorphism of science, and the last one? Let us put the fundamental question: What part of the universe is filled by matter? Let us surround our planetary system with a sphere the radius of which is equal to half of the distance from the sun to the nearest stars: the length of this radius is traversed by a light-ray in one and a half years. The volume of this sphere let us take as the volume of the world. Let us now describe, with the sun as a centre, another, lesser sphere with a radius equal to the distance of our sun to the outermost planet. I admit that the matter of our world, collected in one place, will not take more than one-tenth of the volume of the planetary sphere: I think that this figure is considerably exaggerated. After calculations of volume it will appear that in our world the volume occupied by the matter will be related to the volume of the vacuum as the figure 1 to the number represented by the figure 3 with 13 zeros. This relation is equivalent to the relation of one second to one million years.

According to the calculations of Lord Kelvin, the density of matter corresponding to such a relation would be less than the density of water by ten thousand million times, i.e., it would be in an extreme degree of rarefaction. . . .

Prof. Oumoff gives the example of such a number of balls as correspond to the number of seconds in one million years. Upon one of these balls (corresponding to the matter in the universe) is written all that we know, because all that we know is related to matter. And matter is only one ball among millions and millions of "balls of vacuum."

This is his conclusion; says he:

Matter represents a highly improbable fact in the universe. This event came into existence because small probability does not mean impossibility. But where, and in what manner, are realized more probable events? Is it not in the domain of radiant energy?

The theory of probability includes the immense part of the universe — the vacuum — in the world of becoming. We know that radiant energy possesses the preponderating mass. Among the different phenomena in the world of inter-crossing rays, out of elements attracting one another are not the tiny fragments born which by their congregation compose our material world? Is not the vacuum the laboratory matter? The material world corresponds to that limited horizon which is open to a man who has come out into a field. To his senses life is teeming only within the limits of this horizon; outside of it for the senses of man there is only a vacuum.

I do not desire to start a polemic about those thoughts in Prof. Oumoff's address with which I do not agree. Yet I shall mention and enumerate the questions which in my opinion are raised by the incompatibility of certain principles.

The contrast between the *vacuum* and the *material world* sounds almost naïve after the just quoted words of Minkowsky concerning the necessity of a transfer of attention, on the part of science, from purely physical problems to questions of consciousness. Moreover I do not see any fundamental difference between the material, the mechanical, and the electro-magnetic universe. All this is three-dimensional. In the electro-magnetic universe there is as yet no true transition to the fourth dimension. And Prof. Oumoff makes only one clear attempt to bind the electro-magnetic world with the higher dimensions. He says:

That sheet of paper, written in electro-magnetic symbols, with which we covered the vacuum, it is possible to regard as billions of separate superimposed sheets, but of which each one represents the field of one small electric quantity or charge.

But this is all. The rest is just as three-dimensional as the theory of atoms and the ether.

"We are present at the funeral of the old physics," says Prof. Oumoff, and this is true. But the old physics is losing itself and disappears not in the electro-magnetic theory, but in the idea of a new dimension of space which up to the present has been called time and *motion*.

Truly, the *new physics* will be that in which there will be no *motion*, i.e., there will be no dualism of rest and motion, and no dualism of matter and vacuum.

Understanding the universe as *thought* and *consciousness* we completely divorce ourselves from the idea of a vacuum. And from this standpoint is explained *the small probability* of matter to which Prof. Oumoff referred. Matter, i.e., everything *finite*, is an illusion in an infinite world.*

Among many attempts at the psychological investigation of the fourth dimension I shall note one in the book by Johan Van Manen, *Some Occult Experiences*.

In this book is a remarkable drawing of a four-dimensional figure which the author "saw" by means of his inner vision. This interesting experience Van Manen describes in the following way:

When residing and touring in the North of England, several years ago, I talked and lectured several times on the fourth dimension. One day after having retired to bed, I lay fully awake, thinking out some problems connected with this subject. I tried to visualize or think out the shape of a four-dimensional cube, which I imagined to be the simplest four-dimensional shape. To

---

* The works on Relativity by Dr. A. Einstein make possible a more thorough acquaintance with the scientific (physical) treatment of this subject.

my great astonishment I saw plainly before me first a four-dimensional globe and afterwards a four-dimensional cube, and learned only then from this object-lesson that the globe is the simplest body, and not the cube, as the third-dimensional analogy ought to have told me beforehand. The remarkable thing was that the definite endeavor to see the one thing made me see the other. I saw the forms as before me in the air (though the room was dark), and behind the forms I saw clearly a rift in the curtains through which a glimmer of light filtered into the room. This was a case in which I can clearly fix the impression that the objects seen were outside my head. In most of the other cases I could not say so definitely, as they partake of a dual character, being almost equally felt as outside and inside the brain.

I forego the attempt to describe the fourth-dimensional cube as to its form. Mathematical description would be possible, but would at the same time disintegrate the real impression in its totality. The fourth-dimensional globe can be better described. It was an ordinary three-dimensional globe, out of which, on each side, beginning at its vertical circumference, bent, tapering horns proceeded, which, with a circular bend, united their points above the globe from which they started. The effect is best indicated by circumscribing the numeral 8 by a circle. So three circles are formed, the lower one representing the initial globe, the upper one representing empty  space, and the greater circle circumscribing the whole. If it be now understood that the upper circle does not exist and the lower (small) circle is identical with the outer (large) circle, the impression will have been conveyed, at least to some extent.

I have always been easily able to recall this globe; to recall the cube is far more difficult, and I have to concentrate to get it back.

I have in a like manner had rare visions of the fifth- and sixth-dimensional figures. At least I have felt *as if* the figures I saw were fifth- and sixth-dimensional. In these matters the greatest caution is necessary. I am aware that I have come into contact with these things as far as the physical brain allows it, without denying that beyond what the brain has caught there was something further, *felt* at the time, which was not handed on. The sixth-dimensional figure I cannot describe. All I remember of it is that it gave me at the time an impression in *form* of what we might call diversity in unity, or synthesis in differentiation. The fifth-dimensional vision is best described, or rather hinted at, by saying that it looked like an Alpine relief map, with the singularity that all mountain peaks and the whole landscape represented in the map were *one* mountain, or again in other words as if all the mountains had one single base. This was the difference between the fifth and the sixth, that in the fifth the excrescences were in one sense exteriorized and yet rooted

in the same unit; but in the sixth they were differentiated but not exteriorized; they were only *in different ways* identical with the same base, which was
their whole.

C. W. Leadbeater on a note to these remarkable pages says:

Striking as this drawing is, its value lies chiefly in its suggestiveness to
those who have once seen that which it represents. One can hardly hope that
it will convey a clear idea of the reality to those who have never seen it. It is
difficult to get an animal to understand a picture — apparently because he is
incapable of grasping the idea that perspective on a flat surface is intended to
represent objects which he knows only as solid. The average man is in exactly
the same position with regard to any drawing or model which is intended to
suggest to him the idea of the fourth dimension; and so, clever and suggestive
as this is, I doubt whether it will be of much help to the average reader.

The man who has seen the reality might well be helped by this to bring
into his ordinary life a flash of that higher consciousness; and in that case he
might perhaps be able to supply, in his thought, what must necessarily be
lacking in the physical-plane drawing.

For my part, I may say that the true meaning of Van Manen's "vision" is difficult even to appreciate with the means at our disposal. After
seeing the drawing in his book I at once felt and understood all that it
means, but I disagree somewhat with the author in the interpretation of
his drawing. He says:

"We may also call the total impression that of a ring. I think it was
then that I understood for the first time that so-called fourth-dimensional
sight is sight with reference to a space-conception arising from the visual
perception of density."

This remark though very cautious seems to me dangerous, because it
creates the possibility of the same mistake which stopped Hinton in
many things and which I partly repeated in the first edition of the book
*The Fourth Dimension.** This mistake consists in the possibility of the
construction of some *pseudo fourth dimension*, which lies in reality completely in three dimensions. In my opinion *there is very much of motion*
in the figure. The entire figure appears to me *as a moving one*, continuously generating itself, as though it were at the point of contact of the
acute ends, coming from there and involving back there. But I shall not
analyze and comment upon Van Manen's experience now, leaving it to
readers who have had similar experiences.

* One of P. D. Ouspensky's books. *Transl.*

The "Higher" Dimensions

So far as Van Manen's descriptions of his observations of the "fifth" and "sixth" dimensions are concerned, it seems to me that nothing in them warrants the supposition that they are related to any region *higher* or *more complex* than the four-dimensional world. In my opinion all these are just observations of the region of the fourth dimension. But the similarity to the experience of certain mystics is very remarkable in them, especially those of Jacob Boehme. Moreover the method of *object-lesson* is very interesting — i.e., those *two images* which Van Manen saw and from the comparison of which he deduced his conclusions.

CHAPTER XII

THE ORDER of phenomena is defined for us, first, by the method of apprehending them, and second, by the form of the transition of one order of phenomenon into another.

According to our method of apprehending them and by the form of their transition into one another we discern three orders of phenomena:

Physical phenomena (i.e., all phenomena studied by physics and chemistry); *phenomena of life* (all phenomena studied by biology and its subdivisions); *psychic phenomena* (thoughts, feelings, sensations, etc.).

We know physical phenomena by means of our sense organs or by the aid of apparatus. Many recognized physical phenomena are not observed directly; they are merely projections of the assumed causes of our sensations, or those of the causes of other phenomena. Physics recognizes the existence of many phenomena which have never been observed by the sense organs or by means of apparatus (the temperature of absolute zero etc., for example).

The phenomena of life, as such, are not observed directly. We cannot project them as the cause of definite sensations. But certain *groups of sensations* force us to assume in certain groups of physical phenomena the presence of the phenomena of life. It may be said that a certain grouping of physical phenomena forces us to assume the presence of the phenomena of life. We define the cause of the phenomena of life as a something not capable of being grasped by the senses or by apparatus, and incommensurable with the causes of physical sensations. A sign of the

The Psychic and the Physical

presence of the phenomena of life consists in the power of organisms to reproduce themselves, i.e., the multiplication of them in the same forms, the indivisibility of separate units and their especial adaptability, which is not observed outside of life.

Psychic phenomena are the feelings and the thoughts that we know in ourselves by direct sensation. We assume their existence in others (1) *from analogy* with ourselves; (2) from their manifestation in actions and (3) from that which we gather by the aid of speech. But, as has been shown by certain philosophical theories, it is impossible to establish strictly objectively, the presence of consciousness other than our own. A man establishes this usually because of his inner assurance of its truth.

Physical phenomena transform themselves into one another completely. It is possible to *transform* heat into light, pressure into motion, etc. It is possible to produce any physical phenomenon from other physical phenomena; to produce any chemical combination by the synthetic method, combining the composite parts in proper proportions and under proper physical conditions. Modern physics assumes electro-magnetic phenomena as the basis of all physical phenomena. *But physical phenomena do not transform themselves into the phenomena of life.* By no combination of physical conditions can science create life, just as by chemical synthesis it cannot create living matter — protoplasm. We can tell what amount of coal is necessary to generate the certain amount of heat necessary to transform a given quantity of ice into water; but we cannot tell what amount of coal is necessary to create the vital energy with which one living cell forms another living cell. In similar manner physical, chemical and mechanical phenomena cannot themselves produce the phenomena of consciousness, i.e., of thought. Were it otherwise, *a rotating wheel*, after the expenditure of a certain amount of energy, or after the lapse of a certain time, could *generate an idea*. Yet we know perfectly well that the wheel can go on rotating for millions of years, and no single *idea* will be produced by it at all. Thus we see that the phenomena of motion differ in a fundamental way from the phenomena of life and of consciousness.

The phenomena of life change into other phenomena of life, multiply infinitely, and *transform themselves into physical phenomena,* generating whole series of mechanical and chemical combinations. The phenomena of life manifest themselves to us in physical phenomena, and in the existence of such phenomena.

Psychic phenomena are sensed directly, and having enormous potential force, transform themselves into physical phenomena and into manifestations of life. We know that at the basis of our procreative force lies *desire* — that is, a psychical state, or a phenomenon of consciousness. *Desire* is possessed of enormous potential force. Out of the united desire of a man and of a woman, a whole nation may come into being. At the root of the active, constructive, creative force of man, that can change the course of rivers, unite oceans, cut through mountains, lies desire, i.e., again a psychical state, or a phenomenon of consciousness. Thus psychic phenomena possess even greater unifying force with relation to physical phenomena than do the phenomena of life.

Positive philosophy affirms that all three orders of phenomena proceed from one cause *lying within the sphere of the study of physics*. This cause is called by different names at different times, but it is assumed to be identical with physical energy in general.

Seriously analyzing such an affirmation, it is easily seen to be absolutely arbitrary, and not founded upon anything. Physical phenomena of themselves, inside the limits of our existence and observation, never create the phenomena of life and the phenomena of consciousness. Consequently we may with *greater* right assume that in the phenomena of life and in the phenomena of consciousness there is something which does not exist in physical phenomena.

Moreover, we cannot *measure* physical, biological, and psychic phenomena *by the same unit of measurement*. Or more correctly, we cannot measure the phenomena of life and the phenomena of consciousness at all. It is only the phenomena first mentioned, i.e., the physical, that we fancy we can measure, though this is very doubtful, too.

In any case we undoubtedly know that we can express neither the phenomena of life nor psychic phenomena in the formulæ of physical phenomena; and generally speaking we have for them no formulæ at all.

In order to clarify the relation between phenomena of different kinds, let us examine in detail the laws of their transformation one into another.

First of all it is necessary to consider physical phenomena, and make a detailed study of the conditions and properties of their transformation one into another.

In an essay on Wundt (*The Northern Messenger*, 1888) A. L. Volinsky, elucidating the principles of Wundt's physiological psychology, says:

The actions of sensation are provoked by the actions of irritation. But both these actions need not be at all equal. It is possible to burn a whole city by a spark from a cigarette. It is necessary to understand why this is possible. Place a board upon the edge of some object scalewise, so that it will balance. On both ends of the board put now an equal amount of weights. The weights will not fall: although both of them will tend to fall, they balance one another. If we lift the least weight from one end of the board, then the other end will overbalance, and the board will fall — i.e., the force of gravity which existed before as an invisible tendency, will have become a visible motive force. If we put the board and weights on the earth, the force of gravity will not produce any action, but it will not be eliminated: it will only transform itself into other forces.

Those forces which are only *striving* to produce motion are called *constrained*, or *dead*, forces. The forces which are actually manifesting themselves in certain definite actions are called free, or live forces; but as regards free forces it is necessary to differentiate those forces which are liberating, setting free, from the forces which are liberated, or set free.

An enormous difference exists between the *liberation* of a force and its *transformation* into another.

When one kind of motion transforms itself into another kind, the amount of free force remains the same; and contrariwise, when one force *liberates* another, the amount of free force changes. The free force of an irritation liberates the tied-up forces of a nerve. And this liberation of tied-up forces is proceeding at each point of the nerve. The first motion increases like a fire, like a snow-slide carrying along with it new and ever new drifts. It is for this reason that the action (phenomenon) of sensation need not be exactly equal to the action of irritation.

Let us look more broadly at the relation between liberated and liberating forces in the different kinds of phenomena.

We shall discover that sometimes an almost negligible amount of physical force may liberate an enormous, a colossal amount of physical energy. But *all that we can ever assemble of physical force* is powerless *to liberate* a single iota of that vital energy necessary for the independent existence of a single microscopic living organism.

The force contained in *living organisms*, the vital force, is capable of liberating infinitely greater amounts of vital and also of physical energy than the force of motion.

The microscopic living cell is capable of infinite dissemination, to evolve new species, to cover continents with vegetation, to fill the oceans with seaweed, to build islands out of coral, to deposit powerful layers of coal, etc., etc.

Concerning the latent energy contained in *the phenomena of consciousness*, i.e., in thoughts, feelings, desires, we discover that its potentiality is even more immeasurable, more boundless. From personal experience, from observation, from history, we know that ideas, feelings, desires, manifesting themselves, can liberate enormous quantities of energy, and create infinite series of phenomena. An idea can act for centuries and millenniums and only grow and deepen, evoking ever new series of phenomena, liberating ever fresh energy. We know that *thoughts* continue to live and act when even the very name of the man who created them has been converted into a myth, like the names of the founders of ancient religions, the creators of the immortal poetical works of antiquity — heroes, leaders, prophets. Their words are repeated by innumerable lips, their ideas are studied and commented upon. Their preserved works are translated, printed, read, studied, staged, illustrated. And this is done not only with the masterpieces of men of genius, but some single little verse may live millenniums, making hundreds of men work for it, serve it, in order to transmit it further.

Observe how much of potential energy there is in some little verse of Pushkin or Lermontoff. This energy acts not only upon the feelings of men, but by reason of its very existence it acts upon their will. See how vital and immortal are the words, thoughts and feelings of half-mythical Homer — how much of "motion" each word of his, during the time of its existence, has evoked.

Undoubtedly each thought of a poet contains enormous potential force, like the power confined in a piece of coal or in a living cell, but infinitely more subtle, imponderable and potent.

This remarkable correlation of phenomena may be expressed in the following terms: the farther a given phenomenon is from the visible and sensed — from the physical, the farther it is from matter — the more there is in it of hidden force, the greater the quantity of phenomena it can produce, can leave in its wake, the greater amount of energy it can liberate, and so the less it is dependent upon time.

If we would correlate all of the above with the principle of physics that *the amount of energy is constant*, then we must state more exactly that in the preceding discussion nothing has been said of the *creation* of new energy, but of the *liberation* of latent force. And we have found that the liberating force of life and thought is infinitely greater than the liberating force of mechanical motion and of chemical reactions. *The microscopic living cell is more powerful than a volcano — the idea is more powerful than the geological cataclysm.*

"Energy" a Hypothesis

Having established these differences between phenomena, let us endeavor to discover what phenomena themselves represent, taken by themselves, independently of our receptivity and sensation of them.

We at once discover that we know nothing about them.

We know a phenomenon just as much and just as far as it is *irritation*, i.e., to the extent that it provokes sensation.

The positivistic philosophy sees mechanical motion or electro-magnetic energy as the basis of all phenomena. But the hypothesis of vibrating atoms or of *units of energy* — electrons and cycles of motion, combinations of which create different "phenomena" — is only an hypothesis, built upon a perfectly arbitrary and artificial assumption concerning the existence of the world in time and space. Just as soon as we discover that the conditions of time and space are merely the properties of our sensuous receptivity, we absolutely destroy the validity of the hypothesis of "energy" as the foundation of everything; because time and space are necessary for energy, i.e., it is necessary for time and space to be properties of the world and not properties of consciousness.

Thus in reality we know nothing about *the causes of phenomena*.

We do know that some combinations of causes, acting through the organism upon our consciousness, produce the series of sensations which we recognize as *a green tree*. But we do not know if this perception of a tree corresponds to the real substance of the causes which evoked this sensation.

The question concerning the relation of the phenomenon to the *thing-in-itself*, i.e., to the indwelling reality, has been from far back the chief and most difficult concern of philosophy. Can we, studying phenomena, get at the very cause of them, at the very substance of things? Kant has said definitely: No! — by studying phenomena we do not even approach to the understanding of things in themselves. Recognizing the correctness of Kant's view, if we desire to approach to an understanding of things in themselves, we must seek an entirely different method, an utterly different path from that which positive science, which studies *phenomena*, is treading.

CHAPTER XIII

THERE exist visible and hidden causes of phenomena; there exist also visible and hidden effects.

Let us consider some one example.

In all textbooks on the history of literature we are told that in its time Goethe's *Werther* provoked an epidemic of suicides.

What did provoke these suicides?

Let us imagine that some "scientist" appears, who, being interested in the fact of the increase of suicides, begins to study the first edition of *Werther* according to the method of exact, positive science. He weighs the book, measures it by the most precise instruments, notes the number of its pages, makes a chemical analysis of the paper and the ink, counts the number of lines on every page, the number of letters, and even how many times the letter A is repeated, how many times the letter B, and how many times the interrogation mark is used, and so on. In other words he does everything that the pious Mohammedan performs with relation to the Koran of Mohammed, and on the basis of his investigations writes a treatise on the relation of the letter A of the German alphabet to suicide.

Or let us imagine another scientist who studies the history of painting, and deciding to put it on a scientific basis, starts a lengthy series of analyses of the pigment used in the pictures of famous painters in order to discover the causes of the different impressions produced upon the beholder by different pictures.

Imagine a savage studying a watch. Let us admit that he is a wise and crafty savage. He takes the watch apart and counts all its wheels and screws, counts the number of teeth in each gear, finds out its size and thickness. The only thing that he does not know is *what all these things are for*. He does not know that the hand completes the circuit of the dial

Limitations of Positivism

in half of twenty-four hours, i.e., *that it is possible to tell time by means of a watch.*

All this is "positivism."

We are too familiar with "positivistic" methods, and so fail to realize that they end in absurdities and that if we are seeking *to explain the meaning* of anything, they do not lead to the goal at all.

The difficulty is that for the *explanation of the meaning* positivism is of no use. For it nature is a closed book of which it studies the appearance only.

In the matter of the study of the *operations* of nature, the positive methods have achieved much, as is proven by the innumerable successes of modern technics, including the conquest of the air. But everything in the world has its own definite sphere of action. Positivism is very good when it seeks an answer to the question of *how* something operates under given conditions; but when it makes the attempt to get outside of its definite conditions (space, time, causation), or presumes to affirm that nothing exists outside of these given conditions, then it is transcending its own proper sphere.

It is true that the more serious positive thinkers deny the possibility of including in "positive investigation" the question of *why* and *what for*. But as a matter of fact the positive standpoint is not the only possible one. The usual mistake of positivism consists in its not seeing anything *except itself* — it either considers everything as possible to it, or considers as generally impossible much that is entirely possible, *but not for* positive inquiry.

Humanity will never cease to search, however, for answer to the questions *why*, and *wherefore*.

The positivistic scientist finds himself in the presence of nature almost in the position of a savage in a library of rare and valuable books. For a savage a book is *a thing* of definite size and weight. However long he may ask himself what purpose this strange thing serves, he will never discover the truth from its appearance; and *the contents of the book* will remain for him the *incomprehensible noumenon*. In like manner the contents of nature are incomprehensible to the positivistic scientist.

But if a man *knows* of the existence of the contents of the book — the *noumenon* of life — if he knows that a mysterious meaning is hidden under visible phenomena, there is the possibility that in the long run he will discover the contents.

For success in this it is necessary to grasp the *idea* of the inner contents, i.e., the meaning of the thing in itself.

Tertium Organum

The scientist who discovers little tablets with hieroglyphics, or wedge-shaped inscriptions in an unknown language, deciphers and reads them after great labor. And in order to accomplish this he needs only one thing: it is necessary for him to know that these little signs *represent an inscription.* As long as he regards them simply as an ornament, as the outside embellishment of little tablets, or as an accidental tracing without meaning — up to that time their meaning and significance will be closed to him absolutely. But let him only assume the existence of that meaning and the possibility of its comprehension will be already within sight.

No secret cipher exists which cannot be solved without the aid of any key. *But it is necessary to know that it is a cipher.* This is the first and necessary condition. Lacking this it is impossible to accomplish anything.

The idea of the existence of the visible and the hidden sides of life was known to philosophy long ago. *Phenomena* were regarded as only one aspect of the world, and as being infinitely small compared to the hidden aspect — *seeming,* not existing really, arising in consciousness at the moment of its contact with the real world. Another side, *noumena,* was recognized as really existing in itself, but inaccessible for our receptivity.

But there is no greater error than to regard the world as *divided* into phenomena and noumena — to conceive of phenomena and noumena apart from one another, and susceptible of being separately known. This is philosophic illiteracy, which shows itself most clearly in the dualistic *spiritistic* theories. The division into phenomena and noumena exists only in our minds. The "phenomenal world" is simply our incorrect perception of the world.

As Carl DuPrel has said, *"The world beyond is this world, only perceived strangely."* It would be more accurate to say, that *this world is the world beyond perceived strangely.*

Kant's idea is quite correct, that the study of the phenomenal side of the world will not bring us any nearer to the understanding of "things-in-themselves." The "thing-in-itself" — that is the thing as it exists in itself, *independently of us.* The "phenomenon of the thing" — that is the thing in such semblance as we perceive it.

The example of a book in the hands of an illiterate savage shows us quite clearly that it is sufficient not to know about the existence of the noumenon of a thing (the contents of the book in this case) in order that it shall not manifest itself in phenomena. On the other hand,

Man Not a Mechanism

the knowledge of its existence is sufficient to make possible its discovery with the aid of the very phenomena which, without the knowledge of the noumenon, would be perfectly useless.

Just as it is impossible for a savage to attain to an understanding of the nature of a watch by a study of its phenomenal side — the number of wheels, and the number of teeth in each gear — so also for the positivistic scientist, studying the external, *manifesting* side of life, its secret *raison d'être* and the *aim* of separate manifestations will be forever hidden.

To the savage the watch will be an extremely interesting, complicated, but entirely useless toy. Somewhat after this manner a *man* appears to the scientist-materialist — a mechanism infinitely more complex, but equally unknown as regards the purpose for which it exists and the manner of its creation.

We pictured to ourselves how incomprehensible the functions of *a candle* and of *a coin* would be for a plane-man, studying *two similar circles* on his plane. In like manner the functions of a man are incomprehensible to the scientist, studying him as a *mechanism*. The reason for this is clear. It is because the coin and the candle are not *two similar circles*, but two different objects, having an entirely different use and meaning in that world which is relatively higher than the plane — and man is *not a mechanism*, but something having an aim and meaning in the world relatively higher than the visible one.

The functions of a candle and of a coin in our world are for the imaginary plane-man an inaccessible *noumenon*. It is evident that the phenomenon of a circle cannot give any understanding of the function of a candle, and its difference from the function of a coin. But *two-dimensional knowledge* exists not alone on the plane. Materialistic thought tries to apply it to real life. A curious result follows, the true meaning of which is, unhappily, incomprehensible to many people. One of such applications is "the economic man" — this is quite clearly the two-dimensional and flat being moving in two directions — those of production and consumption — i.e., living upon the plane of *production-consumption*. How is it possible to imagine man in general as such an obviously artificial being? And how is it possible to hope to understand the laws of the life of man, with his complex spiritual aspirations and his great impulse to *know*, to understand everything around about him and within himself — by studying the imaginary laws of the imaginary being upon an imaginary plane? The inventors of this theory alone possess the secret of the answer to this question. But the economic theory of human life attracts men as do all simple theories giving a short answer to a series of complicated questions. And we are ourselves too entangled in materialistic theories to see anything beyond them.

Positivistic science does not really deny the theory of phenomena and noumena, it only affirms, in opposition to Kant, that in studying phenomena we are gradually approaching to noumena. The noumena of phenomena science considers to be the motion of atoms and the ether, or the vibrations of electrons; it conceives of the universe as a whirl of mechanical motion or the field of manifestation of electro-magnetic energy taking on the "phenomenal tint" for us on their reception by the organs of sense.

"Positivism" affirms that the phenomena of life and psychic phenomena are simply the functions of physical phenomena, that without physical phenomena the phenomena of life, thought and emotion cannot exist and that they represent only certain complex combinations of the foregoing; and furthermore that all these three kinds of phenomena are one and the same thing in substance — and the *higher*, i.e., the phenomena of life and of consciousness, are only different expressions of the *lower*, i.e., of one and the same physico-mechanical or electro-magnetic energy.

But to all this it is possible to answer one thing. If it were true it would have been proven long ago. Nothing is easier than to prove the energetic hypothesis of life and the psyche. Just *create life and thought* by the mechanical method. Materialism and energetics are those "obvious" theories which *cannot be true without proofs,* because they cannot *not* have proofs if they contain even a little grain of truth.

But there are no proofs at the disposition of these theories; quite the reverse: the infinitely greater potentiality of the phenomena of life and the psyche compared with physical phenomena assures us of the exact opposite.

The simple fact, above shown, of the enormous liberating, unbinding force of psychic phenomena is sufficient to establish quite really and firmly the problem of *the world of the hidden.*

And the world of the hidden cannot be the world of unconscious mechanical motion, of unconscious development of electro-magnetic forces. The positivistic theory admits the possibility of explaining the *higher* through the *lower,* the *invisible* through the *visible.* But it has been shown at the very beginning that this is the explanation of one unknown by another unknown. There is still less justification for explaining the *known* through the *unknown*. Yet that "lower" (matter and motion) through which the positivists strive to explain the "higher" (life and thought) *is itself unknown*. Consequently it is impossible to explain and define anything else in terms of it, while the *higher*, i.e., the *thought*, this is our sole *known*: it is this alone that we do know, that we are conscious of in ourselves, that we can neither mistake nor doubt. And if thought can evoke or *unbind* physical energy, and motion can *never* create or unbind thought (out of a revolving wheel no thought ever arose) so of course we shall strive to define, not the higher in terms of the lower, but the lower in terms of the higher. If the invisible, like *the contents of a book* or *the purpose of a watch*, defines by itself the visible, so also we shall endeavor to understand not the visible, but the invisible.

Starting from a false assumption concerning the *mechanicality* of the noumenal side of nature, positive science, upon which the view of the world of the intelligent majority of contemporary humanity is founded, makes still another mistake in regard to cause and effect, or the law of functions — that is, it mistakes what is cause, and what is effect.

Just as the two-dimensional plane-man thinks of all phenomena touching his consciousness as lying on one plane, so the positivistic method strives to interpret upon one plane all phenomena of different orders, i.e., to interpret all visible phenomena as the effects of antecedent visible phenomena, and as the inevitable cause of subsequent visible phenomena. In other words, it sees in causal and functional interdependence merely phenomena proceeding upon the surface, and studies the visible world, or the phenomena of the visible world, not admitting that causes can enter into this world which are not contained in it or that the phenomena of this world can possess functions extending beyond it.

But this could be true only in case there were no phenomena of life and of thought in the world, or if the phenomena of life and thought were really *derivatives* from physical phenomena, and did not possess infinitely greater latent force than they. Then only should we have the right to consider the chains of phenomena in their physical or visible sequence alone, as positivistic philosophy does. But taking into consideration the phenomena of life and thought we shall inevitably recognize that the chain of phenomena often translates itself from a sequence purely physical to a biological sequence, i.e., one in which there is much of the hidden and invisible to us — or to a psychical sequence where there is even more of the hidden; but during reverse translations from biological and psychical spheres into physical sequences actions proceed often, if not always, from regions which are hidden from us; i.e., the cause of the visible is the invisible. In consequence of this we must admit that it is impossible to consider the chains of sequences in the world of physical phenomena only. When such a sequence touches the life of a man or that of a human society, we perceive clearly that it escapes from the "physical sphere" and returns into it. Regarding the matter from this standpoint we see that, just as in the life of one man and in the life of a society there are many streams, at times appearing on the surface and spouting up in boisterous torrents, and at other times disappearing deep underground, hidden from view, but only waiting for their moment to appear again on the surface, so do we observe in the world continuous chains of phenomena and we perceive how these chains shift from one order of phenomena to another without a break. We observe how the phenomena of consciousness — thoughts, feelings, desires — are accompanied by physiological phenomena — creating them perhaps — and inaugurate a series of purely physical phenomena; and we see how physical phenomena, becoming the object of sensations of sight, hearing, touch, smell and the like, induce physiological phenomena, and then psychological. But looking at life from that side, we see only physical phenomena, and having assured ourselves that it is the only reality we may not notice the others at all. Herein appears the enormous power of suggestion in current ideas. To a sincere positivist any metaphysical argument proving the unreality of matter or energy seems sophistry. It strikes him as a thing unnecessary, disagreeable, hindering a logical train of thought, an assault without aim or meaning on that which in his opinion is firmly established, alone immutable, lying at the foundation of everything. He vexedly fans away from himself all "idealistic" or "mystical" theories as he would a buzzing mosquito.

But the fact is that *thought* and *energy* are different in substance and cannot be *one and the same thing*, because they are different sides of one and the same thing. For if we open the cranium of a living man in order to observe all the vibrations of the cells of the gray matter of the brain, and all the quivering white fibres, *in spite of everything there will be merely motion*, i.e., the manifestation of energy, and thought will remain somewhere beyond the limits of investigation, retreating like a shadow at every approach. The "positivist," when he begins to realize this, feels that the ground is quaking underneath his feet, feels that by his method he will *never* approach to the *thought*. Then he sees clearly the necessity for a new method. *As soon as he begins to think about it* he begins quite unexpectedly to notice things around him which he did not see before. His eyes begin to open to that which he did not wish to see before. The walls which he had erected around himself begin to fall one after another, and behind the falling walls infinite horizons of *possible knowledge,* hitherto undreamed of, unroll before him.

Thereupon he completely alters his view of everything surrounding him. He understands that *the visible* is produced by *the invisible;* and that without understanding the invisible it is impossible to understand the visible. His "positivism" begins to totter and, if he is a man with a bold thought, then in some splendid moment he will perceive those things which he was wont to regard as real and true to be unreal and false, and those things regarded as false to be real and true.

First of all he will see that *manifested* physical phenomena often hide themselves, like a stream that has gone underground. Yet they do not disappear altogether, but continue to exist in latent form in some minds, in someone's memory, in the words or books of someone, just as the future harvest is latent in the seeds. And thereafter they again burst into light; out of this latent state they come into an apparent one, making a roar, reverberation, motion.

We observe such transitions of the invisible into the visible in the personal life of man, in the life of peoples, and in the history of humanity. These chains of events go on continuously, interweaving among themselves, entering one into another, sometimes hidden from our eyes, and sometimes visible.

I find an admirable description of this idea in the chapter on "Karma" in *Light on the Path* by Mabel Collins.*

Consider with me that the individual existence is a rope which stretches from the infinite to the infinite, and has no end and no commencement, neither is it capable of being broken. This rope is formed of innumerable fine threads, which, lying closely together, form its thickness . . . and remember that the threads are living — are like electric wires; more, are like quivering nerves. . . .

But eventually the long strands, the living threads which in their unbroken continuity form the individual, pass out of the shadow into the shine. . . .

This illustration presents but a small portion — a single side of the truth: it is less than a fragment. Yet dwell on it; by its aid you may be led to perceive more. What it is necessary first to understand is not that the future is formed by any separate acts of the present, but that the whole of the future

* Theosophical Publishing Co., London, 1912, pp. 96–98.

is in unbroken continuity with the present, as the present is with the past. In the plane, from one point of view, the illustration of the rope is correct.

The passages quoted show us that the idea of karma, developed in remote antiquity by Hindu philosophy, embodies the idea of the unbroken consecutiveness of phenomena. Each phenomenon, no matter how insignificant, is a link of an infinite and unbroken chain, extending from *the past* into *the future,* passing from one sphere into another, sometimes *manifesting* as physical phenomena, sometimes *hiding* in the phenomena of consciousness.

If we regard karma from the standpoint of our theory of time and space of many dimensions, then *the connection between distant events* will cease to be wonderful and incomprehensible. If events most distant from one another in relation to time *touch one another in the fourth dimension,* this means that they are proceeding simultaneously as cause and effect, and the walls dividing them are just an illusion which our weak intellect cannot conquer. Things are united, not by time, but by an inner connection, an inner correlation. And time cannot separate those things which are inwardly near, following one from another. Certain other properties of these things force us to think of them as being separated by the ocean of time. But we know that this ocean does not exist *in reality* and we begin to understand how and why the events of one millennium can *directly* influence the events of another millennium.

The hidden activity of events becomes comprehensible to us. We understand that the events must become hidden in order to preserve for us the illusion of time.

We know this — know that the events of today were the ideas and feelings of yesterday — and that the events of tomorrow are lying in someone's irritation, in someone's hunger, in someone's suffering, and possibly still more in someone's imagination, in someone's fantasy, in someone's dreams.

We know all this, yet nevertheless our "positive" science obstinately seeks to establish correlations between visible phenomena only, i.e., to regard each visible or physical phenomenon as the effect of some other physical phenomenon *only,* which is also visible.

This tendency to regard everything upon one plane, the unwillingness to recognize anything outside of that plane, horribly narrows our view of life, prevents our grasping it in its entirety — and taken in conjunction with the materialistic attempts to account for *the higher* as a function of *the lower,* appears as the principal impediment to the development of our knowledge, the chief cause of the dissatisfaction with science, the complaints about the bankruptcy of science, and its actual bankruptcy in many of its relations.

The dissatisfaction with science is perfectly well grounded, and the complaints about its insolvency are entirely just, because science has really entered a *cul de sac* out of which there is no escape, and the official recognition of the fact that the direction it has taken is entirely the wrong one, is only a question of time.

We may say — not as an assumption, but as an affirmation — that the world of physical phenomena in itself represents the section, as it were, of another world, existing *right here*, and the events of which are proceeding *right here*, but invisibly to us. There is nothing more miraculous or supernatural than life. Consider the street of a great city, in all its details. An enormous diversity of facts will result. But how much is hidden underneath these facts of that which it is impossible to see at all! What desires, passions, thoughts, greed, covetousness; how much of suffering both petty and great; how much of deceit, falsity; how much of lying; how many invisible threads — sympathies, antipathies, interests — bind this street with the entire world, with all the past and with all the future. If we realize this imaginatively, then it will become clear that it is impossible to study the street *by that which is visible* alone. It is necessary to plunge into the depths. The complex and enormous *phenomena* of the street will not reveal its infinite noumenon, which is bound up both with eternity and with time, with the past and with the future, and with the entire world.

Therefore we have a full right to regard the visible phenomenal world as a section of some other infinitely more complex world, manifesting itself at a given moment in the first one.

And this world of noumena is infinite and incomprehensible for us, just as the three-dimensional world, in all its manifoldness of function, is incomprehensible to the two-dimensional being. The nearest approach to "truth" which is possible for a man is contained in the saying: *everything has an infinite variety of meanings, and to know them all is impossible*. In other words, "truth," as we understand it, i.e., *the finite definition*, is possible only in a finite series of phenomena. In an infinite series it will certainly become its own opposite.

Hegel has given utterance to this last thought: "Every idea, extended into infinity, becomes its own opposite."

In this *change of meaning* is contained the cause of the incomprehensibility to man of the noumenal world. The substance of a thing, i.e., the *thing-in-itself*, contains an infinite quantity of meanings and functions of something which it is impossible to grasp with our mind. And in addition to this it involves a change of meaning of one and the same thing. In one meaning it represents an enormous whole, including within itself a great number of things; in another meaning it is an insignificant part of a great whole. Our mind cannot bind all this into one; therefore, the substance of *a thing* recedes from us according to the measure of our knowledge, just as a shadow flees before us. *Light on the Path* says:

"You will enter the light, but you will never touch the flame."

This means, that *all knowledge* is relative. We can never grasp *all the meanings* of any one thing, because in order to grasp them all, it is necessary for us to grasp *the whole world*, with all the variety of meanings contained in *it*.

The principal difference between the phenomenal and noumenal aspects of the world is contained in the fact that the first one is *always limited*, always finite; it includes those properties of a given thing which we can generally know *as phenomena*: the second, or noumenal aspect, is always unlimited, *always infinite*. And we can never say where the hidden functions and the hidden meanings of a given thing end. Properly speaking, they end nowhere. They may vary infinitely, i.e., may seem various, ever new from some new standpoint, but they cannot utterly vanish, any more than they can cease, come to an end.

All that is highest to which we shall come in the understanding of the meaning, the significance, of *the soul* of any phenomenon, will *again* have another meaning, from another, still higher standpoint, in still broader generalization — *and there is no end to it!* In this is the majesty and the horror of infinity.

Let us also remember that the world as we know it does not represent anything stable. It must change with the slightest change in the forms of our knowledge. Phenomena which appear to us as unrelated can be seen by some other more inclusive consciousness as parts of a single whole. Phenomena which appear to us as similar may reveal themselves as entirely different. Phenomena which appear to us as complete and indivisible, may be in reality exceedingly complex, may include within themselves different elements, having nothing in common. And all these together may be one whole in a category quite incomprehensible to us.

From "the Other Side"

Therefore, beyond our view of things another view is possible — a view, as it were, from another world, from *"over there,"* from "the other side."

Now "over there" does not mean some other place, but a new method of knowledge, a new understanding. And should we regard phenomena not as isolated, but bound together with inter-crossing chains of things and events, we would begin to regard them not *from over here,* but from *over there.*

CHAPTER XIV

IT seems to us that we see something and understand something. But in reality all that proceeds around us we sense only very confusedly, just as a snail senses confusedly the sunlight, the darkness, and the rain.

Sometimes in things we sense confusedly their difference in function, i.e., their *real* difference.

On one occasion I was crossing the Neva with one of my friends, A, with whom I happened to have had many conversations upon the themes touched on in this book. We had been talking, but both fell silent as we approached the fortress, gazing up at its walls and making probably the same reflection. "Right there are also factory chimneys!" said A. Behind the walls of the fortress indeed appeared some brick chimneys blackened by smoke.

On his saying this, I too sensed *the difference between* the chimneys and the prison walls *with unusual clearness* and like an electric shock. I realized *the difference between the very bricks themselves*, and it seemed to me that A realized this difference also.

Later in conversation with A, I recalled this episode, and he told me that not only then, but *always*, he sensed these differences and was deeply convinced of their reality. "Positivism assures itself that a stone is a stone and nothing more," he said, "but any simple woman or child knows perfectly that a stone from the wall of a church and one from a prison wall are different things."

It seems to me also, that in considering a given phenomenon in connection with all the chains of sequences of which it is a link, we shall

Substance and Shadow

see that *the subjective sensation* of the difference between two physically similar objects — which we are accustomed to think of only as poetic expression, *metaphor*, and the reality of which we deny — *is entirely real*; we shall see that these objects are *really different*, just as different as the candle and the coin which appear as similar circles (moving lines) in the two-dimensional world of the plane-man. We shall see that things of the same material constitution but different in their functions are *really different*, and that this difference goes so deep as to *make different* the very material which is physically the same. There are differences in stone, in wood, in iron, in paper, which no chemistry will ever detect: but these differences exist, and there are men who feel and understand them.

The mast of a ship, a gallows, a crucifix at a cross-roads on the steppes — these may be made of the same kind of wood, but in reality they are *different* objects made of *different material*. That which we see, touch, investigate, is nothing more than "the circles on the plane" made by the coin and the candle. They are only the *shadows* of real things, *the substance of which is contained in their function*. The shadow of a sailor, of a hangman, and of an ascetic may be quite similar — it is impossible to distinguish them by their shadows, just as it is impossible to find any difference between the wood of a mast, of a gallows and of a cross by chemical analysis. But they are different men and different objects — their *shadows only* are equal and similar.

And if we take men as we know them — the sailor, the hangman, the ascetic: men who seem to us similar and *equal* — and consider them from the standpoint of their differences in function, we shall see that in reality they are entirely different and that there is nothing in common between them. They are quite different beings, belonging to different categories, to different planes of the world between which there are no bridges, no avenues at all. These men seem to us equal and similar because in most cases we see only the shadows of real facts. The "souls" of these men are actually quite different, different not only in their quality, their magnitude, their "age," as some people like now to put it, but as different *in the very nature, origin and purpose of their existence* as things belonging to entirely different categories can be.

When we shall begin to understand this, the general concept *man* will take on a different meaning.

And this relation holds in the observation of all phenomena. The mast, the gallows, the cross — these are things belonging to such different categories, the atoms of such different objects (known only by their functions), that there cannot be a question of any similarity at all. Our misfortune consists in the fact that we regard the chemical constitution of a thing as its *most real* attribute, while as a matter of fact its true attributes must be sought for in its functions. Could we broaden and deepen our vision of the chains of causation the links of which are forged by our action and our conduct; could we learn to see them not only in their narrow relation to the life of man — *to our personal life* — but in their broad cosmical meaning; could we succeed in finding and establishing a connection between the simple phenomena of our life and the life of the cosmos; then without doubt in these "simplest" phenomena would be unveiled for us an infinity of the new and the unexpected.

For example, in this way we may come to know something entirely new about those simple physical phenomena which we are accustomed to regard as natural and obvious and about which we think we know something. Then, unexpectedly, we may find that we know nothing, that everything heretofore known about them is only an incorrect deduction from incorrect premises. There may be revealed to us something infinitely great and immeasurably important in such phenomena as the expansion and contraction of solids, electrical phenomena, heat, light, sound, the movements of the planets, the coming of day and of night, the change of seasons, a thunderstorm, heat-lightning, etc., etc. Generally speaking, we may find explained in the most unexpected manner the properties of phenomena which we used to accept as given things, as not containing anything within themselves that we could not see and understand.

The constancy, the time, the periodicity or unperiodicity of phenomena may take on quite a new meaning and significance for us. The new and the unexpected may reveal itself in the *transition* of some phenomena into others. Birth, death, the life of a man, his relations with other men; love, enmity, sympathies, antipathies, desires, passions — these may unexpectedly receive illumination by an entirely new light. It is impossible now to imagine the nature of this *newness* which we shall sense in familiar things, and once felt it will be difficult to understand.

But it is really only our inaptitude to feel and understand this "newness" which divides us from it, because we are *living* in it and amidst it. Our senses, however, are too primitive, our concepts are too crude, for that fine differentiation of phenomena which must unfold itself to us in higher space. Our minds, our powers of correlation and association are sufficiently elastic for the grasping of new relations. Therefore, the first emotion at the rising of the curtain on "that world" — i.e., this our world, but free of those limitations under which we usually regard it — must be of *wonderment*, and this wonderment must grow greater and greater according to our better acquaintance with it. And the better we know a certain thing or a certain relation of things — the nearer, the more familiar they are to us — the greater will be our wonder at the new and the unexpected therein revealed.

Desiring to understand the *noumenal world* we must search for *the hidden meaning* in everything. At present we are too heavily enchained by the habit of the positivistic method of searching always for the *visible* cause and the *visible* effect. Under this weight of positivistic habit it is extremely difficult for us to comprehend certain ideas. Among other things we have difficulty in understanding *the reality of the difference* in the noumenal world between objects of our world which are *similar*, but different in function.

But if we desire to approach to an understanding of the noumenal world, we must try with all our might to *notice* all those seeming, "subjective" differences between objects which astonish us sometimes, of which we are often *painfully aware* — those differences expressed in the symbols and metaphors of art which are often revelations of the world of reality. Such differences are the realities of the noumenal world, far more real than all *maya* (illusion) of our phenomena.

We should endeavor to notice these realities and to develop within ourselves the ability to feel them, because exactly in this manner and only by such a method do we put ourselves in contact with the noumenal world or the world of causes.

I find an interesting example of the understanding of the *hidden* meaning of phenomena contained in *The Occult World* in the letter of a Hindu occultist to the author of the book, A. P. Sinnett.

We see a vast difference between the two qualities of two equal amounts of energy expended by two men, of whom one, let us suppose, *is on his way* to his daily quiet work, and another *on his way* to denounce a fellow creature at the police station, while the men of science see none; and we — not they — see a specific difference between the energy in the motion of the wind and that of a revolving wheel.

Every thought of man upon being evolved passes into the inner world, and becomes an active entity by associating itself, coalescing, we might term it, with an elemental — that is to say, with one of the semi-intelligent forces of the kingdom.

Tertium Organum

If we ignore the last part of this quotation for the moment, and consider only the first part, we shall easily see that the "man of science" does not recognize the difference in the quality of the energy spent by two men going, one to his work, and another to denounce someone. For the man of science this difference is negligible: science does not sense it and does not recognize it. But perhaps the difference is much deeper and consists not in the difference between modes of energy but in the difference between *men*, one of whom is able to develop energy of one sort and another that of a different sort. Now we have *a form of knowledge* which senses this difference perfectly, knows and understands it. I am speaking of art. The musician, the painter, the sculptor well understand that it is possible to walk differently — and even impossible not to walk differently: a workman and a spy cannot walk alike.

Better than all *the actor* understands this, or at least he should understand it better.

The poet understands that the mast of a ship, the gallows, and the cross are made of *different wood*. He understands the difference between the stone from a church wall and the stone from a prison wall. He hears "the voices of stones," understands the whisperings of ancient walls, of tumuli, of mountains, rivers, woods and plains. He hears *"the voice of the silence,"* understands the psychological difference between silences, knows that *one silence can differ from another*. And this *poetical* understanding of the world should be developed, strengthened and fortified, because only by its aid do we come in contact with the true world of reality. In the real world, behind phenomena which appear to us similar, often stand noumena so different that only by our blindness is it possible to account for our idea of the similarity of those phenomena.

Through such a false idea the current belief in the similarity and equality of men must have arisen. In reality the difference between a "hangman," a "sailor," and an "ascetic" is not an accidental difference of position, state and heredity, as materialism tries to assure us; nor is it a difference between the stages of one and the same evolution, as theosophy affirms; but it is a deep and IMPASSABLE difference — such as exists between murder, work and prayer — involving entirely different worlds. The representatives of these worlds may seem to us to be similar MEN, only because we see, not them, but their shadows only.

It is necessary to accustom oneself to the thought that this difference is not metaphysical but entirely real, more real than many *visible* differences between things and between phenomena.

All art, in essence, consists of the understanding and representation

Art and the Occult

of these elusive differences. The phenomenal world is merely a means for the artist — just as colors are for the painter, and sounds for the musician — a means for the understanding of the noumenal world and for the expression of that understanding. At the present stage of our development we possess nothing so powerful, as an instrument of knowledge of the world of causes, as art. The mystery of life dwells in the fact that the *noumenon*, i.e., the hidden meaning and the hidden function of a thing, is reflected in its *phenomenon*. A phenomenon is merely the reflection of a noumenon in our sphere. THE PHENOMENON IS THE IMAGE OF THE NOUMENON. It is *possible* to know the noumenon by the phenomenon. But in this field the chemical reagents and spectroscopes can accomplish nothing. Only that fine apparatus which is called *the soul of an artist* can understand and feel the reflection of the noumenon in the phenomenon. In art it is necessary to study "occultism" — the hidden side of life. The artist must be a clairvoyant: he must see that which others do not see; he must be a magician: must possess the power to make others see that which they do not themselves see, but which he does see.

Art sees more and farther than we do. As was said before, we usually see nothing, we merely *feel our way*; therefore we do not notice those differences between things which cannot be expressed in terms of chemistry or physics. But art is *the beginning of vision*; it sees vastly more than the most perfect apparatus can discover; and it senses the infinite invisible facets of that crystal, one facet of which we call man.

The truth is that this earth is the scene of a drama of which we only perceive scattered portions, and in which the greater number of the actors are invisible to us.

Thus says the theosophical writer, Mabel Collins, the author of *Light on the Path*, in a little book, *Illusions*. And this is very true: we *see* only a little.

But art sees farther than merely human sight, and therefore concerning certain sides of life art alone can speak, and has the right to speak.

A remarkable attempt to portray our relation to the "noumenal world" — to that "great life" — is found in Book VII of Plato's *Republic*.*

* "The Dialogues of Plato," Transl. by B. Jowett, Vol. II, pp. 341–345, Chas. Scribner's Sons, N. Y. 1911.

Behold! human beings living in a sort of underground den; they have been there from their childhood, and have their legs and necks chained — the chains are arranged in such a manner as to prevent them from turning round their heads. At a distance above and behind them the light of a fire is blazing, and between the fire and the prisoners there is a raised way; and you will see, if you look, a low wall built along the way, like the screen which mario-nette players have before them, over which they show the puppets. Imagine men passing along the wall carrying vessels, which appear over the wall; also figures of men and animals, made of wood and stone and various materials; and some of the passengers, as you would expect, are talking, and some of them are silent!

That is a strange image, he said, and they are strange prisoners.

Like ourselves, I replied; and they see only their own shadows, or the shadows of one another, which the fire throws on the opposite wall of the cave?

True, he said; how could they see anything but the shadows if they were never allowed to move their heads?

And of the objects which are being carried in like manner they would only see the shadows?

Yes, he said.

And if they were able to talk with one another, would they not suppose that they were naming what was actually before them?

Very true.

And suppose further that the prison had an echo which came from the other side, would they not be sure to fancy that the voice which they heard was that of a passing shadow?

No question, he replied.

There can be no question, I said, that the truth would be to them just nothing but the shadows of the images.

That is certain.

And now look again and see how they are released and cured of their folly. At first, when any one of them is liberated and compelled suddenly to go up and turn his neck around and walk and look at the light, he will suffer sharp pains; the glare will distress him and he will be unable to see the reali-ties of which in his former state he had seen the shadows; and then imagine someone saying to him, that what he saw before was an illusion, but that now he is approaching real being and has a truer sight and vision of more real things, — what will be his reply? And you may further imagine that his in-structor is pointing to the objects as they pass and requiring him to name them, — will he not be in a difficulty? Will he not fancy that the shadows which he formerly saw are truer than the objects which are now shown to him?

Far truer.

And if he is compelled to look at the light, will he not have a pain in his eyes which will make him turn away to take refuge in the object of vision which he can see, and which he will conceive to be clearer than the things which are now being shown to him?

True, he said.

And suppose once more, that he is reluctantly dragged up a steep and rugged ascent, and held fast and forced into the presence of the sun himself, do you not think that he will be pained and irritated, and when he approaches the light he will have his eyes dazzled, and will not be able to see any of the realities which are now affirmed to be the truth?

Not all in a moment, he said.

He will require to get accustomed to the sight of the upper world. And first he will see the shadows best, next the reflections of men and other objects in the water, and then the objects themselves; next he will gaze upon the light of the moon and the stars; and he will see the sky and the stars by night, better than the sun, or the light of the sun, by day?

Certainly.

And at last he will be able to see the sun, and not mere reflections of him in the water, but he will see him as he is in his own proper place, and not in another, and he will contemplate his nature.

Certainly.

And after this he will reason that the sun is he who gives the seasons and the years, and is the guardian of all that is in the visible world, and in a certain way the cause of all things which he and his fellows have been accustomed to behold?

Clearly, he said, he would come to the other first and to this afterwards.

And when he remembered his old habitation, and the wisdom of the den and his fellow-prisoners, do you not suppose that he would felicitate himself on the change, and pity them?

Certainly, he would.

And if they were in the habit of conferring honors on those who were quickest to observe and remember and foretell which of the shadows went before, and which followed after, and which were together, do you think that he would care for such honors and glories, or envy the possessors of them?

Would he not say with Homer, —

"Better to be a poor man, and have a poor master," and endure anything, than to think and live after their manner?

Yes, he said, I think that he would rather suffer anything than live after their manner.

Imagine once more, I said, that such an one coming suddenly out of the sun were to be replaced in his old situation, is he not certain to have his eyes full of darkness?

Very true, he said.

And if there were a contest, and he had to compete in measuring the shadows with the prisoners who have never moved out of the den, during the time that his sight is weak, and before his eyes are steady (and the time which would be needed to acquire this new habit of sight might be very considerable), would he not be ridiculous? Men would say of him that up he went and down he comes without his eyes; and that there was no use in even thinking of ascending: and if anyone tried to loose another and lead him up to the light, let them only catch the offender in the act, and they would put him to death.

No question, he said.

This allegory, I said, you may now append to the previous argument; the prison is the world of sight, the light of the fire is the sun, the ascent and vision of the things above you may truly regard as the upward progress of the soul into the intellectual world.

And you will understand that those who attain to this beatific vision are unwilling to descend to human affairs; but their souls are ever hastening into the upper world in which they desire to dwell. And is there anything surprising in one who passes from divine contemplations to human things, misbehaving himself in a ridiculous manner.

There is nothing surprising in that, he replied.

Any one who has common sense will remember that the bewilderments of the eyes are of two kinds, and arise from two causes, either from coming out of the light or from going into the light, which is true of the mind's eye, quite as much as of the bodily eye; and he who remembers this when he sees the soul of any one whose vision is perplexed and weak, will not be too ready to laugh; he will first ask whether that soul has come out of the brighter life, and is unable to see because unaccustomed to the dark, or having turned from darkness to the day is dazzled by excess of light. And then he will count one happy in his condition and state of being.

CHAPTER XV

THERE is not a single side of life which is not capable of revealing to us an infinity of the new and the unexpected, if we approach it with the *knowledge* that it is not exhausted by its visibility, that beyond this visibility there is a whole "invisible world" — a world of to us new and incomprehensible forces and relations. The *knowledge* of the existence of this invisible world: this is the first key to it.

A wealth of "newness" unfolds to us in the most mysterious sides of our existence, in those sides through which we come into direct contact with *eternity* — in love and in death. In Hindu mythology love and death are the two faces of *one deity. Siva*, god of the creative force of nature, is at the same time the god of violent death, of murder and destruction. His wife is *Parvati*, goddess of beauty, love and happiness, and she is also *Kali* or *Durga* — goddess of evil, of misfortune, of sickness and of death. Together *Siva* and *Kali* are the gods of wisdom, the gods of the knowledge of good and evil.

In the beginning of his book, *The Drama of Love and Death*,* Edward Carpenter very well defines our relation to these deeply incomprehensible and enigmatical sides of existence:

Love and death move through this world of ours like things apart — underrunning it truly, and everywhere present, yet seeming to belong to some other mode of existence.

And further:

These figures, Love and Death, move through the world like closest friends indeed, never far separate, and together dominating it in a kind of triumphant superiority; and yet like bitterest enemies, dogging each other's footsteps, undoing each other's work, fighting for the bodies and souls of mankind.

* Mitchell Kennerly, 1912, New York and London.

Tertium Organum

In these few words is shown the contents of the enigma which confronts us, encompasses us, creates and annihilates us. But man's relation to the two aspects of this enigma is not identical. Strange as it may seem, *the face of death* has ever been more attractive to the mystical imagination of men than *the face of love*. There have always been many attempts to understand and define the hidden meaning of death; all religions, all religious doctrines begin with giving to man this or that idea about death. It is impossible to construct any system of world-contemplation without some definition of death; and there are numerous systems such as contemporary spiritism which consist almost entirely of "views upon death," of doctrines about death and post-mortem existence. (In one of his articles, V. V. Rosanoff * observes that *all religions* consist in substance of teachings about death.)

But the problem of love, in the contemporary way of looking at the world, is regarded as something given, as something already *understood* and known. Different systems contribute little that is enlightening to an understanding of love. So although in reality love is for us the same enigma as is death, yet for some strange reason we think about it less. We seem to have developed certain cut and dried standards in regard to an understanding of love, and men thoughtlessly accept this or that standard. Art, which from its very nature should have much to say on this subject, gives a great deal of attention to love; love ever has been, and perhaps still is, the principal theme of art. But even art chiefly confines itself merely to descriptions and to the psychological analysis of love, seldom touching those infinite and eternal depths which love contains for man.

In reality love is a *cosmic phenomenon*, in which men, humanity, are merely accidents: a cosmic phenomenon which has nothing to do with either the lives or the souls of men, any more than because the sun is shining, by its light men may go about their little affairs, and may utilize it for their own purposes. If men would only understand this, even with a part of their consciousness, a new world would open, and to look on life from all our usual angles would become very strange.

For then they would understand that love is something else, and of quite a different order from the petty phenomena of earthly life.

Perhaps love is a world of strange spirits who at times take up their abode in men, subduing them to themselves, making them tools for the accomplishment of their inscrutable purposes. Perhaps it is some particular region of the inner world wherein the souls of men sometimes

* A Russian journalist and author. *Transl.*

Love not a Material Fact

enter, and where they live according to the laws of that world, while their bodies remain on earth, bound by the laws of earth. Perhaps it is an alchemical work of some Great Master wherein the souls and bodies of men play the rôle of elements out of which is compounded *a philosopher's stone, or an elixir of life,* or some mysterious magnetic force necessary to someone for some incomprehensible purpose.

Love in relation to our life is a deity, sometimes terrible, sometimes benevolent, but never subservient to us, never consenting to serve our purposes. Men strive to subordinate love to themselves, to warp it to the uses of their every-day mode of life, and to their souls' uses; but it is impossible to subordinate love to anything, and it mercilessly revenges itself upon those little mortals who would subordinate God to themselves and make Him serve them. It confuses all their calculations, and forces them to do things which confound themselves, forcing them to serve *itself,* to do what *it* wants.

Mistaken about the *origin* of love, men are mistaken about its *result.* Positivistic and spiritistic morality equally recognize in love only one possible result — children, the propagation of the species. But this objective result, which may or may not be, is in any case an effect of the outer, objective side of love, of the material fact of impregnation. If it is possible to see in love nothing more than this material fact and the desire for it, so be it; but in reality love consists not at all in a material fact, and the results of it — except material ones — may manifest themselves on quite another plane. This other plane, upon which love acts, and the ignored, hidden results of love, are not difficult to understand, even from the strictly positivistic, scientific standpoint.

To science, which studies life from this side, the purpose of love is the continuation of life. More exactly, love is a link in the chain of facts supporting the continuation of life. The force which attracts the two sexes to each other is acting in the interests of the continuation of the species, and is accordingly created by the forms of the continuation of the species. But if we regard love in this way, then it is impossible not to recognize that there is *much more of this force than is necessary.* Herein lies the key to the correct understanding of the true nature of love. There is more of this force than is necessary, infinitely more. In reality only an infinitesimal part of love's force incarnate in humanity is utilized for the purpose of the continuation of the species. But where does the major part of that force go?

We know that nothing can be lost. If energy *exists,* then it must transform itself into something. Now if a merely negligible percentage of energy goes into the creation of the future by begetting, then the remainder must go into the creation of the future also, but in another way. We have in the physical world many cases in which the *direct* function is affected by a very small percentage of the consumed energy, and the greater part is spent without return, as it were. But of course this greater part of energy does not disappear, is not wasted, but accomplishes other results quite different from the direct function.

Take the example of a common candle. It gives light, but it also gives considerably more heat than light. Light is the direct function of a candle, heat the indirect, but we get more heat than light. A candle is a furnace adapted to the purpose of lighting. In order to give light a candle must burn. Combustion is a necessary condition for the receiving of light from a candle; it is impossible to ignore this combustion; but the same combustion gives heat. At first thought it appears that the heat from a candle is spent unproductively; sometimes it is superfluous, unpleasant, annoying; if a room is lighted by candles it will soon grow excessively hot. But the fact remains that light is received *from a candle only because of combustion* — by the development of heat and the incandescence of volatilized gases.

The same thing is true in the case of love. We may say that a merely negligible part of love's energy goes *into posterity*; the greater part is spent by the fathers and mothers on their personal emotions as it were. But this also is necessary. Without this expenditure the principal thing could not be achieved. Only *because* of these at first sight collateral results of love, only because of all this tempest of emotions, feelings, effervescences, desires, thoughts, dreams, fantasies, inner creations; only because of the beauty which it creates, can love fulfil its immediate function.

Moreover — and this perhaps is the most important — the superfluous energy is not wasted at all, but is transformed into other forms of energy, possible to discover. Generally speaking, the significance of the indirect results may very often be of more importance than the significance of direct ones. And since we are able to trace how the energy of love transforms itself into instincts, ideas, creative forces on different planes of life; into symbols of art, song, music, poetry; so can we easily imagine how the same energy may transform itself into a higher order of intuition, into a higher consciousness which will reveal to us a marvelous and mysterious world.

In all living nature (and perhaps also in that which we consider as dead) *love* is the motive force which drives the creative activity in the most diverse directions.

Love a Creative Force

In springtime with the first awakening of love's emotions the birds begin *to sing*, and *build nests*.

Of course a positivist would strive to explain all this very simply: singing acts as an attraction between the females and the males, and so forth. But even a positivist will not be in a position to deny that there is a good deal more of this singing than is necessary for "the continuation of the species." For a positivist, indeed, "singing" is merely "an accident," a "by-product." But in reality it may be that this singing is *the principal function of a given species*, the realization of its existence, the purpose pursued by nature in creating this species; and that this singing is *necessary*, not so much to attract the females, as for some general harmony of nature which we only rarely and imperfectly sense.

Thus in this case we observe that what appears to be a collateral function of love, from the standpoint of the individual, may serve as a principal function of the species.

Furthermore, there are no fledglings as yet: there is even no intimation of them, but "homes" are prepared for them nevertheless. Love inspires this orgy of activity, and instinct directs it, because it is expedient from the standpoint of the species. At the first awakening of love this work begins. One and the same desire creates a new generation and those conditions under which this new generation will live. One and the same desire urges forward creative activity in all directions, brings the pairs together for the birth of a new generation, and makes them *build* and *create* for this same future generation.

We observe the same thing in the world of men: there too love is the creative force. And the creative activity of love does not manifest itself in one direction only, but in many ways. It is indeed probable that by the spur of love, *Eros*, humanity is aroused to the fulfilment of its *principal function*, of which we know nothing, but only at times by glimpses hazily perceive.

But even without reference to the purpose of the existence of humanity, within the limits of the knowable we must recognize that all the creative activity of humanity results from love. *Our* entire world revolves around love as its centre.

Love unfolds in a human being traits of his which he never knew in himself. In love there is much both of the Stone Age and of the Witches' Sabbath. By anything less than love many men cannot be induced to commit a crime, to be guilty of a treason, to reanimate in themselves such feelings as they thought to have killed out long ago. In love is hidden an infinity of egoism, vanity and selfishness. Love is the potent force that tears off all masks, and men who run away from love do so in order that they may preserve their masks.

If creation, *the birth of ideas*, is the light which comes from love, then this light comes from *a great fire*. In this eternally burning fire in which humanity and all the world are being incessantly purified, all the forces of the human spirit and of genius are being evolved and refined; and perhaps indeed, from this same fire or by its aid a new force will arise which shall deliver from the chains of matter all who follow where it leads.

Speaking not figuratively, but literally, it may be said that love, being the most powerful of all emotions, unveils in the soul of man all its qualities patent and latent; and it may also unfold those *new* potencies which even now constitute the object of occultism and mysticism — the development of powers in the human soul so deeply hidden that by the majority of men their very existence is denied.*

In the majority of cases love, as it exists in modern life, has become a trifling away of feelings, of sensations. It is difficult, in the conditions which govern life in the world, to imagine such a love as will not interfere with mystical aspirations. Temples of love and the mystical celebration of love's mysteries exist in reality no longer: there is the "every-day manner of life," and psychological labyrinths from which those who rise a little above the ordinary level can only desire to run away.

For this reason certain fine forms of asceticism are developing quite naturally. This asceticism does not slander love, does not blaspheme against it, does not try to convince itself that love is an abomination from which it is necessary to run away. It is Platonism rather than asceticism. It recognizes that love is the sun, but often does not see its way to live in the sunlight, and so considers it better not to see the sun at all, to divine it in the soul only, rather than receive its light through darkened or smoked glasses.

In general, however, love represents for men too great an enigma; and often the denial of love and asceticism take on strange and unnatural forms, even with persons who are quite sincere, but unable to under-

* In the first Russian edition of this book, in those sketches which took the place of the present chapter, among other things I made the attempt to classify love, and to differentiate between "love" (individualized feeling) and "sexual emotion" (not individualized and undiscriminating in its longing for the satisfaction of the purely physical desire). But it seems to me now that this division, like all similar divisions, is unsatisfactory. *The difference is not in facts but in men.*

On earth there are living two entirely different *races* of men; and the difficulty of making psychological distinctions depends, in great measure, upon the fact that we endeavor to impose on *all men* common characteristics which they do not possess.

Voluptuousness

stand the great *mystical* aspect of love. When one encounters these perversions of love, one involuntarily calls to mind the words of Zarathustra: *

Voluptuousness: unto all hair-shirted despisers of the body, a string and stake; and cursed as "the world" by all *backworldsmen:* for it mocketh and befooleth all erring, misinferring teachers.

Voluptuousness: to the rabble the slow fire at which it is burnt: to all wormy wood, to all stinking rags, the prepared heat and stew furnace.

Voluptuousness: to free hearts, a thing innocent and free, the garden-happiness of the earth, all the future's thanks-overflow to the present.

Voluptuousness: only to the withered a sweet poison: to the lion-willed, however, the great cordial, and the reverently saved wine of wines.

Voluptuousness: the great symbolic happiness of a higher happiness and highest hope. For to many is marriage promised and more than marriage — to many that are more unknown to each other than man and woman — and who hath fully understood *how unknown* to each other are man and woman.

I have dwelt so long on the subject of the understanding of love because it has the most vital significance; because to the majority of men, approaching the threshold of the great mystery, much is closed or opened to them in this way, and because for many this question represents the greatest obstacle.

In love the most important element is *that which is not,* which *absolutely* does not exist from the usual worldly, materialistic point of view.

In this sensing of that which is not, and in the contact through it with the world of the wondrous, i.e., truly real, consists the principal element of love in human life.

It is a well-known psychological fact that in moments of powerful emotion, of great joy or great suffering, everything happening round about a man seems to him *unreal* — a dream. This is the beginning of the soul's awakening. When a man in a dream begins to be conscious of the fact that he is asleep and that what he sees is a dream, then he is waking up; so also the soul, beginning to be conscious of the fact that all visible life is a dream, approaches its awakening. And the more powerful, the brighter the inner emotions are, so much the more quickly will the moment of consciousness of the unreality of life come.

It is very interesting to consider love and men's relation to love in the

* F. Nietzsche, "Thus spake Zarathustra," Boni and Liveright, New York, pp. 195, 196.

light of that method and those analogies which we have already applied to the comparative study of different dimensions.

Again it is necessary to imagine a world of plane beings, observing phenomena entering their plane from another unknowable world (such as the change of the color of lines on a plane, in reality depending upon the rotation through the plane of a wheel with many-colored spokes). The plane beings believe that the phenomena arise within the limits of their plane, from causes also belonging to the same plane, and that they are finished there. Also, all similar phenomena are to them identical, such as two circles which in reality belong to two entirely different objects.

On this foundation they erect their science and their morality. Yet if they would decide to discard their "two-dimensional" psychology and try to understand the true substance of these phenomena, then *with the aid* and by means of these phenomena they could sever their connection with their plane, arise, fly up above it, and discover a great unknown world.

The question of love holds exactly the same place in our life.

Only he who can see considerably beyond *the facts* discerns love's real meaning; and it is possible to illumine these very facts by the light of that which lies behind them.

And he who is able to see beyond the "facts" begins to discern much of "newness" *in love and through love.*

I shall quote in this connection a poem in prose by Edward Carpenter, from the book *Towards Democracy.*

THE OCEAN OF SEX

To hold in continence the great sea, the great ocean of Sex, within one,
With flux and reflux pressing on the bounds of the body, the beloved genitals,
Vibrating, swaying emotional to the star-glint of the eyes of all human beings,
Reflecting Heaven and all Creatures,
How wonderful!

Scarcely a figure, male or female, approaches, but a tremor travels across it.
As when on the cliff which bounds the edge of a pond someone moves, then in the bowels of the water also there is a mirrored movement,
So on the edge of this Ocean.
The glory of the human form, even faintly outlined under the trees or by the shore, convulses it with far reminiscences;
(Yet strong and solid the sea-banks, not lightly overpassed);

Love and Death Linked

Till maybe to the touch, to the approach, to the incantation of the eyes of one,

It bursts forth, uncontrollable.

O wonderful ocean of Sex,

Ocean of millions and millions of tiny seed-like human forms contained (if they be truly contained) within each person,

Mirror of the very universe,

Sacred temple and innermost shrine of each body, Ocean-river flowing ever on through the great trunk and branches of Humanity,

From which after all the individual only springs like a leaf-bud!

Ocean which we so wonderfully contain (if indeed we do not contain thee), and yet who containest us!

Sometimes when I feel and know thee within, and identify myself with thee,

Do I understand that I also am of the dateless brood of Heaven and Eternity.

Returning to that from which I started, the relation between the fundamental laws of our existence, *love* and *death*, the true mutual correlation of which remains enigmatical and incomprehensible to us, I shall merely recall Schopenhauer's words with which he ends his *Counsels and Maxims*.

I should point out how Beginning and End meet together, and how closely and intimately Eros is connected with Death; how Orcus, or Amenthes, as the Egyptians called him, is not only the receiver but the giver of all things . . . Death is the great reservoir of Life. Everything comes from Orcus — everything that is alive now and was once there. Could we but understand the great trick by which that is done, all the world would be clear.*

* Transl. by T. B. Saunders, M. A. Macmillan Co., New York.

CHAPTER XVI

We know what man is only imperfectly; our conceptions regarding him are extremely fallacious and easily create new illusions. First of all, we are inclined to regard man as a certain unity, and to regard the different parts and functions of *man* as being bound together, and dependent upon one another. Moreover, in the physical apparatus, in man visible, we see the cause of all his properties and actions. In reality, man is a very complicated something, and complicated in various meanings of the word. Many sides of the life of a man are not bound together among themselves at all, or are bound only by the fact that they belong to one man; but the life of man goes on simultaneously on different planes, as it were, while the phenomena of one plane only at times and partially touch those of another, and may not themselves touch at all. And the relations of the same man to the various sides of himself and to other men are entirely dissimilar.

Man includes within himself all three of the above-mentioned orders of phenomena, i.e., he represents in himself the combination of physical phenomena with those of life and psychic phenomena. And the mutual relations between these three orders of phenomena are infinitely more complex than we are accustomed to think. Psychic phenomena we feel, sense and are conscious of *in ourselves*; physical phenomena and the phenomena of life we observe and make conclusions about on the basis of experience. We do not sense the psychic phenomena of *others*, i.e., the thoughts, feelings and desires of another man; but the fact that they exist in him we conclude from what he says, and by analogy with ourselves. We know that in ourselves certain actions, certain thoughts, and feelings proceed, and when we observe the same actions in another man, we conclude that he has thought and felt like us. Analogy with ourselves — this is our sole criterion and method of reasoning and drawing conclusions about the psychic life in other men if we cannot communicate with them, or do not wish to believe in what they tell us about themselves.

Suppose that I should live among men without the possibility of communicating with them and having no way to make conclusions based upon analogy; in that case I should be surrounded by moving and acting automatons, the cause, purpose and meaning of whose actions would be perfectly incomprehensible to me. Perhaps I would explain their actions by "molecular motion," perhaps by the "influence of the planets," perhaps by "spiritism," i.e., by the influence of "spirits," possibly by "chance" or by a haphazard combination of causes — but in any case I should not and could not see *the psychic life* in the depth of these men's actions.

Concerning the existence of thought and feeling I can usually only conclude by analogy with myself. I know that certain phenomena are connected in me with my possession of thought and feeling. When I see the same phenomena in another man I conclude that he also possesses thought and feeling. But I cannot convince myself *directly* of the existence of psychic life in another man. Studying man from one side only I should stand in the same position in relation to him as, according to Kant, we stand with relation to the world surrounding us. We know merely the form of our knowledge of it. The *world-in-itself* we do not know.

Thus the psyche, with all its functions and with all its contents — I have two methods — analogy with myself, and intercourse with him by the *exchange of thoughts*. Without this, man is for me a phenomenon merely, a moving automaton.

The noumenon of a man is his psyche together with everything this psyche includes within itself and that with which it unites him.

In "man" are opened to us both worlds, though the noumenal world is open only slightly, because it is cognized by us through the phenomenal.

Noumenal means apprehended by the mind; and the characteristic property of *the things of the noumenal world* is that *they cannot be comprehended by the same method by which the things of the phenomenal world are comprehended*. We may speculate about the things of the noumenal world; we may discover them by a process of reasoning, and by means of analogy; we may feel them, and enter into some sort of communion with them; but we can neither see, hear, touch, weigh, measure them; nor can we photograph them or decompose them into chemical elements or number their vibrations.

Thus, the psyche, with all its functions and with all its contents — thoughts, feelings, desires, will — does not relate itself to the world of phenomena. We cannot know even a single element of the psyche *objectively*. Emotion as such is a thing which it is impossible to see, just as it is impossible to see *the value of a coin*. You can see the stamp upon a coin, but you will never see *its value*. It is just as impossible to photograph thought as it is to imagine "Egyptian darkness" in a vial. To think otherwise, to experiment with the photographing of thought, simply means to be unable to think logically. On a phonographic record are the tracings of the needle, elevations and depressions, but *there is no sound*. He who holds a phonographic record to his ear, hoping *to hear* something, will be sure to listen in vain.

Including within himself *two worlds*, the phenomenal and the noumenal, man gives us the opportunity to understand in what relation these worlds stand to one another everywhere throughout nature. It is necessary however to remember, that defining a noumenon in terms of the psyche, we take but one of its infinity of aspects.

We have already arrived at the conclusion that the *noumenon* of a thing consists in *its function* in another sphere — in its meaning which is incomprehensible in a given section of the world.* Next we came to the conclusion that the number of meanings of one and the same thing in different sections of the world must be infinitely great and infinitely various, that it must become its own opposite, return again to the beginning (from our standpoint), etc., etc., infinitely expanding, contracting again, and so forth.

It is necessary to remember that the noumenon and the phenomenon *are not different things*, but merely different aspects of *one and the same*

---

* The expression "section of the world" is taken as an indicator of the unreality of the forms of each section. The world is infinite, and all forms are infinite, but to grasp them with the finite brain-consciousness, i.e., by consciousness reflected in the brain, we must imagine the infinite forms as being finite, and these are "sections of the world." The world is one, but the number of possible sections is infinite. Let us imagine an apple: it is one, but we may imagine an infinite number of sections in all directions and these sections will differ from one another. If instead of an apple we take a more complicated body, for instance the body of some animal: then the sections taken in different directions will be even more unlike one another.

Man's Psyche is his Function

thing. Thus, each phenomenon is *the finite expression*, in the sphere of our knowledge through the organs of sense, *of something infinite*.

A phenomenon is the three-dimensional expression of a given noumenon.

This three-dimensionality depends upon the three-dimensional forms of our knowledge, i.e., speaking simply, upon our brains, nerves, eyes, and finger-tips.

In "man" we have found that one side of his noumenon is his psychic life, and that therefore in the psyche lies the beginning of the solution of the riddle of the functions and meanings of man which are incomprehensible from an outside point of view. What is the psyche of man if it is not his function — incomprehensible in the three-dimensional section of the world? Truly, if we shall study and observe man by all accessible means, objectively, from without, we shall never discover his psyche and shall never define the function of his consciousness. We must first of all *become aware of* the existence of our own psyche, and then either begin a conversation (by signs, gestures, words) with another man, begin to exchange thoughts with him, and from his answers deduce the conclusion that he possesses the same thing that we do — or come to the conclusion about it from external indications (actions similar to ours in similar circumstances). By the *direct method* of objective investigation, without the help of *speech*, or without the help of conclusions based upon *analogy*, we shall not discover the psyche in another man. That which is inaccessible to the direct method of investigation, *but exists*, is NOUMENAL. Consequently we shall not be in a position to define the functions and meanings of man in another section of the world than that world of Euclidian geometry, solely accessible to the "direct methods of investigation." Therefore we have a perfect right to regard "the psyche of man" as his function in some section of the world different from that *three-dimensional* section wherein "the body of man" functions.

Having established this much we may ask ourselves the question: Have we not the right to make a reverse conclusion, and regard as *a psyche of its own kind* the to us unknown function of the "world" and of "things" outside of their three-dimensional section?

Our usual positivistic view regards psychic life as *a function of the brain*. Without a brain we cannot imagine rationality.

Max Nordau, when he wanted to imagine the world's consciousness (in *Paradoxes*), was obliged to say that we cannot be certain that somewhere in the infinite space of the universe *is not repeated on a grandiose scale the same combination of physical and chemical elements as constitutes our brains.* This is very characteristic and typical of "positive science." Desiring to imagine the "world's consciousness" positivism is first of all forced to imagine *a gigantic brain.* Does not this at once savor of the two-dimensional or plane world? Surely the idea of a gigantic brain somewhere beyond the stars reveals the appalling poverty and impotence of positivistic thought. This thought cannot leave its usual grooves; it has no wings for a soaring flight.

Let us imagine that some curious inhabitant of Europe in the seventeenth century should try to foresee the means of transportation in the twentieth century, and should picture to himself an enormous stage-coach, large as an hotel, harnessed to one thousand horses; he would be pretty near to the truth, but also at the same time infinitely far from it. And yet even in his time some minds which foresaw along correct lines already existed: already the idea of the steam engine had been broached and models were appearing.

The thought expressed by Nordau reminds one of a favorite concept of popular philosophy relating to an accidentally caught idea, that the planets and satellites of the solar system are merely molecules of some tremendous organism, an insignificant part of which that system represents.

"Perhaps the entire universe is located on the tip of the little finger of some great being," says such a philosophizer, "and perhaps our molecules are also worlds." The deuce! Perhaps on my little finger there are several universes too! And such a philosophizer gets frightened. But all such reasonings are merely the gigantic *stage-coach* over again.* This is the way a little girl thought, about whom I was reading, if I mistake not, in *The Theosophical Review.* The girl was sitting near the fireplace, and beside her slept a cat. "Well, the cat is sleeping," the girl reflected, "perhaps she sees in a dream that she is not a cat, but a little girl. And maybe *I am not a little girl at all, but a cat, and only see in a dream that I am a little girl. . . .*" The next moment the house resounds with a violent cry, and the parents of the little girl have a hard time to convince her that she is not a cat but really a little girl.

---

* The incorrectness here is not in the idea itself, but in a literal analogy. The thought itself, that molecules are worlds and worlds are but molecules, deserves attention and study.

Higher and Lower Phenomena

All this shows that it is necessary to philosophize with a certain amount of skill. Our thought is encompassed by many blind alleys, and positivism, always attempting to apply the rule of proportion, is in itself such a blind alley.

Our analysis of phenomena, the relation which we have shown to exist between physical phenomena and those of life and of the psyche, permits us to assert *quite definitely* that psychic phenomena cannot be a function of physical phenomena — or phenomena of a lower order. We established that the higher cannot be a function of the lower. And this division into higher and lower is also based upon the clear fact of the different potentialities of various orders of phenomena — of the different amount of *latent force* contained in them (or liberated by them). And of course we have the right to call those phenomena *the higher* which possess immeasurably greater potentiality, immeasurably more latent force; and to call those *the lower* which possess less potentiality, less latent force.

The phenomena of life are *the higher* in comparison with physical phenomena.

Psychic phenomena are *the higher*, in comparison with the phenomena of life and physical phenomena.

Which must be the function *of which* is clear.

Without making a palpable logical mistake we cannot declare life and the psyche to be dependent functionally upon physical phenomena, i.e., to be a *result* of physical phenomena. The truth is quite the opposite of this: everything forces us to recognize physical phenomena as the result of life, and life (in a biological sense) as the result of some form of psychic life, which is perhaps unknown to us.

But of *which* life, and of *which* psyche? Here lies the question. Of course it would be absurd to regard our planetary sphere as a function of the vegetable and animal life *proceeding upon it* — and the visible stellar universe as a function of the *human* psyche. But nothing of this sort is meant. In the occult understanding of things we speak always of *another* life and *another* psyche, the particular manifestation of which is our life and our psyche. It is important to establish *the general principle* that physical phenomena, being *the lower*, depend upon the phenomena of life and of the psyche, which are *higher*.

If we admit this principle as established, then it is possible to proceed further.

Tertium Organum

The first question which arises is this: In what relation does the psychic life of man stand to his body and his brain?

This question has been answered differently in different times. Psychic life has been regarded as a direct function of the brain (*"Thought is the motion of brain substance"*), thus of course denying any possibility of thought without the existence of a brain. Then followed an attempt to establish *a parallelism* between psychic activity and the activity of the brain. But the nature of this parallelism has always remained obscure. Yes, evidently, the brain works parallel to thinking and feeling: an arrestment or a disorder of the activity of the brain brings as a consequence a visible arrestment or disorder of psychic activity. But after all the activity of the brain is *merely motion,* i.e., an objective phenomenon, whereas the activity of the psyche is a phenomenon objectively undefinable, and at the same time *more powerful* than anything objective. How shall we reconcile all this?

Let us endeavor to consider the activity of the brain and the activity of the psyche from the standpoint of the existence of those two data, the "world" and "consciousness," accepted by us at the very beginning.

If we consider the brain from the standpoint of consciousness, then the brain will be part of the "world," i.e., part of the outer world lying outside of consciousness. Therefore the psyche and the brain are different things. But the psyche, as experience and observation shows, can act only through the brain. The brain is that necessary prism, passing through which, part of the psyche manifests itself to us as *intellect.* Or to put it a little differently, *the brain is a mirror, reflecting psychic life in our three-dimensional section of the world.* This last means that in our three-dimensional section of the world *not all* of the psyche (the true dimensions of which we do not know) is acting, but only so much of it as can be reflected in a brain. It is clear that if the mirror be broken, then the image will be broken too, or if the mirror be injured or imperfect, then the reflection will be blurred or distorted. But there is absolutely no reason to believe that when the mirror is broken the object which it reflects is thereby destroyed, i.e., *psychic life* in the given case.

The psyche cannot suffer from any disorder of the brain, but *the manifestations* of it may suffer very much or may even disappear from the field of our observation altogether. Therefore it is clear that a disorder in the activity of the brain causes an enfeeblement or a distortion, or even a complete disappearance of the psychic faculties manifesting in our sphere.

The idea of the comparison between a three-dimensional body and a four-dimensional one enables us to affirm that not all the psychic activity goes through the brain, but a part of it only.*

Each of us is in reality an abiding physical entity far more extensive than he knows — an individuality which can never express itself completely through any corporeal manifestation. The self manifests through the organism; but there is always some part of the self unmanifested.†

The "positivist" will remain unconvinced. He will say: prove to me that thought can act without a brain, then I will believe it.

I shall answer him by the question: WHAT, in the given case, will constitute a proof?

There are no proofs and there can not be any. The existence of the psyche *without a brain* (without a body), if that be possible, is for us a fact which cannot *be proven* like a physical fact.

And if my opponent will reason sincerely, then he will be convinced there can be no proof, because *he himself has no means of being convinced of the existence of a psyche acting independently of a brain.* Let us assume that the thought of a *dead* man (i.e., of a man whose brain has ceased to act) continues to function. How can we convince ourselves of this? *By no possible means whatever.* We have means of communication (speech, writing) with beings which are in conditions similar to our own — i.e., acting through brains; concerning the existence of the psyche of *those same* beings we can conclude by analogy with ourselves; but concerning the existence of the psychic life of other beings, *whether they do or they do not exist is immaterial,* we can not by ordinary means convince ourselves *that they exist.*

It is exactly this that gives us a key to the understanding of the true relation of psychic life to the brain. Our psyche being a reflection from the brain, we can observe only those reflections which are similar to itself. We have before established that we can make conclusions concerning the psychic life of other beings from the *exchange of thoughts with them* and

* Frederick Myers, "Essay on the Subliminal Consciousness," as quoted in William James' "The Varieties of Religious Experience," Longmans, Green & Co., New York, p. 512.

† In all the above it would be more correct to substitute for the word *brain* the word *body* — organism. The present trend of scientific psychology leads to an understanding of the psychic importance of diverse physiological functions, previously unknown and even now but little investigated. The psychic life is connected not with the brain only, but with the entire body, all its organs, all its tissues. The study of the activity of glands, and of many other things with which science is now concerning itself, shows that the brain is by no means the only conductor of the psychic activity of man.

from analogies with ourselves. Now we may add to this, that *for this very reason we can know only* about the existence of psychic lives *similar to our own*, and we can know any other at all, whether they exist or not, *unless we ourselves enter their plane*.

Should we ever realize our psychic life, not only as it is reflected from a brain, but in a condition more universal, simultaneously with this the possibility would open up of discovering beings with a psychic life independent of the brain analogical to ourselves, if such exist in nature.

But do such beings exist or not? How can we gain information on this point with our thought *such as it is now?*

Observing the world from our standpoint, we perceive in it actions proceeding from rational conscious causes, such as the work of a man seems to us; and other actions proceeding from the unconscious blind forces of nature, such as the movement of waves, the ebbing and flowing of the tide, the descent of great rivers, etc., etc.

In such a division of observed actions into rational and mechanical there is something naïve, even from the positivistic standpoint. For if we have learned anything from the study of nature, if the positivistic method has given us anything at all, then it is the assurance of the necessity for the *uniformity* of phenomena. We know, and with great certainty, that things basically similar cannot proceed from dissimilar causes. Our scientific philosophy knows this too. Therefore it also regards the foregoing division as naïve, and conscious of the impossibility of such dualism — that one part of observed phenomena proceeds from rational and conscious causes and another part from unreasoned and unconscious ones — positivistic philosophy finds it possible to explain *everything* as proceeding from mechanical causes.

Scientific observation holds that the seeming rationality of human actions is an illusion and a self-deception. Man is a toy in the hands of elemental forces. He is merely a transforming station of forces. All that which as it seems to him, *he is doing,* is in reality done instead by external forces which enter him through air, food, sunlight. Man does not perform a single action by himself. He is merely a prism in which a line of action is refracted in a certain manner. But just as the beam of light does not proceed from the prism, so action does not proceed from the reason of man.

The "theoretical experiment" of certain German psycho-physiologists is usually advanced in confirmation of this. They affirmed that if it were possible, from the time of his birth, to deprive a man of ALL EXTERNAL IMPRESSIONS: light, sound, touch, heat, cold, etc., and at the same time preserve him alive, then such a man would not be able to perform EVEN THE MOST INSIGNIFICANT ACTION.

From this it follows that man is an automaton, like that *automaton* projected by the American inventor Tesla, which, obeying electric currents and vibrations coming from a great distance without wires, was calculated to execute a whole series of complicated movements.

It follows from this that *all the actions of a man* depend upon outer impulses. For the smallest reflex, outer irritation is necessary. For more complex action a whole series of preceding complex irritations is necessary. Sometimes between the irritation and the action a considerable time elapses, and a man does not feel any connection between the two. Therefore he regards his actions as voluntary, though in reality there are no voluntary actions at all — man cannot do anything by himself, just as a stone cannot jump voluntarily: it is necessary that something should throw it up. Man needs something to give him an impulse, and then he will develop exactly as much force as such an impulse (and all preceding impulses) put into him and no trifle more. Such is the teaching of positivism.

From the STANDPOINT OF LOGIC such a theory is more correct than the theory of two classes of actions — REASONED AND UNREASONED. It at least establishes the principle of NECESSARY UNIFORMITY. It is really impossible to suppose that in an immense machine certain parts move according to their own desire and reasoning; there must be something uniform — either all parts of the machine possess a consciousness of their function and act according to this consciousness, or all are worked from one motor and are driven by one transmission. The enormous service performed by positivism is that it established this principle of uniformity. It is left to us to define in what this uniformity consists.

The positivistic hypothesis of the world considers that the basis of *everything* is unconscious *energy*, which arose from unknown causes at a time that is not known. This energy, after it has passed through a whole series of invisible electro-magnetic and physico-chemical processes, is expressed for us in visible and sensed motion, then in growth, i.e., in the phenomena of life, and at last in psychic phenomena.

This view has been already investigated and the conclusion reached that it is impossible to regard physical phenomena as the cause of PSYCHIC PHENOMENA, while on the other hand, psychic phenomena serve as an undoubted cause for a great number of the physical phenomena observed by us. The observed process of origination of psychic phenomena under the influence of outside mechanical impulses does not at all mean that physical phenomena create psychic phenomena. Such do not constitute the cause, but are merely a shock, disturbing the balance. In order that outer shocks may evoke psychic phenomena an organism is necessary, i.e., a complex and animated life. The cause of psychic life lies in the organism, its animatedness, which can be defined as a potential of psychic life.

Then, from the very essence of the idea of motion — which is the foundation of the physico-mechanical world — was deduced the conclusion that motion is not an entirely obvious truth, that the idea of motion arose in us because of the limitation and incompleteness of our sense of space (a slit through which we observe the world). And it was established, not that the idea of time is deduced from the observation of motion, but that the idea of motion results from our "time-sense" — and that the idea of motion is quite definitely *the function of the "time-sense,"* which in itself is a limit or boundary of the space-sense belonging to a being of a given psyche. It was also established that the idea of motion could arise out of a comparison between two different fields of consciousness. And in general, all analysis of the fundamental categories of our knowledge of the world — space and time — showed that we have absolutely no data whatever for accepting motion as the fundamental principle of the world.

And if this is so — if it is impossible to assume behind the scenes of the creation of the world the presence of an unconscious mechanical motor — then it is necessary to consider the world as living and rational. Because one or the other of two things must be true: either it is mechanical and dead — "accidental" — or it is living and animated. There can be nothing dead in living nature and there can be nothing living in dead nature.

Nature exhibits a continual progress, starting from the mechanical and chemical activity of the inorganic world, proceeding to the vegetable, with its dull enjoyment of self, from that to the animal world, where intelligence and consciousness began at first very weak, and only after many intermediate stages attaining its last great development in man, whose intellect is nature's crowning point, the goal of all her efforts, the most perfect and difficult of all her works.

So writes Schopenhauer in his *Counsels and Maxims*, and indeed it is very effectively expressed, but we have no foundation whatsoever for regarding man as *the summit* of that which nature has created. This is only THE HIGHEST THAT WE KNOW.

Dualism Self-annihilated

Positivism would be absolutely correct in its picture of the world, there would not be even one deficiency, *if there were no reason in the world, anywhere or at any time.* Then it would be necessary, *nolens volens*, to regard the universe as *an accidentally self-created mechanical toy in space.* But the fact of the existence of psychic life "spoils all the statistics." It is impossible to exclude it.

We are either forced to admit the existence of two principles — "spirit" and "matter" — or to select one of them.

Then dualism annihilates itself, because if we admit the separate existence of spirit and matter, and reason further on this basis, it will be inevitably necessary to conclude, either that spirit is unreal and matter real; or that matter is unreal and spirit real — i.e., either that spirit is material or that matter is spiritual. Consequently it is necessary to select some one thing — spirit or matter.

But to think really MONISTICALLY is considerably more difficult than it seems. I have met many men who have called themselves "monists," and sincerely considered themselves as such, but in reality they never departed from the most naive dualism, and no spark of understanding of the world's unity ever flashed upon them.

Positivism, regarding "motion" or "energy" as the basis of everything, can never be "monistic." It is impossible to annihilate the fact of psychic life. If it were possible not to take this fact into consideration at all, then everything would be splendid, and the universe could be something like an accidentally self-created mechanical toy. But to its sorrow, positivism cannot deny the existence of the psyche. It can only try to degrade it as low as possible, calling it the *reflection* of reality, the substance of which consists of motion.

But how deal with the fact that the "reflection" possesses in this case an infinitely greater potentiality than the "reality"? How can this be? From what does this reality reflect, or what is it refracted in, that in its reflected state it possesses infinitely greater potentiality than in its original state?

The consistent "materialist-monist" will be forced to say that "reality" reflects from itself, i.e., "one motion" reflects from another motion. But this is merely dialectics, and fails to make clear the nature of psychic life, for it is *something other* than motion.

No matter how hard we may try to define thought in terms of *motion*, we nevertheless know that they are *two different things*, different as regards our receptivity of them, belonging to different worlds, incommensurable, capable of existing simultaneously. Moreover, thought can exist without *motion*, but motion cannot exist without thought, because out of the psyche comes the necessary condition of motion — time: no psychic life — no time, as it exists for us; no time — no motion.

We cannot escape this fact, and *thinking logically*, we must inevitably recognize *two principles*. But if we begin to consider the very recognition of two principles as *illogical*, then we must recognize THOUGHT *as a single principle*, and *motion* as AN ILLUSION OF THOUGHT.

But what does this mean? It means that there can be no "monistic materialism." Materialism can be *only* dualistic, i.e., it must recognize *two principles*: motion and thought.

Here a new difficulty arises.

Our concepts are limited by language. Our language is *deeply* dualistic. This is indeed a terrible obstacle. I showed previously how language retards our thought, making it impossible to express the relations of a *being* universe. In our language only *an eternally becoming* universe exists. The "Eternal Now" cannot be expressed in language.

Thus our language pictures to us beforehand a false universe — *dual*, when in reality it is *one*; and *eternally becoming* when it is in reality *eternally being*.

And if we come to realize the degree to which our language falsifies the real view of the world, then the understanding of this fact will enable us to see that it is not only difficult, but even *absolutely impossible* to express in language the correct relation of the things of the real world.

This difficulty can be conquered only by the formation of new concepts and by extended analogies.

Later on the principles and methods of this expansion of what we already have, and what we can extract from our stores of knowledge will be made clear. For the present it is only important to establish one thing — THE NECESSITY FOR UNIFORMITY: the monism of the universe.

As a matter of *principle* it is not important which one we regard as *first cause*, spirit or matter. It is essential to recognize their unity.

— *But what then is matter?*

From one point of view, it is a *logical concept*, i.e., a form of *thinking*. Nobody ever saw *matter*, nor will he ever — it is possible only to *think* matter. From another point of view it is an illusion accepted for reality. Even more truly, it is the incorrectly perceived form of that which exists in reality. Matter is a section of *something*; a non-existent, imaginary section. But that of which matter is a section, exists. This is the real, *four-dimensional* world.

Wood, the substance from which this table (for example) is made, exists; but the true nature of its existence we do not know. All that we know about it is just the form of our receptivity of it. And if we should cease to exist, it would continue to exist, but only for a receptivity acting similarly to ours. But *in itself* this substance exists in some other way — how, *we do not know*. Certainly not in space and time, for we ourselves impose these forms upon it. Probably *all similar wood*, of different centuries, and different parts of the world, constitutes one mass — one body — perhaps *one being*. Certainly that substance (or that part of it) of which this table is made, has no *separate existence apart from our receptivity*. We fail to understand that a particular *thing* is merely an artificial *definition* by our senses, of some indefinable cause infinitely surpassing that *thing*.

But a thing may acquire its own individual and unique soul; and in that case the thing exists quite independently of our receptivity. Many things possess such souls, *especially old things* — old houses, old books, works of art, etc.

But what ground have we for thinking that there is psychic life in the world other than our human one, that of animals and of plants?

First of all, of course, the thought that everything in the world is alive and animated and that manifestations of life and animatedness would naturally exist on all planes and in all forms. But we can discern the psychic life only in forms analogous to ours.

The question stands in this way: how could we know about the existence of the psychic life of other sections of the world if they exist?

By two methods: through COMMUNICATION, EXCHANGE OF THOUGHTS, and through CONCLUSIONS BY ANALOGY.

For the first, it is necessary that our psyche should become similar to theirs, should transcend the limits of the three-dimensional world, i.e., it is necessary to change the form of receptivity and perception.

The second may result as a consequence of the *gradual* expansion of the faculty of drawing inferences by analogy. By trying to think out of the usual categories, by trying to look at things and at ourselves from a new angle and simultaneously from many sides, by trying to liberate our thinking from its accustomed categories of perception in space and time, little by little we begin to notice analogies between things which we did not notice before. Our mind grows, and with it grows the power to discover analogies. This ability, with each new step attained, expands and enriches the mind. Each minute we advance more rapidly, each new step makes the next more easy. Our psyche becomes *different*. Then, applying to ourselves this expanded ability to construct analogies, and looking about we suddenly perceive all around ourselves a psychic life the existence of which we were previously unaware. And we understand the reason for this unawareness: this psychic life belongs to another plane, and not to that to which our psychic life is native. Thus in this case *the ability to discover new analogies* is the beginning of changes, which translate us into another plane of existence.

The thought of a man begins to penetrate into the world of *noumena*, which is in affinity with it. Then his point of view changes likewise with regard to the things and events of the *phenomenal world*. Phenomena may suddenly assume, to his eyes, quite a different grouping. As already said, *similar* things may be *different* from one another in reality, different things may be similar; quite separate, disconnected things may be part of one great whole, *of some entirely new category*; and things which appear inextricably united in one, constituting one whole, may in reality be manifestations of *different* beings having nothing in common among themselves, even knowing nothing whatever about the existence of one another. *Such* indeed may be any *whole* of our world — man, animal, planet, planetary system — i.e., consisting of different psychic lives, a battlefield as it were of warring entities.

In each *whole* of our world we perceive a multitude of *opposing* tendencies, aspirations, efforts. Each aggregate is as it were an arena of struggle for multitudes of *opposing* forces, each of which acts *by itself*, is directed *to its own goal*, usually to the disruption of the whole. But the *interaction* of these forces represents the life of the whole; and in everything *something* is always acting which limits the activity of separate tendencies. This *something* is the psychic life of the whole. We cannot establish the existence of *such a life* by analogy with ourselves, or by intercourse with it, or by exchange of thoughts, but *a new path* opens before us. We perceive a certain separate and quite definite function (the preservation of *the whole*). Behind this function we infer a certain separate *something*. A separate something having a definite function is impossible without a separate psychic life. If *the whole* possesses its own psychic life then the separate tendencies or forces must also possess a psychic life of their own. A body or organism is the point of intersection of such lines of forces, a place of meeting, perhaps *a battle-field*. Our "I" is also that *battlefield* on which this or that emotion, this or that habit or inclination gains an advantage, subjecting to itself all of the rest at every given moment, and indentifying itself with the I. Our I is *a being*, having *its own* life, imperfectly conscious of that of which it itself consists, and identifying itself with this or another portion of itself. Have we any warrant for supposing that the organs and members of a body, *thoughts* and *emotions*, are BEINGS also? We have, because we know that there exists *nothing* purely mechanical; and any something, having *a separate function*, MUST BE *animated* and can be called *a being*.

All the beings assumed by us to exist *in the world of many dimensions*, cannot know one another, i.e., cannot know that we are binding them together in different wholes in our phenomenal world, just as in general they cannot know our phenomenal world and its relations. But they must know *themselves*, although it is impossible for us to define the degree of clearness of this consciousness. It may be clearer than ours, and it may be more vague — dreamlike, as it were. Between these beings there may be a continuous but imperfectly perceived *exchange of thoughts*, analogous to the exchange of substance in a living organism. They may experience certain *feelings* in common, certain *thoughts* may arise in them spontaneously as it were, under the influence of general causes. Upon the lines of this inner communion they must divide themselves into different *wholes* of some categories to us entirely incomprehensible, or only guessed at. The essence of each such separate being must consist in its *knowledge* of itself, and its nearest functions and relations; it must feel things analogous to itself, and must have the faculty of telling about itself and them, i.e., this consciousness must always behold *a picture of itself* and its conditioning relations. It is eternally studying this picture and instantly communicating it to another being coming into communion with it.

Whether these consciousnesses in sections of the world other than ours exist or not, we, under *the existing conditions of our receptivity*, cannot say. They can be sensed only by the changed psyche. Our usual receptivity and thinking are too absorbed by the sensations of the phenomenal world, and by themselves, and therefore do not reflect impressions coming to them from other beings, or reflect them so weakly that they are not fixed there in any intelligible form. Moreover we do not recognize the fact that we are in constant communion with the *noumena* of all surrounding things, near and remote, with beings like ourselves and others entirely different, with the life of everything in the world and of all the world. But if the impressions coming from other beings are so forceful that the consciousness feels them, then our mind immediately projects them into the outer world of phenomena and seeks for their cause in the phenomenal world, exactly in the same manner that a two-dimensional being, inhabiting a plane, seeks in its plane for the cause of the impressions which come from a higher world.

Our psyche is limited by its phenomenal receptivity, i.e., it is surrounded by itself. The world of phenomena, i.e., the form of its own perception, surrounds it as a ring, or as a wall, and it sees nothing save this wall.

But if the psyche succeeds in escaping out of this limiting circle, it will invariably see much that is new in the world.

If we will separate self-elements in our perception, writes Hinton [A New Era of Thought, pp. 36, 37], then it will be found that the deadness which we ascribe to the external world is not really there, but is put in by us because of our own limitations. It is really the self-elements in our knowledge which make us talk of mechanical necessity, dead matter. When our limitations fall, we behold the spirit of the world as we behold the spirit of a friend — something which is discerned in and through the material presentation of a body to us.

Our thought means are sufficient at present to show us human souls; but all except human beings is, as far as science is concerned, inanimate. Our self-element must be got rid of from our perception, and this will be changed.

But is the unknowableness of the noumenal world as absolute for us as it sometimes seems?

In *The Critique of Pure Reason* and in other writings, Kant denied the possibility of "spiritual sight." But in *Dreams of a Ghost-seer* he not only admitted this possibility, but gave to it one of the best definitions which we have ever had up to now. He clearly affirms:

I confess that I am very much inclined to assert the existence of immaterial natures in the world, and to put my soul itself into that class of beings. These immaterial beings . . . are immediately united with each other, they might form, perhaps, a great whole which might be called the immaterial world. Every man is a being of two worlds: of the incorporeal world and of the material world . . . and *it will be proved* I don't know where or when, that the human soul also in this life forms an indissoluble communion with all immaterial natures of the spirit-world, that, alternately, it acts upon and receives impressions from that world of which nevertheless it is not conscious while it is still man and as long as everything is in proper condition . . .

We should, therefore, have to regard the human soul as being conjoined in its present life with two worlds at the same time, of which it clearly perceives only the material world, in so far as it is conjoined with a body, and thus forms a personal unit. . . .

It is therefore, indeed, one subject, which is thus at the same time a member of the visible and of the invisible world, but not one and the same person; for on account of their different quality, the conceptions of the one world are not ideas associated with those of the other world; thus, what I think as a spirit, is not remembered by me as a man, and, conversely, my state as a man does not at all enter into the conception of myself as a spirit.

Birth, life, death are the states of soul only . . . Consequently, our body only is perishable, the essence of us is not perishable, and must have been existent during that time when our body had no existence. The life of the man is dual. It consists of two lives — one animal and one spiritual. The first life is the life of man, and man needs a body to live this life. The second life is *the life of spirit*; his soul lives in that life separately from the body, and must live on in it after the separation from the body.

In an essay on Kant in *The Northern Messenger* (1888, Russian), A. L. Volinsky says that both in V*orlesungen*, and also in *Dreams of a Ghost-seer*, Kant denied the possibility of one thing only — the possibility of the physical receptivity of spiritual phenomena.

Thus Kant admitted not only the possibility of the existence of a spiritual *conscious* world, but also the possibility of communion with it.

Hegel built all his philosophy upon the possibility of a direct knowledge of truth, upon spiritual vision.

Approaching the question of two worlds from the psychological standpoint, from the standpoint of the theory of knowledge, let us firmly establish the principle that before we can hope to comprehend anything in the region of *noumena*, we must define *everything that it is possible to define* of the world of many dimensions by a purely intellectual method, by a process of reasoning. It is highly probable that by this method we cannot define very much. Perhaps our definitions will be too crude, will not quite correspond to the fine differentiation of relations in the noumenal world: all this is possible and must be taken into consideration. Nevertheless we shall define what we can, and at the outset make as clear as possible *what the noumenal world cannot be*; then what it *can* be — show what relations are impossible in it, and what are possible.

This is necessary in order that we, coming in contact with the real world, may discriminate between it and the phenomenal world, and what is more important, that we may not mistake simple reflections of the phenomenal world for the noumenal. We do not know the world of causes; we are confined in the jail of the phenomenal world simply because we do not know how to discern where one ends and where the other begins.

We are in constant touch with the world of causes, we live in it, because our psyche and our incomprehensible function in the world are part of it or a reflection of it. But we do not see or know it because we either deny it — consider that *everything existing* is phenomenal, and that nothing exists except the phenomenal — or we recognize it, but try to comprehend it in the forms of the three-dimensional phenomenal world; or lastly, we search for it and find it not, because we lose our way amid the deceits and illusions of the *reflected* phenomenal world which we mistakenly accept for the noumenal world.

In this dwells the tragedy of our spiritual questings: *we do not know what we are searching for.* And the only method by which we can escape this tragedy consists in a preliminary *intellectual* definition of the properties *of that of which we are in search.* Without such definitions, going merely by indefinite feelings, we shall not approach the world of causes or else *we shall get lost on its borderland.*

Spinoza understood this, saying that he could not speak of God, *not knowing his attributes.*

When I studied Euclid, I learned first of all that the sum of three angles of a triangle was equal to two right angles, and this property of a triangle was entirely comprehensible to me, although I did not know its many other properties. But so far as spirits and ghosts are concerned, I do not know even one of their attributes, but constantly hear different fantastic tales about them in which it is impossible to discover any truth.

We have established certain criteria which permit us to deal with the world of noumena or the "world of spirits." These we shall make use of now.

First of all we may say that *the world of noumena* cannot be three-dimensional and that there cannot be anything three-dimensional in it, i.e., commensurable with physical objects, similar to them in outside appearance, *having form* — there cannot be anything having extension in space and changing in time. And most important, there cannot be anything dead or inanimate. In the world of causes everything must be alive, because it is life itself: the soul of the world.

Let us remember also that *the world of causes* is the world of the marvelous; that what appears simple to us can never be real. The *real* appears to us as the marvelous. We do not believe in it, we do not recognize it; and therefore we do not feel the *mysteries* of which life is so full.

The simple is only that which is unreal. The real must seem marvelous.

The mystery of time penetrates all. It is felt in every stone, which perhaps might have witnessed the glacial period, seen the ichthyosaurus and the mammoth. It is felt in the approaching day, which we do not see, but which possibly sees us, which perchance is our last day; or on the other hand is the day of some transformation the nature of which we do not ourselves now know.

The mystery of thought creates all. As soon as we shall understand that thought is not a "function of motion," but that motion itself is only a function of thought — and shall begin to feel the depth of THIS MYSTERY — we shall perceive that the entire phenomenal world is some gigantic hallucination, which fails to frighten us, and does not drive us to think that we are mad simply because we have become accustomed to it.

The mystery of infinity — the greatest of all mysteries — it tells us that all the visible universe and its galaxies of stars *have no dimension:* that in relation to infinity *they are equal to a point*, a mathematical point which has no extension whatever, and that points which are not measurable for us may have a different extension and different dimensions.

In "positive" thinking we make the effort TO FORGET ABOUT ALL THIS: NOT TO THINK ABOUT IT.

At some future time positivism will be defined as a system by the aid of which it was possible not to think of real things and to limit oneself to the region of the unreal and illusory.

CHAPTER XVII

IF rationality exists in the world, then it must permeate everything, although manifesting itself variously.

We have accustomed ourselves to ascribe animism and rationality in this or that form to those things only which we designate as "beings," i.e., to those whom we find analogous to ourselves in the functions which define ANIMISM in our eyes.

Inanimate objects and mechanical phenomena are to us lifeless and irrational.

But this cannot be so.

It is only for our limited mind, for our limited power of communion with other minds, for our limited skill in analogy that rationality and psychic life in general manifest only in certain classes of living creatures, alongside of which a long series of dead things and mechanical phenomena exist.

But if we could not converse among ourselves, if every one of us could not infer the existence of rationality and of psychic life in another by analogy with himself, then everyone would consider himself alone to be alive and animated, and he would relegate all the rest of humankind to mechanical, "dead" nature.

In other words, we recognize as animated only those beings which have psychic life accessible to our observation in three-dimensional sections of the world, i.e., beings whose psyche is analogous to ours. About other consciousness we do not know and cannot know. All "beings" whose psychic does not manifest itself in the three-dimensional section of the world are inaccessible to us. If they contact our life at all, then *we necessarily regard* their manifestations as those of dead and unconscious nature. Our power of analogy is limited to *this section*. We cannot think logically outside of the conditions of the three-dimensional

Nature is Conscious

section. Therefore everything that lives, thinks and feels in a manner not analogous to us must appear dead and mechanical.

But sometimes we vaguely feel an intense *life* manifesting in the phenomena of nature, and sense a vivid emotionality the manifestations of which constitute the phenomena of (to us) inanimate nature. What I wish to convey is that behind the *phenomena* of visible manifestations is felt the noumena of emotion.

In *electrical discharges,* in thunder and lightning, in the rush and howling of the wind, are seen flashes of the sensuous-nervous shudderings of some gigantic organism.

A strange individuality which is all their own is sensed in certain days. There are days brimming with the marvelous and the mystic, days having each its own individual and unique consciousness, its own emotions, its own thoughts. One may almost commune with these days. And they will tell you that they live a long, long time, perhaps eternally, and that they have known and seen many, many things.

In the processional of the year; in the iridescent leaves of autumn, with their memory-laden smell; in the first snow, frosting the fields and communicating a strange freshness and sensitiveness to the air; in the spring freshets, in the warming sun, in the awakening but still naked branches through which gleams the turquoise sky; in the white nights of the north, and in the dark, humid, warm tropical nights spangled with stars — in all these are the thoughts, the emotions, the forms, peculiar to itself alone, of some great consciousness; or better, all this is *the expression* of the emotions, thoughts and forms of consciousness of a mysterious being — Nature.

There can be nothing dead or mechanical in nature. If in general life and feeling exist, they must exist in all. Life and rationality make up the world.

If we consider nature *from our side,* from the side of phenomena, then it is necessary to say that each thing, each phenomenon, possesses a psyche of its own.

A MOUNTAIN, A TREE, A RIVER, THE FISH WITHIN THE RIVER, DEW AND RAIN, PLANET, FIRE — each separately must possess a psyche of its own.

If we consider nature *from the other side,* from the side of noumena, then it is necessary to say that each thing and each phenomenon of our world is a manifestation in our section of a rationality incomprehensible to us, belonging to another section, the same having *there* functions incomprehensible to us. In that section of space, one rationality is such and its function is such that it manifests itself *here* as *a mountain*, some other manifests as *a tree*, a third as *a little fish*, and so forth.

The phenomena of our world are very different from one another. If they are nothing else but manifestations in our section of different rational beings, then these beings must be *very different* too.

Between *the psyche of a mountain* and *the psyche of a man* there must be *the same difference* as between a mountain and a man.

We have already admitted the possibility of different existences. We said that a house exists, and that a man exists, and that an idea exists also — but they all exist differently. If we pursue this thought, then we shall discover many kinds of *different existences*.

The fantasy of fairy tales, making all the world animate, ascribes to mountains, rivers, forests a psychic life similar to that of men. But this is just as untrue as the complete denial of consciousness to inanimate nature. Noumena are as distinct and various as phenomena, which are their manifestation in our three-dimensional sphere.

Each stone, each grain of sand, each planet has its *noumenon*, consisting of life and of psyche, binding them into certain *wholes* incomprehensible to us.

The *activity of life* of separate units may vary greatly. The degree of the activity of life can be determined from the standpoint of its power of reproducing itself. In inorganic, mineral nature, this activity is so insignificant that units of this nature *accessible to our observation* do not reproduce themselves, although it may only seem so to us because of the narrowness of our view in time and space. Perhaps if that view embraced hundreds of thousands of years and our entire planet simultaneously, we might then see *the growth* of minerals and metals.

Were we to observe, *from the inside*, one cubic centimeter of the human body, knowing nothing of the existence of the entire body and of the man himself, then the phenomena going on in this little cube of flesh would seem like elemental phenomena in inanimate nature.

But in any case, *for us* phenomena are divided into living and mechanical, and visible objects are divided into organic and inorganic. The latter are partitioned without resistance, remaining as they were before. It is possible to break a stone in halves, and then there will be two stones. But if one were to cut a snail in two, then there would not be two snails. This means that the psyche of the stone is very simple, primitive — so simple that it may be fractured without change of state. But a snail consists of living cells. Each living cell is a complex being, considerably more intricate than that of a stone. The body of the snail possesses the power to move, to nourish itself, feel pleasure and pain, seek the first and avoid the last; and most important of all, it possesses the faculty to multiply, to create new forms similar to itself, to involve inorganic substance within these forms, subduing physical laws to its service. The snail is a *complex centre* of transmutation of some physical energies into others. This centre possesses a consciousness of its own. It is for this reason that the snail is indivisible. Its psyche is infinitely higher than that of the stone. The snail has the *consciousness of form*, i.e., the form of a snail is conscious of itself, as it were. The form of a stone is not conscious of itself.

In organic nature where we see life, it is easier to assume the existence of a psyche. In the snail, a living creature, we already admit without difficulty a certain kind of psyche. But life belongs not alone to separate, individual organisms — anything indivisible is a living being. Each cell in an organism is a living being and it must have a certain psychic life.

Each combination of cells having a definite function is a living being also. Another higher combination — the organ — is a living being no less, and possesses a psychic life of its own.

Invisibility in our sphere is the sign of a definite function. If a given phenomenon in our plane is *a manifestation* of that which exists on another plane, then on our side evidently, indivisibility corresponds to *individuality* on that other side. Divisibility on our side shows divisibility on that side. The rationality of the divisible can express itself in a collective, non-individual reason only.

But even a complete organism is *merely a section* of a certain magnitude, of what we may call the life of this organism from birth to death. We may imagine this *life* as a body of four dimensions extended in time. The three-dimensional physical body is merely a section of the four-dimensional body, *Linga-Sharîra*. The image of the man which we know, his "personality," is also merely a section of his true personality, which undoubtedly has its separate psychic life. Therefore we may assume in man three psychic lives: first, the *psychic life of the body*, which manifests itself in instincts, and in the constant work of the body; second, his *personality*, a complex and constantly changing I, which we know, and in which we are conscious of ourselves; third, the consciousness of *all life* — a greater and higher I. In our state of development these *three* psychic lives know one another only very imperfectly, communicating under narcosis only, in trance, in ecstasy, in sleep, in hypnotic and mediumistic states, i.e., in other states of consciousness.

In addition to our own psychic lives, with which we are indissolubly bound, but which we do not know, we are surrounded by various *other psychic lives* which we do not know either. These lives we often *feel*, they are composed of our lives. We enter into these lives as their component parts, just as into our life enter different other lives. These lives are good or evil spirits, helping us or precipitating evil. *Family*, clan, nation, race — any aggregate to which we belong (such an aggregate undoubtedly possesses a life of its own), any group of men having its separate function and feeling its inner connection and unity, such as a philosophical school, a "church," a sect, a masonic order, a society, a party, etc., etc., is undoubtedly a living being possessing a certain rationality. A nation, a people, is a living being; humanity is a living being also. This is the *Grand Man*, ADAM KADMON of the Kabalists. ADAM KADMON is a being living in men, uniting in himself the lives of all men. Upon this subject, H. P. Blavatsky, in her great work, *The Secret Doctrine* (Vol. III, p. 146), has this to say:

. . . "It is not *the Adam of dust* (of Chapter II) who is thus made in the divine image, but the Divine Androgyne (of Chapter I), or Adam Kadmon."

ADAM KADMON IS HUMANITY, or humankind — *Homo Sapiens* — the SPHYNX, i.e., "the being with the body of an animal and the face of a superman."

Entering as a component part into different great and little lives man himself consists of an innumerable number of great and little I's. Many of the I's living in him do not even know one another, just as men who live in the same house may not know one another. Expressed in terms of this analogy, it may be said that "man" has much in common with *a house* filled with inhabitants the most diverse. Or better, he is like a great ocean liner on which are many transient passengers, each going to his own place for his own purpose, each uniting in himself elements the most diverse. And each separate unit in the population of this steamer orientates himself, involuntarily and unconsciously regards himself as the very centre of the steamer. This is a fairly true presentment of a human being.

Perhaps it would be more correct to compare a man with some little separate place on earth, living a life of its own; with a forest lake, full of the most diverse life, reflecting the sun and stars, and hiding in its depths some incomprehensible phantasm, perhaps an undine, or a water-sprite.

If we abandon analogies and return to facts, so far as these are accessible to our observation, it then becomes necessary to begin with several somewhat artificial divisions of the human being. The old division into

Body, Soul, Spirit

body, soul and spirit, has in itself a certain authenticity, but leads often to confusion, because when such a division is attempted disagreements immediately arise as to where the body ends and where the soul begins, where the soul ends and the spirit begins, and so forth. There are no strict limits at all, nor can there be. In addition to this, confusion enters in by reason of the *opposition* of body, soul and spirit, which are recognized in this case as *inimical* principles. This is entirely erroneous also, because the body is the expression of the soul, and the soul of the spirit.

The very terms, body, soul and spirit need explanation. The "body" is the physical body with its (to us) little understood mind; the soul — the *psyche* studied by scientific psychology — is the reflected activity which is guided by impressions received from the external world and from the body. The "spirit" comprises those higher principles which guide, or under certain conditions may guide, the soul-life.

Thus a human being contains in itself the following three categories.

First: *the body* — the region of instincts, and the inner "instinctive" consciousnesses of the differet organs, parts of the body, and the entire organism.

Second: *the soul* — consisting of sensations, perceptions, conceptions, thoughts, emotions and desires.

Third: *the region of the unknown* — consciousness, will, and the one I, i.e., those things which in ordinary man are in potentiality only.

Under the usual conditions of the average man the extremely misty focus of his consciousness is confined to the *psyche* perpetually going from one object to another.

> *I wish to eat.*
> *I read a newspaper.*
> *I wait for a letter.*

Only rarely does it touch the regions which give access to the religious, esthetic and moral emotions, and to the higher intellect, which expresses itself in abstract thinking, united with the moral and esthetic sense, i.e., the sense of the necessity of the *co-ordination* of thought, feeling, word and action.

In saying "I," a man means, of course, not the total complex of all these regions, but that which in a given moment is in the focus of his consciousness. "*I wish*" (or more correctly, simply "wish," because man very seldom says *I* wish): these words (or this word), playing the most important rôle in the life of man, usually refer not at all to every side of his being simultaneously, but merely to some small and insignificant facet, which at a given moment holds the focus of consciousness and subjects to itself all the rest, until it in turn is forced out by another equally insignificant facet.

In the psyche of man there occurs a continual shifting of view from one subject to another. Through the focus of receptivity runs a continuous cinematographical film of feelings and impressions, and each separate impression defines the I of a given moment.

From this point of view the psyche of man has often been compared to a dark, sleeping town in the midst of which night-guards with lanterns slowly move about, each lighting up a little circle around himself. This is a perfectly true analogy. In each given moment there are several such unsteadily lighted circles in the focus, and all the rest is enveloped in darkness.

Each such little lighted circle represents an I, living its own life, sometimes very short. And there is continuous movement, either fast or slow, moving out into the light more of new and still new objects, or else old ones from the region of memory, or tormentingly revolving in a circle of the same fixed ideas.

This continuous motion going on in our psyche, this uninterrupted running over of the light from one I to another, perhaps explains the phenomenon of motion in the outer visible world.

We know already by our *intellect*, that there is no such motion. We know that *everything exists* in infinite spaces of time, nothing is made, nothing becomes, *all is*. But we do not see everything at once, and therefore *it seems to us* that everything moves, grows, is becoming. We do not see everything at once, either in the outer world, or in the inner world; thence arises the illusion of motion. For example, as we ride past a house the house turns behind us; but if we could see it, not with our eyes, not in perspective, but by some sort of vision, simultaneously from all sides, from below and from above and from the inside, we should no longer see that illusory motion, but would see the house entirely immobile, just as it is in reality. Mentally, we know that the house did not move.

It is just the same with everything else. The motion, growth, "becoming," which is going on all around us in the world is no more real than the motion of a house which we are riding by, or the motion of trees and fields relative to the windows of a rapidly moving railway car.

Motion goes on inside of us, and it creates the illusion of motion round about us. The lighted circle runs quickly from one I to another — from one object, from one idea, from one perception or image to another: within the focus of consciousness rapidly changing I's succeed one another, a little of the light of consciousness going over from one I to another. This is the true motion which alone exists in the world. Should this motion stop, should all I's simultaneously enter the focus of receptivity, should the light so expand as to illumine all at once that which is usually lighted bit by bit and gradually, and could a man grasp simultaneously by his reason all that ever entered or will enter his receptivity and all that which is never clearly illumined by thought (producing its action on the psyche nevertheless) — then would a man behold himself in the midst of an *immobile universe*, in which there would exist simultaneously everything that lies usually in the remote depths of memory, in the past; all that lies at a remote distance from him; all that lies in the future.

C. H. Hinton very well says, in regard to beings of other sections of the world:

By the same process by which we know about the existence of other men around us, we may know of the high intelligences by whom we are surrounded. We feel them but we do not realize them.

To realize them it will be necessary to develop our power of perception.

The power of seeing with our bodily eye is limited to the three-dimensional section. But the inner eye is not thus limited; we can organize our power of seeing in higher space, and we can form conceptions of realities in this higher space.

And this affords the groundwork for the perception and study of these other beings than man.

We are, with reference to the higher things of life, like blind and puzzled children. We know that we are members of one body, limbs of one vine; but we cannot discern, except by instinct and feeling, what that body is, what the vine is.

Our problem consists in the diminution of the limitations of our perception.

Nature consists of many entities toward the apprehension of which we strive.

For this purpose *new conceptions* have to be formed first, and vast fields of observation shall be unified under one common law. The real history of progress *lies in the growth of new conceptions*.

When the new conception is formed it is found to be quite simple and natural. We ask ourselves what we have gained; and we answer: nothing; we have simply removed an obvious limitation.

Tertium Organum

The question may be put: In what way do we come into contact with these higher beings at present? And evidently the answer is: *In those ways in which we tend to form organic unions* — unions in which the activities of individuals coalesce in a living way.

The coherence of a military empire or of a subjugated population, presenting no natural nucleus of growth, is not one through which we should hope to grow into direct contact with our higher destinies. But in friendship, in voluntary associations and above all in the family, we tend towards our greater life.

Just as, to explore the distant stars of the heavens, a particular material arrangement is necessary which we call a telescope, so to explore the nature of the beings who are higher than we, a mental arrangement is necessary. We must prepare a more extended power of looking. We want a structure developed inside the skull for the one purpose which an exterior telescope will do for the other.

This animism of nature takes the most diverse directions. *This tree* is a living being. The *birch tree* in general — *the species* is a living being. A birch tree forest is a living being also. A forest in which there are trees of different kinds, grass, flowers, ants, beetles, birds, beasts — this is a living being too, living by the life of everything composing it, thinking and feeling for all of which it consists.

This idea is very interestingly expressed in the essay of P. Florensky, *The Humanitarian Roots of Idealism. (The Theological Messenger,* 1909, II, p. 288. In Russian.)

Are there many people who regard a forest not merely as a collective proper noun and rhetorical embodiment, i.e., as a pure fiction, but as something unique, living? . . . The real unity is a unity of self-consciousness. . . . Are there many who recognize unity in a forest, i.e., the living soul of a forest taken as a whole — voodoo, wood-demon, Old Nick? Do you consent to recognize undines and water-sprites — those souls of the aquatic element?

The activities of the life of such a composite being as a forest is not the same as the activity of *different species* of plants and animals, and the activity of the life of a species is again different from the life of separate individuals.

Moreover, the diversity of the functions expressed in different life-activities reveals the differences existing between the psychic lives of different "organisms." The life-activity of a single leaf of a birch tree, is of course an infinitely lower form of activity than the life of *the tree*. The activity of the life of the tree is not such as the activity of the life of the species, and the life of *the species* is not such as the life of the forest.

The functions of these four "lives" are entirely different, and their rationality must be correspondingly different also.

The rationality of a single cell of the human body must be as much lower in comparison with the rationality of the body — i.e., with the "physical consciousness of man" — as its life-activity is lower in comparison with the life-activity of the entire organism.

Therefore, from a certain standpoint, we may regard the noumenon of a phenomenon as the soul of that phenomenon, i.e., we may say that the hidden *soul of a phenomenon* is its noumenon. The concept of *the soul of a phenomenon* or the *noumenon of a phenomenon* includes within itself both life and rationality together with their functions in sections of the world incomprehensible to us; and the manifestation of those in our sphere constitutes a phenomenon.

The idea of an animistic universe leads inevitably to the idea of a "World-Soul" — a "Being" whose manifestation is this visible universe.

The idea of the "World-Soul" was very picturesquely understood in the ancient religions of India. The mystical poem, The *Bhagavad Gîtâ* gives a remarkable presentment of *Mahadevi*, i.e., the great *Deva* whose life is this world.

Thus Krishna propounded his teaching to his disciples . . . preparing them for an apprehension of those high spiritual truths which unfold before his inner sight in a moment of illumination.

When he spoke of Mahadeva his voice became very deep, and his face was illuminated by an inner light.

Once Arjuna, in an impulse of boldness, said to him:

Let us see Mahadeva in his divine form. May we behold him?

And then Krishna . . . began to speak of a being who breathes in every creature, has an hundred-fold and a thousand-fold forms, many-faced, many-eyed, facing everywhere, and who surpasses everything created by infinity, who envelops in his body the whole world, things still and animate. If the radiance of a thousand suns should burst forth suddenly in the sky, it would not compare with the radiance of that Mighty Spirit.

When Krishna spoke thus of Mahadeva, a beam of light of such tremendous force shone in his eyes, that his disciples could not endure the radiance of that light, and fell at Krishna's feet. From very fear the hair rose on Arjuna's head, and bowing low he said: Thy words are terrible, we cannot look upon such a being as Thou evokest before our eyes. His form makes us tremble.*

* "The Great Initiates," by E. Schure.

In an interesting book of lectures by Prof. William James, A *Pluralistic Universe*, there is a lecture on Fechner, devoted to "a conscious universe."

Ordinary monistic idealism leaves everything intermediary out. It recognizes only extremes, as if, after the first rude face of the phenomenal world in all its particularity, nothing but the supreme in all its perfection could be found. First, you and I, just as we are in this room; and the moment we get below that surface, the unutterable itself! Doesn't this show a singularly indigent imagination? Isn't this brave universe made on a richer pattern, with room in it for a long hierarchy of beings? Materialistic science makes it infinitely richer in terms, with its molecules, and ether, and electrons and what not. Absolute idealism, thinking of reality only under intellectual forms, knows not what to do with bodies of any grade, and can make no use of any psycho-physical analogy or correspondence.

Fechner, from whose writings Prof. James makes copious quotations, upheld quite a different view-point. Fechner's ideas are so near to those which have been presented in the previous chapters that we shall dwell upon them more extensively.

I use the words of Prof. James:

The original sin, according to Fechner, of both our popular and scientific thinking, is our inveterate habit of regarding the spiritual not as the rule but as an exception in the midst of nature. Instead of believing our life to be fed at the breasts of the greater life, our individuality to be sustained by the greater individuality, which must necessarily have more consciousness and more independence than all that it brings forth, we habitually treat whatever lies outside of our life as so much slag and ashes of life only.

Or if we believe in Divine Spirit, we fancy it on the one side as bodiless, and nature as soulless on the other.

What comfort, or peace, Fechner asks, can come from such a doctrine? The flowers wither at its breath, the stars turn into stone; our own body grows unworthy of our spirit and sinks to a tenement for carnal senses only. The book of nature turns into a volume on mechanics, in which whatever has life is treated as a sort of anomaly; a great chasm of separation yawns between us and all that is higher than ourselves; and God becomes a thinnest of abstractions.

Fechner's great instrument for verifying the daylight view is analogy. . . . *Bain defines genius as the power of seeing analogies.*

The number that Fechner could perceive was prodigious; *but he insisted on the differences as well.* Neglect to make allowance for these, he said, is the common fallacy in analogical reasoning.

According to Fechner

Most of us, for example, reasoning justly that, since all the minds we know are connected with bodies, therefore God's mind should be connected with a body, proceed to suppose that that body must be just an animal body over again, and paint an altogether human picture of God. But all that the analogy comports is *a* body — the particular features of our body are adaptations to a habitat so different from God's that if God have a physical body at all, it must be utterly different from ours in structure.

The vaster orders of mind go with the vaster orders of body. The entire earth on which we live must have, according to Fechner, its own collective consciousness. So must each sun, moon, planet; so must the whole solar system have its own wider consciousness, on which the consciousness of our earth plays one part. So has the entire starry system as such its consciousness; and if that starry system be not the sum of all that *IS*, materially considered, then that whole system, along with whatever else may be, is the body of that absolutely totalized consciousness of the universe to which men give the name of God. Speculatively Fechner is thus a monist in his theology; but there is room in his universe for every grade of spiritual being between man and the final all-inclusive God.

The earth-soul he passionately believes in; he treats the earth as our special human guardian angel; we can pray to the earth as men pray to their saints.

His most important conclusion is, that the constitution of the world is identical throughout. In ourselves, visual consciousness goes with our eyes, tactile consciousness with our skin. But although neither skin nor eye knows aught of the sensations of the other, they come together and figure in some sort of relation and combination in the more inclusive consciousness which each of us names his *self*. Quite similarly, then, says Fechner, we must suppose that my consciousness of myself and yours of yourself, although in their immediacy they keep separate and know nothing of each other, are yet known and used together in a higher consciousness, that of the human race, say, into which they enter as constituent parts.

Similarly, the whole human and animal kingdom come together as conditions of a consciousness of still wider scope. This combines in the soul of the earth with the consciousness of the vegetable kingdom, which in turn contributes its share of experience to that of the whole solar system, etc.

The supposition of an earth-consciousness meets a strong instinctive prejudice. All the consciousness we directly know seems tied to brains. But our brain, which primarily serves to correlate our muscular reactions with the external objects on which we depend, performs a function which the earth performs in an entirely different way. She has no proper muscles or limbs of her own, and the only objects external to her are the other stars. To these her whole mass reacts by most exquisite alterations in its total gait, and by still more exquisite vibratory responses in its substance. Her ocean reflects the lights of heaven as on a mighty mirror, her atmosphere refracts them like a monstrous lens, the clouds and snow-fields combine them into white, the woods and flowers disperse them into colors. Polarization, interference, absorption awaken sensibilities in matter of which our senses are too coarse to take any note.

For these cosmic relations of hers, then, she no more needs a special brain than she needs eyes or ears. Our brains do indeed unify and correlate innumerable functions. Our eyes know nothing of sound, our ears nothing of light, but having brains, we can feel sound and light together, and compare them . . . . . . Must every higher means of unification between things be a literal brain-fibre? Cannot the earth-mind know otherwise the contents of our minds together?

In a striking page Fechner relates one of his moments of direct vision of truth.

"On a certain morning I went out to walk. The fields were green, the birds sang, the dew glistened, the smoke was rising, here and there a man appeared, a light as of transfiguration lay on all things. It was only a little bit of earth; it was only one moment of her existence; and yet as my look embraced her more and more it seemed to me not only so beautiful an idea, but so true and clear a fact, that she is an angel — an angel carrying me along with her into Heaven. . . . I asked myself how the opinions of men could ever have so spun themselves away from life so far as to deem the earth only a dry clod . . . But such an experience as this passes for fantasy. The earth is a globular body, and what more she may be, one can find in mineralogical cabinets."

The special thought of Fechner's is his belief that the more inclusive forms of consciousness are in part *constituted* by the more limited forms. Not that they are the mere sum of the more limited forms. As our mind is not the bare sum of our sights plus our sounds, plus our pains, but in adding these terms together it also finds relations among them and weaves them into schemes and forms and objects of which no one sense in its separate estate knows anything, so the earth-soul traces relations between the contents of my mind and the contents of yours of which neither of our separate minds is conscious. It has schemes, forms, and objects proportionate to its wider field, which our mental fields are far too narrow to cognize. By ourselves we are simply out of relation with each other, for we are both of us there, and *different* from each other, which is a positive relation. What we are without knowing, it knows that we are. It is as if the total universe of inner life had a sort of grain or direction, a sort of valvular structure, permitting knowledge to flow in one way only, so that the wider might always have the narrower under observation, but never the narrower the wider.

Fechner likens our individual persons on the earth unto so many sense-organs of the earth-soul. We add to its perceptive life. . . . It absorbs our perceptions into its larger sphere of knowledge, and combines them with the other data there. The memories and conceptual relations that have spun themselves round the perceptions of a certain person remain in the larger earth-life as distinct as ever, and form new relations. . . ."

Fechner's ideas are expounded in his book, *Zendavesta.*

I have made such a lengthy quotation from Prof. James' book in order to show that the ideas of the animism and of the rationality of the world are neither new nor paradoxical. It is a natural and logical necessity, resulting from a broader view of the world than that which we usually permit ourselves to hold.

Logically we must either recognize life and rationality in everything, in all "dead nature," or deny them completely, even IN OURSELVES.

CHAPTER XVIII

THE MEANING OF LIFE — this is the eternal theme of human meditation. All philosophical systems, all religious teachings strive to find and give to men the answer to this question. Some say that the meaning of life is in service, in the surrender of self, in self-sacrifice, in the sacrifice of everything, *even life itself*. Others declare that the meaning of life is in the delight of it, relieved against "the expectation of the final horror of death." Some say that the meaning of life is perfection, and the creation of a better future *beyond the grave*, or in future lives for ourselves. Others say that the meaning of life is in the approach to *non-existence*: still others, that the meaning of life is in the perfection of the race, in the organization of life on earth; while there are those who deny the possibility of even attempting to know its meaning.

The fault of all these explanations consists in the fact that they all attempt to discover the meaning of life *outside of itself*, either in the future of humanity, or in some problematical existence beyond the grave, or again in the evolution of the *Ego* throughout many successive incarnations — always in something *outside* of the present life of man. But if instead of thus speculating about it, men would simply look within themselves, then they would see that in reality the *meaning of life* is not after all so obscure. IT CONSISTS IN KNOWLEDGE. All life, through all its facts, events and incidents, excitements and attractions, inevitably leads us TO THE KNOWLEDGE OF SOMETHING. All life-experience is KNOWLEDGE. The most powerful emotion in man is his yearning toward the unknown. EVEN IN LOVE, the most powerful of all attractions, to which everything is sacrificed, is this yearning toward the unknown, toward the NEW — *curiosity.*

The Persian poet-philosopher, Al-Ghazzali, says: *"The highest function of man's soul is the perception of truth."* *

In the very beginning of this book PSYCHIC LIFE AND THE WORLD were recognized as existing. The world is everything that exists. The function of psychic life may be defined as *the realization of existence.*

Man realizes his existence and the existence of the world, a part of which he is. His relation to himself and to the world is called knowledge. The expansion and deepening of his relation to himself and to the world is the expansion of knowledge.

All the soul-properties of man, all the elements of his psyche — sensations, perceptions, conceptions, ideas, judgments, reasonings, feelings, emotions, even creation — all these are the INSTRUMENTS OF KNOWLEDGE which the I possesses.

Feelings — from the simple emotions up to the most complex, such as esthetic, religious and moral emotion — and creation, from the creation of a savage making a stone hatchet for himself up to the creation of a Beethoven, indeed are means of *knowledge.*

Only to our narrow HUMAN view do they appear to serve other purposes — the preservation of life, the construction of something, or merely pleasure. In reality all this *conduces* to knowledge.

Evolutionists, followers of Darwin, say that the struggle for existence and the selection of the fittest created in the mind and feeling of contemporary man — that mind and feeling SERVE LIFE, preserve the life of separate individuals and of the species — and that *beyond this* they have no meaning in themselves. But it is possible to answer this with the same arguments before advanced against the *mechanicality* of the universe; namely, that if rationality exists, then nothing exists except rationality. The struggle for existence and the survival of the fittest, if they truly play such a rôle in the creation of life, are also not merely accidents, but products of a mind, CONCERNING WHICH WE DO NOT KNOW; and they also conduce, like everything else, TO A KNOWLEDGE.

But we do not realize, do not discern the presence of rationality in the phenomena and laws of nature. This happens because we study always not the whole but the part, and we do not divine that whole which we wish to study — by studying the little finger of a man we cannot discover his reason. It is the same way in our relation to nature: we study always the little finger of nature. When we come to realize this and

* Al-Ghazzali, "The Alchemy of Happiness."

shall understand that EVERY LIFE IS THE MANIFESTATION OF A PART OF SOME WHOLE, then only the possibility of knowledge of that whole opens to us.

In order to comprehend the rationality of a given whole, it is necessary to understand the character of the whole and its functions. Thus the function of man is knowledge; but without understanding "man" as a whole, it is impossible to understand his function.

To understand our psyche, the function of which is knowledge, it is necessary to clear up our relation to life.

In Chapter X an attempt was made — a very artificial one, founded upon the analogy with a world of two-dimensional beings — to define *life* as motion in a sphere higher in dimensionality in comparison with ours. From this standpoint every separate life is as it were the manifestation in our sphere of a part of one of the rational entities of another sphere. These rationalities look in upon us, as it were, in these lives which we see. When a man dies, *one eye of the Universe closes*, says Fechner. Every separate human life is a moment of the life of some *great being*, which lives *in us*. The life of every separate tree is a moment of the life of a being, "species" or "family." The rationalities of these *higher* beings do not exist independently of these lower lives. They are two sides of one and the same thing. Every *single* human psyche, in some other section of the world, may produce the illusion of *many* lives.

This is difficult to illustrate by an example. But if we take Hinton's spiral, passing through a plane, and the point running in circles on the plane (see p. 70), and conceive of the spiral as the psyche, then the moving point of intersection of the spiral with the plane will be life. This example illustrates a possible relation between the psyche and life.

To us, life and the psyche are different and separate from each other, because we are inept at seeing, inept at looking at things. And this in turn depends upon the fact that it is very difficult for us to step outside the frames of our *divisions*. We see the life of a tree, *of this tree*; and if we are told that the life of a tree is a manifestation of some psychic life, then we understand it in such a way that the life of *this tree* is the manifestation of the psychic life of *this tree*. But this is of course an absurdity resulting from "three-dimensional thinking" — the "Euclidian" mind. The life of this tree is a manifestation of the *psychic life of the species*, or family, or perhaps of the psychic life of *the entire vegetable kingdom*.

In exactly the same way, our separate *lives* are manifestations of some great rational entity. We find the proof of this in the fact that our lives have no other meaning at all aside from that *process of acquiring knowl-*

A False Dualism

edge performed by us. A thoughtful man ceases to feel painfully the absence of meaning in life only when he realizes this, and begins to strive consciously for that for which he strove unconsciously before.

This process of acquiring knowledge, representing *our function in the world*, is performed not by the intellect only, but by our entire organism, by all the body, by all the life, and by all the life of human society, its organizations, its institutions, by all culture and all civilization; by that which we know of humanity and, still more, by that which we do not know. And we acquire the knowledge of that which we deserve to know.

If we declare in regard to the intellectual side of man that its purpose is knowledge this will evoke no doubts. All agree that the human intellect together with everything subjected to its functions is for the purpose of knowledge — although often the faculty of knowledge is considered as serving only utilitarian ends. But concerning the emotions: joy, sorrow, rage, fear, love, hatred, pride, compassion, jealousy; concerning the sense of beauty, esthetic pleasure and artistic creation; concerning the moral sense; concerning all religious emotions: faith, hope, veneration, etc., etc., — concerning all human activity — things are not so clear. We usually do not see that all emotions, and *all* human activity serve knowledge. How do *fear*, or *love*, or *work* serve knowledge? It seems to us that by *emotions* we feel; by work — create. *Feeling* and *creation* seem to us as something different from *knowledge*. Concerning work, creative power, creation, we are rather inclined to think that they *demand* knowledge, and if they serve it, do so only indirectly. In the same way it is incomprehensible how *religious emotions* serve knowledge.

Usually *the emotional* is opposed to *the intellectual* — "heart" to "mind." Some place "cold reason" or intellect over against feelings, emotions, esthetic pleasure; and from these they separate the moral sense, the religious sense, and "spirituality."

The misunderstanding here lies in the interpretation of the words *intellect* and *emotion*.

Between intellect and emotion there is no sharp distinction. Intellect, considered as a whole, is also emotion. But in every-day language, and in "conversational psychology" *reason* is contrasted with *feeling; will* is considered as a separate and independent faculty; moralists consider *moral feeling* as entirely distinct from all these; religionists consider *spirituality* separately from *faith*.

One often hears such expressions as: reason mastered feeling; will mastered desire; the sense of duty mastered passion; spirituality mastered intellectuality; faith conquered reason. But all these are merely the incorrect expressions of conversational psychology; just as incorrect as are the expressions "sunrise" and "sunset." In reality in the soul of man nothing exists save emotions. And the soul life of man is either a struggle or a harmonious adjustment between different emotions. Spinoza saw this quite clearly when he said that emotion can be mastered only by another more powerful emotion, and by *nothing else*. Reason, will, feeling, duty, faith, spirituality, mastering some other emotion, can conquer only by force of the *emotional element* contained in them. The ascetic who kills all desires and passions in himself, kills them by the *desire* for salvation. A man renouncing all the pleasures of the world, renounces them because of the delight of sacrifice, of renunciation. A soldier dying at his post through his *sense of duty* or habit of obedience, does so because the emotion of *devotion*, or *faithfulness*, is more powerful in him than all other things. A man whose moral sense prompts him to overcome passion in himself, does so because the moral sense (i.e., emotion) is more powerful than all his other feelings, other emotions. In substance all this is perfectly clear and simple, but it has become confused and confusing simply because men, calling different degrees of one and the same thing by diverse names, began to see *fundamental differences* where there were only *differences in degree*.

Will is the resultant of desires. We call that man *strong-willed* in whom the *will* proceeds on definite lines, without turning aside; and we call that man *weak-willed* in whom the line of the will takes a zigzag course, turning aside here or there under the influence of every new desire. But this does not mean that *will* and *desire* are something opposite; quite the reverse, they are one and the same, because the will is composed of desires.

Reason cannot conquer feeling, because feeling can be conquered only by feeling. Reason can only give thoughts and pictures, evoking feelings *which* will conquer the feeling of a given moment. Spirituality is not opposed to "intellectuality" or "emotionality." It is only THEIR HIGHER FLIGHT. Reason has no limits: only the human, "Euclidian" mind, the mind devoid of emotions, is limited.

But what is "reason"?

It is the inner aspect of any given being. In the earth's animal kingdom, in all animals lower than man, we see *passive reason*. But with the appearance of *concepts* it becomes active, and part of it begins to work as intellect. The animal is conscious through his sensation and emotions.

The Emotions·are Organs of Knowledge

The intellect is present in the animal only in an embryonic state, as an *emotion of curiosity*, a pleasure of knowing.

In man the growth of consciousness consists in the growth of the intellect and the accompanying growth of the higher emotions — esthetic, religious, moral — which according to the measures of their growth become more and more *intellectualized*, while simultaneously with this the intellect is assimilating emotionality, ceasing to be "cold."

Thus "spirituality" is a fusion of the intellect with the higher emotions. The intellect is spiritualized from the emotions; the emotions are *spiritualized* from the intellect.

The functions of the rational faculty are not limited, but not often does the human intellect rise to its highest form. At the same time it is incorrect to say that the highest form of human knowledge will not be intellectual, but of a different character; only this higher reason is entirely unrestricted by *logical concepts* and by Euclidian modes of thought. We are likely to hear a great deal concerning this from the standpoint of *mathematics*, which as a matter of fact transcended the reasoning of logic long ago. But it achieved this *by the aid of the intellect*. A new order of receptivity grows in the soil of the intellect and of the higher emotions, but it is not created by them. A tree grows in the earth, but it is not created by the earth. A seed is necessary. This seed may be in the soul, or absent from it. When it is there it can be cultivated or it can be choked; when it is not there it is impossible to replace it with anything else. The soul (if a soul it may be called) lacking that seed, i.e., inept to feel and reflect the world of the wondrous, will never put forth the living sprout, but will always reflect the phenomenal world, and that alone.

At the present stage of his development man comprehends many things by means of his intellect, but at the same time he comprehends many things by means of his emotions. In no case are emotions merely organs of feeling *for feeling's* sake: they are all organs of knowledge. In every emotion man knows something that he could not know without its aid — something that he could know by no other emotion, by no effort of the intellect. If we consider the emotional nature of man as self-contained, as serving *life* and not serving *knowledge* we shall never understand its true content and significance. Emotions serve knowledge. There are things and relations which can be known only emotionally, and only through *a given emotion*.

To understand the psychology of *play*, it is necessary to experience the emotions of the player; to understand the psychology of *the hunt*, it is necessary to experience the emotions of the hunter; the psychology of a man in love is incomprehensible to him who is indifferent; the state of mind of Archimedes when he jumped out of the bath tub is incomprehensible to the staid citizen, who would look on such a performance as a sign of insanity; the feelings of the globe-trotter, delightedly breathing in the sea air and sweeping with his eyes the wide horizon, is incomprehensible to the sedentary stay-at-home. The feeling of a believer is incomprehensible to an unbeliever, and to a believer the feeling of an unbeliever is quite as strange. Men understand one another so imperfectly because they live always by *different* emotions. And when they feel similar emotions simultaneously, then and then only do they understand one another. The proverbial philosophy of the people knows this very well: "A FULL MAN DOES NOT UNDERSTAND A HUNGRY ONE," it says. "A drunkard is no comrade for a sober man." "One rogue recognizes another."

In this mutual understanding or in the illusion of mutual understanding — in this immersion in similar emotions — lies one of the principal charms of love. The French novelist, de Maupassant, has written very delightfully about this in his little story *Solitude*. The same illusion explains the secret power of alcohol over the human soul, for alcohol creates the illusion of *a communion of souls*, and induces similar fantasies *simultaneously*, in two or several men.

Emotions are the stained-glass windows of the soul; colored glasses through which the soul looks at the world. Each such glass assists in finding in the contemplated object the same or similar colors, but it also prevents the finding of opposite ones. Therefore it has been correctly said that a one-sided emotional illumination cannot give a correct perception of an object. Nothing gives one such a clear idea of things as the emotions, yet nothing deludes one so much.

Every emotion has a meaning for its existence, although its *value* from the standpoint of knowledge varies. Certain emotions are important and necessary for the life of knowledge and certain emotions hinder rather than help one to understand.

Theoretically all emotions are an aid to knowledge; all emotions arose *because* of the knowing of one or another thing. Let us consider one of the most elementary emotions — say THE EMOTION OF FEAR. Undoubtedly there are relations which can be known *only through fear*. The man who never experienced the sensation of fear will never understand many things in life and in nature; he will never understand many of the controlling motives in the life of man. (What else but the fear of hunger and cold forces the majority of men to work?) He will never understand many things in the animal world. For example, he will not understand the relation of mammals to reptiles. A snake excites a feeling of repulsion and fear in all mammals. By this *repulsion* and *fear* the mammal knows the nature of the snake and the relation of that nature to its own, and knows it correctly, but strictly personally, and only from its own standpoint. But what the snake is in itself the animal never knows by the emotion of fear. What the snake is *in itself* — not in the philosophical meaning of the *thing-in-itself* (nor from the standpoint of the man or animal whom it has bitten or may bite) but simply from the standpoint of zoölogy — THIS CAN BE KNOWN BY THE INTELLECT ONLY.

Emotions unite with the different I's of our psyche. Emotions apparently the same may be united with the very small I's and with the very great and lofty I's; and so the rôle and meaning of such emotions in life may be very different. The continual shifting of emotions, each of which calls itself I and strives to establish power over man, is the chief obstacle to the establishment of a *constant* I. And particularly does this interfere when the emotions are manifesting in and passing through the regions of the psyche connected with a certain kind of self-consciousness and self-assertion. These are the so-called *personal emotions*.

The sign of the growth of the emotions is the liberation of them from the *personal* element, and their sublimation on the higher planes. The liberation from personal elements augments the cognizing power of the emotions, because the more there are of pseudo-personal elements in emotion the greater the possibility of delusion. Personal emotion is always *partial*, always *unjust*, by reason of the one fact that it opposes *itself* to all the rest.

Thus the cognitive power of the emotions is greater in proportion as there is less of *self-elements* in a given emotion, i.e., more consciousness that this emotion is not the I.

We have seen before in studying *space* and its laws, that the evolution of knowledge consists in a gradual withdrawing from oneself. Hinton expresses this very well. He says that only by *withdrawing from ourselves* do we begin to comprehend the world as it is. The entire system of mental exercises with colored cubes invented by Hinton aims at the training of consciousness to look at things from other than the pseudo-personal standpoint.

When we study a block of cubes, writes Hinton, (say a cube consisting of 27 lesser cubes) we first of all learn it by starting from a particular cube and axis, and learning how 26 others come with regard to that cube. . . . We learn the block with regard to this axis, so that we can mentally conceive the disposition of every cube as it comes regarded from one point of view. Next we suppose ourselves to be in another cube at the extremity of another axis; and looking from this axis, we learn the aspect of all the cubes, and so on.

Thus we impress on the feelings what the block of cubes is like from every axis. In this way we get a knowledge of the block of cubes.

Now, to get the knowledge of humanity, we must study it from the standpoint of the individuals composing it.

The egotist may be compared with the man who knows a cube from one standpoint only.

Those who feel superficially with a great many people, are like those learners who have a slight acquaintance with a block of cubes from many points of view.

Those who have a few deep attachments are like those who know them well from only one or two points of view.

And after all, perhaps the difference between the good and the rest of us, lies rather in the former *being aware*. There is something outside them which draws them to it, which they *see*, while we *do not*.*

Just as it is incorrect in relation to oneself to evaluate everything from the standpoint of one emotion, contrasting it with all the rest, so is it correspondingly incorrect in relation to the world and men to evaluate everything from the standpoint of one's own accidental I, contrasting oneself of a given moment with the rest.

Thus the problem of correct emotional knowledge consists in the fact that one shall *feel* in relation to the world and men *from some standpoint other than the personal*. And the broader the circle becomes *for which* a person feels, the deeper becomes the knowledge which his emotions yield. But not all emotions are of equal potency in liberating from *self-elements*. Certain emotions from their very nature are *disruptive*, separative, alienating, forcing man to feel himself as individualized and separate; such are hatred, fear, jealousy, pride, envy. These are emotions of a *materialistic order*, forcing a belief in matter. And there are emotions which are unitive, harmonizing, making man feel himself to be a part of some great whole; such are love, sympathy, friendship, compassion, love of country, love of nature, love of humanity. These emotions lead man out of the material world and show him the truth of the world of the wondrous. Emotions of this character liberate him more easily from self-elements than those of the former class. Nevertheless there can be a quite *impersonal* pride — the pride in an heroic deed accomplished by *another*

* C. H. Hinton, "A New Era of Thought," pp. 77, 78.

Pure and Impure Emotions

man. There can even be *impersonal* envy, when we envy a man who has conquered himself, conquered his *personal* desire to live, sacrificed himself for that which everyone considers to be right and just, but which we cannot bring ourselves to do, cannot even think of doing, *because of weakness, of love of life*. There can be *impersonal* hatred — of injustice, of brute force, anger against stupidity, dullness; aversion to nastiness, to hypocrisy. These feelings undoubtedly elevate and purify the soul of man and help him to *see* things which he would not otherwise see.

Christ driving the money-changers out of the temple, or expressing his opinion about the Pharisees, was not entirely meek and mild; and there are cases wherein meekness and mildness are not virtues at all. Emotions of love, sympathy, pity transform themselves very readily into sentimentality, into weakness; and thus transformed they contribute of course to *nescience*, i.e., *matter*. The difficulty of dividing emotions into categories is increased by the fact that all emotions of the higher order, without exception, can also be personal and then their action partakes of the nature of this class.

There is a division of emotions into *pure* and *impure*. We all know this, we all use these words, but understand little of what they mean. Truly, what does "pure" or "impure" mean with reference to feeling?

Common morality divides, a priori, all emotions into pure and impure according to certain outward signs, just as Noah divided the animals in his ark. All "fleshly desires" fall into the category of the "impure." In reality indeed, "fleshly desires" are just as pure as is everything in nature. Nevertheless emotions are pure and impure. We know very well that there is truth in this classification. But where is it, and what does it mean?

Only an analysis of emotions from the standpoint of knowledge can give the key to this.

Impure emotion — this is quite the same thing as impure glass, impure water, or impure sound, i.e., emotion which is *not* pure, but containing sediments, deposits, or echoes of other emotions: IMPURE — MIXED. Impure emotion gives obscure, *not pure* knowledge, just as impure glass gives a confused image. Pure emotion gives a clear pure image of that for the knowledge of which it is intended.

This is the only possible decision of the question. The arrival at this conclusion saves us from the common mistake of moralists who divide arbitrarily all emotion into "moral" and "immoral." But if we try for a moment to separate emotions from their usual moral frames, then we see that matters are considerably simpler, that there are no *in their nature* pure emotions, nor impure *in their nature*, but that each emotion will be pure or impure according to whether or not there are admixtures of other emotions in it.

There can be a pure sensuality, the sensuality of the *Song of Songs*, which initiates into the sensation of cosmic life and gives the power to hear the beating pulse of nature. And there can be an impure sensuality, mixed with other emotions good or bad from a moral standpoint but equally making muddy the fundamental feeling.

There can be pure sympathy, and there can be sympathy mixed with calculation to receive something for one's sympathy. There can be pure love of knowledge, a thirst for knowledge for its own sake, and there can be an inclination to knowledge wherein considerations of *utility* or *profit* assume the chief importance.

In their outer manifestation pure and impure emotions may differ very little. Two men may be playing chess, acting outwardly very similarly, but in one will burn self-love, desire of victory, and he will be full of different unpleasant feelings toward his rival — fear, envy of a clever move, spite, jealousy, animosity, or schemes to win, while the other will simply solve a complex mathematical problem which lies before him, not thinking about his rival at all.

The emotion of the first man will be impure, if only because it contains much of the mixed. The emotion of the second will be pure. The meaning of this is of course perfectly clear.

Examples of a similar division of outwardly similar emotions may be constantly seen in the esthetic, literary, scientific, public and even the spiritual and religious activities of men. In all regions of this activity only complete victory over the pseudo-personal elements leads a man to the correct understanding of the world and of himself. All emotions colored by such SELF-ELEMENTS are like concave, convex, or otherwise curved glasses which refract rays incorrectly and distort the image of the world.

Therefore the problem of emotional knowledge consists in a corresponding preparation of the emotions which serve as organs of knowledge.

> Become as little children . . . and
> Blessed are the pure in heart. . . .

In these evangelical words is expressed first of all the idea of the purification of the emotions. It is impossible to know through impure emotions. Therefore in the interests of a correct understanding of the world and of the self, man should undertake the purification and the elevation of his emotions.

This last leads to an entirely new view of *morality*. That morality the aim of which is to establish a system of correct relations toward the emotions, and to assist in their purification and elevation, ceases in our eyes to be some wearisome and self-limiting exercise in virtue. Morality — this is a form of esthetics.

That which is *not moral* is first of all not beautiful, because not concordant, not harmonious.

We see all the enormous meaning that morality may have in our life; we see the meaning morality has *for knowledge,* for the reason that there are emotions *by which we know,* and there are *emotions* by which we delude ourselves. If morality can actually help us to analyze these, then its value is indisputable from the standpoint of knowledge.

Current popular psychology knows very well that malice, hatred, anger, jealousy BLIND a man, DARKEN his reason; it knows that fear DRIVES ONE INSANE, etc., etc.

But we also know that *every emotion* may serve either knowledge or nescience.

Let us consider such an emotion — valuable and capable of high development — as *the pleasure of activity*. This emotion is a powerful motive force in culture, and of service in the perfection of life and in the evolution of all higher faculties of man. But it is also the cause of an infinite number of his delusions and *faux pas* for which he afterwards *pays bitterly*. In the passion of activity man is easily inclined to forget the *aim* that started him to act; to accept the activity itself for the aim and even to *sacrifice the aim* in order to preserve the activity. This is seen with especial clearness in the activity of various spiritual movements. Man, starting out in one direction, turns in the opposite one without himself noticing it, and often descends into the abyss thinking that he is scaling the heights.

There is nothing more contradictory, more paradoxical than the man *who is enticed away by activity*. We have become so accustomed to "man" that the strange perversions to which he is sometimes subject fail to startle us as curiosities.

Violence in the name of freedom; violence in the name of love; the Gospel of Christianity with sword in hand; the stakes of the Inquisition for the glory of a God of Mercy; the oppression of thought and speech on the part of the ministers of *religion* — all these are incarnated absurdities of which humanity only is capable.

Tertium Organum

A correct understanding of *morality* can preserve us in some degree from such perversions of thought. In our life in general there is not much morality. European culture has gone along the path of intellectual development. The intellect invented and organized without considering the moral meaning of its own activity. Out of this arose the paradox that the crown of European culture is the "dreadnaught."

Many people realize all this, and on account of it assume a negative attitude to all culture. But this is unjust. European culture created much other than dreadnaughts that is new and valuable, facilitating life. The elaboration of the *principles* of freedom and right; the abolition of slavery (though these are indeed nominal); the victory of man in many regions where nature presented to him a hostile front; the methods for the distribution of thought, the press; the miracles of contemporary medicine and surgery — all these are indisputably real conquests, and it is impossible not to take them into consideration. *But there is no morality in them,* i.e., there is no truth but too much of falsehood. We are satisfied with mere principles as such; we are content to think that eventually they will be introduced into life, and we neither marvel nor are disturbed at the thought that we ourselves (i.e., cultured humanity), developing beautiful principles, continually deny and controvert them in our lives. The man of European culture invents with equal readiness a machine gun and a new surgical apparatus. European culture began from the life of the savage, taking this life as an example as it were and starting to develop *all its sides* to the uttermost without thinking of their moral aspects. The savage crushed the head of his enemy with a simple club. We invented for this purpose complicated devices, making possible the crushing of hundreds and thousands of heads at once. Therefore such a thing as this happened: aerial navigation, toward which men had looked forward for millenniums, finally achieved, is used first of all for purposes of war.

Morality should be the co-ordination and the necessity for the co-ordination of all sides of life, i.e., of the actions of man and humanity with the higher emotions and the higher comprehensions of the intellect. From this point of view the statement previously made, that morality is a form of esthetics, becomes clear. Esthetics — the sense of beauty — is the *sensation* of the relation of parts to a whole, and the perception of the necessity for a certain harmonious relation. And morality is the same. Those actions, thoughts and feelings are not moral which are not co-ordinated, which are not harmonious with the higher understanding and the higher sensations accessible to man. The introduction of morality into our life would make it less paradoxical, less contradictory, more logical and — most important — more *civilized*; because now our vaunted civilization is much compromised by "dreadnaughts," i.e., war and everything that goes with it, as well as many things of "peaceful" life such as the death penalty, prisons, etc.

Morality, or moral esthetics in such a sense as is here shown, is necessary to us. Without it we too easily forget that the *word* has after all a certain relation to the act. We are interested in many things, we enter into many things, but for some strange reason we fail to note the incongruity between our spiritual life and our life on earth. Thus we create two lives. In one we are preternaturally strict with ourselves, analyze with great care every idea before we discuss it; in the other we permit with extreme ease any compromises, and easily keep from seeing that which we do not care to see. Moreover, we reconcile ourselves to this division. We do not find it necessary seriously to introduce into our lives our higher ideals, and almost accept as a principle the division of the "real" from the "spiritual." All of the indecencies of our life have arisen as a result of this; all of those infinite falsifications of our life — falsifications of the press, art, drama, science, politics — falsifications in which we suffocate as in a fetid swamp, but which we ourselves create, because we and none other are servants and ministers of those falsifications. We have no sense of the *necessity* to introduce our ideals into life, to introduce them *into our daily activity*, and we even admit the possibility that this activity may go counter to our spiritual quests, in accordance with one of those established standards the harm of which we recognize, but for which no one holds himself responsible because he did not create them himself. We have no *sense of personal responsibility*, no boldness, and we are even without the consciousness of their necessity.

All this would be very sad and hopeless if the concept "we" were not so dubious. In reality, the correctness of the very expression "we" is subject to grave doubt. The enormous majority of the population of this globe is engaged in effect in destroying, disfiguring, and falsifying the ideas of the minority. The majority is without ideas. It is incapable of understanding the ideas of the minority, and left to itself it must inevitably disfigure and destroy. Imagine a menagerie full of monkeys. In this menagerie a *man* is working. The monkeys observe his movements and try to imitate him but they can imitate only his visible movements; the meaning and aim of these movements are closed to them; therefore their actions will have quite another result. And should the monkeys escape from their cages and get hold of the man's tools, then perhaps they will destroy all his work, and inflict great damage on themselves as well. But they will never be able to create anything. Therefore *a man* would make a great mistake if he referred to their "work," and spoke of them as "we." Creation and destruction — or more correctly, the ability to create or the ability only to destroy — are the principal signs of the two types of men.

Morality is necessary to "man": only by regarding everything from the standpoint of morality is it possible to differentiate unmistakably the work of man from the activity of apes. But at the same time delusions are nowhere more easily created than in the region of morality. Allured by *his own particular morality* and moral gospel, a man forgets the *aim* of moral perfection, forgets that this aim consists in knowledge. He begins to see an aim in *morality itself*. Then occurs the a priori division of the emotions into good and bad, "moral" and "immoral." The correct understanding of the aim and meaning of the emotions is lost along with this. Man is charmed with his "niceness." He desires that everyone else should be just as nice as he, or as that remote ideal created by himself. Then appears delight in morality for morality's sake, a sort of moral sport — the exercise of morality for morality's sake. A man under these circumstances begins to be afraid of everything. Everywhere, in all manifestations of life, something "immoral" begins to appear to him, threatening to dethrone him or others from that height to which they have risen or may rise. This develops a preternaturally suspicious attitude toward the morality of others. In an ardor of proselytism, desiring to popularize his moral views, he begins quite definitely to regard everything which is not in accord with his morality as hostile to it. All this becomes "black" in his eyes. Starting with the idea of utter freedom, by arguments, by compromises, he very easily convinces himself that it is necessary to fight freedom. He already begins to admit a censure of thought. The free expression of opinions contrary to his own seems to him inadmissible. All this may be done with the best intentions, but the results of it are very well known.

There is no tyranny more ferocious than the tyranny of morality. Everything is sacrificed to it. And of course there is nothing so blind as such tyranny, as such "morality."

Nevertheless humanity needs morality, but of a different kind — such as is founded on the *real* data of superior knowledge. Humanity is passionately seeking for this, and perhaps will find it. Then on the basis of this *new morality* will occur a great division, and those few who will be able to follow it will begin to rule others, or they will disappear altogether. In any case, because of this new morality and those forces which it will engender, the contradictions of life will disappear, and those biped animals which constitute the majority of humanity will have no opportunity to pose as men any longer.

The organized forms of intellectual knowledge are: *science*, founded upon observation, calculation and experience; and *philosophy*, founded upon the speculative method of reasoning and drawing conclusions.

The organized forms of emotional knowledge are: *religion* and *art*. Religious teachings, taking on the character of different "cults" as they depart from the original "revelation," are founded entirely upon the emotional nature of man. Magnificent temples, the gorgeous vestments of priests and acolytes, the solemn ritual of worship, processions, sacrifices, singing, music, dances — all these have as their aim the attuning of man in a certain way, the evoking in him of certain definite feelings. The same purpose is served by religious myths, legends, stories of the lives of heroes and saints, prophecies, apocalypses — they all act upon the imagination, upon the feelings, although they fail to fulfil their original purpose, which is to transmit ideas, i.e., to serve knowledge.

The aim of it is to give *God* to man, to give him morality, i.e., to give him an accessible knowledge of the mysterious side of the world. Religion may deviate from its true aim, may serve *earthly* interests and purposes, but its foundation is the search for truth, for God.

Art serves *beauty*, i.e., emotional knowledge of its own kind. Art discovers beauty in everything, and compels man to feel it and therefore *to know*. Art is a powerful instrument of knowledge of the noumenal world: mysterious depths, each one more amazing than the last, open to the vision of man when he holds in his hands this magical key. But let him *only think* that this mystery is not for knowledge but for pleasure in it, and all the charm disappears at once. Just as soon as art begins to take delight in that beauty which is already *found*, instead of *the search for new beauty* an arrestment occurs and art becomes a superfluous estheticism, encompassing man's vision like a wall. The aim of art is *the search for beauty*, just as the aim of religion is the search for God and truth. And exactly as art stops, so religion stops also as soon as it ceases *to search* for God and truth, thinking it has found them. This idea is expressed in the precept: *Seek . . . the kingdom of God and his righteousness. . . .* It does not say, find; but merely, seek!

Science, philosophy, religion and art are forms of knowledge. The method of science is experiment; the method of philosophy is speculation; the method of religion and art is moral or esthetic *emotional* inspiration. But both science and philosophy, religion and art, begin to serve *true knowledge* only when in them commence to manifest the sensing and finding of some inner property in things. In general it is quite possible to say — and perhaps it will be most true to fact — that the aim of even purely intellectual systems of philosophy and science consists not at all in the giving to man of certain data of knowledge, but in the raising of man to such a height of thinking and feeling as to enable him to pass to those new and higher forms of knowledge to which art and religion approach more nearly. It is necessary however to remember that these very divisions into science, philosophy, religion and art betray the poverty and incompleteness of each. A complete religion unites in itself religion, art, philosophy and science; a complete art equally unites them, while a complete science or a complete philosophy comprehends religion and art. A religion which contradicts science, and a science which contradicts religion are both equally false.

CHAPTER XIX

Having established the *principle* of the possible unification of the forms of our knowledge, let us discover if this unification is not somewhere realized; how it may be realized; and whether it will be realized *in a form entirely new,* or in one of the existing forms which shall include all others in itself.

For this we shall return to the fundamental principles of our knowledge, and compare the possible chances for the development of different paths, i.e., we shall try to find out as best we may that path which leads to the new knowledge, and in the shortest time.

Up to a certain point we have already established this regarding the *emotional path;* the growth of the emotions, their purification and their liberation from the materialistic elements of *possession and fear of loss* must lead to super-personal knowledge and to intuition.

But how can the intellectual path lead to the new forms of knowledge?

First of all, what is the new knowledge?

The new knowledge is *direct knowledge,* by an inner sense. I feel my own pain directly; the new knowledge can give me the power to *sense,* as mine, the pain of another man. Thus the new knowledge is the expansion of a direct experience. The question is, can the expansion of objective knowledge be founded upon this new experience? Let us analyze the nature of objective knowledge.

Our objective knowledge is contained in science and philosophy. *Inner experience* science has always regarded as *a thing given,* which cannot be changed, but as something "doubtful," standing in need of verification and affirmation by the objective method. Science has studied

Tertium Organum

the world as an objective phenomenon, and it has striven to study the psyche and its properties as such another objective phenomenon.

In another quarter, the study of the psyche from the inside, so to speak, was proceeding simultaneously with this, but to this study no great significance was ever attached. The limits of inner knowledge, i.e., the limits of the psyche, were considered to be strictly definite, established, and unchangeable. Only for objective knowledge, founded upon identical inner experience, was the possibility of expansion admitted.

Let us discover if there is not some mistake here: is the expansion of objective knowledge, founded upon a limited experience, really possible, and are the possibilities of experience really limited?

Developing science, i.e., objective knowledge, is encountering obstacles everywhere. Science studies phenomena; just as soon as it attempts to discover *causes*, it is confronted with the wall of the unknown, and *to it* unknowable. The question narrows itself down to this: is this unknowable absolutely unknowable, or is it so only for the methods of our science?

At the present time the situation is just this: the number of unknown facts in every region of scientific knowledge is rapidly increasing; and the unknown threatens to swallow the known — or the accepted as known. One might define the progress of science, especially latterly, as a very rapid growth of *the regions of nescience*.

Nescience of course existed before, and not in less degree than at present. But before, it was not so clearly recognized — at that time science did not know *what it does not know*. Now it knows this more and more, and more and more knows its *conditionality*. A little more, and in every separate branch of science *that which it does not know* will become greater than *that which it knows*.

In every department science itself is beginning to repudiate its own foundations. A little more, and science in its entirety will ask, "Where am I?"

Positive thinking — which conceived of its problem as the deducing of general conclusions from the findings of each separate science and all of them combined — will feel itself compelled to deduce conclusions from that which science does not know. Then all the world will see before it the colossus with feet of clay, or rather without any feet at all, but with a formidable misty body, hanging in the air.

For a long time philosophy has realized the lack of feet of this colos-

Limitations of Positivism

sus, but the majority of cultivated mankind is still hypnotized by positivism, which sees something in place of those feet. However, it will be necessary to part company with this illusion very soon. Mathematics, lying at the very foundation of positive knowledge, and to which exact science always pointed with pride, as to its subject and vassal, is in reality now denying all positivism. Mathematics was included in the cycle of positive sciences only by mistake, and soon indeed mathematics will become the principal weapon AGAINST POSITIVISM.

By positivism I mean, in this connection, that system which affirms, in contradiction to Kant, that the study of phenomena *can* bring us nearer to things in themselves, i.e., which affirms that by going along the path of the study of phenomena we can come to an understanding of causes, and — this is important — which regards physico-mechanical phenomena as the cause of biological and psychic phenomena.

The usual positivistic view denies the existence of *the hidden side of life*, i.e., it finds that the hidden side consists of electro-magnetic phenomena and opens to us only little by little — and that the progress of science consists in the gradual unveiling of the hidden.

"This is not known *as yet*," says the positivist, when his attention is called to something 'hidden,' "*but it will be known*. Science, going by the same path that it has gone up to now, will discover this also. Five hundred years ago, Europe did not know of the existence of America; seventy years ago we did not know of the existence of bacteria; twenty-five years ago we did not know of the existence of radium. But America, bacteria and radium are all discovered now. Similarly and by the same methods, and by such methods only, will be discovered everything that is to be discovered. The apparatuses are being perfected, the methods, processes and observations are being refined. That which we did not even suspect a hundred years ago, has now become a generally known and generally understood fact. Everything that is possible to be known will become known after this manner."

Thus do the adherents of the positivistic viewpoints speak, but at the foundation of these reasonings lies a deep delusion.

The affirmation of positivism would be quite true did positivism move uniformly in all directions of the unknown; if sealed doors did not exist for it; if in the multitude of questions the *principal* questions did not remain just as obscure as in those times when science did not exist at all. We see that enormous regions are closed utterly to science, that it *never* penetrated into them, and worst of all it made *not a single step* in the direction of those regions.

There are multitudes of problems the solving of which science *has not even attempted*; problems in the presence of which the contemporary scientist, armed with all his science, is as helpless as a savage or a four-year-old child.

Such are the problems of life and death, the problems of space and time, the mystery of consciousness, etc., etc.

We all know this, and the only thing we can do is to try *not to think* about the existence of these problems, to forget about them. We do so as a rule, but this does not annihilate them. They continue to exist, and at any given moment we may turn to them and try on them the rigidity and force of our *scientific method*. And every time, at such an attempt, we find that our scientific method is not equal to these problems. By its aid we can discover the chemical composition of remote stars; can photograph the skeleton within the human body, invisible to the human eye; can invent a floating mine which can be controlled from a distance by means of electrical waves, and can in this way annihilate in a moment hundreds of lives; but by the aid of this method we cannot tell what the man standing beside us is thinking about. Not matter how much we may weigh, sound or photograph a man, we shall *never* know his thoughts *unless he himself tells them to us*. BUT THIS IS TRULY QUITE A DIFFERENT METHOD.

The sphere of action of the method of exact science is strictly limited. This sphere is the world of the immediate experience accessible for man. In the world lying beyond the domain of usual experience exact science with its methods has *never* penetrated and *will never penetrate*.

The expansion of objective knowledge is possible only in case direct experience is expanded. But in spite of all the growth of objective knowledge science has made not one step in this direction and the border-line of experience remains *in the same place*. Could *science* take a single step in this direction, were we able to feel or sense differently, then we might admit that science might move and take two, three, ten, and ten thousand steps. But it has taken *not even one*, and it is therefore reasonable to believe that it will never take it. The world outside the experience of the five senses is closed to objective investigation, and for this quite definite causes exist.

By no means everything that exists can be detected by any of five senses.

Objective existence is a very narrowly defined form of existence, and does not by any means exhaust or comprehend existence as a whole. The mistake of positivism consists in the fact that it has recognized as really existing only that which exists objectively, and it has even begun to deny *the very existence of all the rest.*

But what is objectivity?

We can define it in this way: because of the properties of *our* receptivity, or because of *the conditions* under which our psyche works, we segregate *a small number of facts* into a definite group. This group of facts represents in itself the objective world, and is accessible to the investigation of science. But in no case does this group represent in itself EVERYTHING THAT IS EXISTING. Extension in space and existence in time constitute the first condition of objective existence. And yet the forms of the extension of a thing in space, and those of its existence in time are created by the cognizing subject, and do not belong to the thing itself. Matter is first of all *three-dimensional.* This three-dimensionality is the form of our receptivity. Matter of four dimensions would imply a change in the form of our receptivity.

Materiality is the condition of existence in space and time, i.e., a condition of existence under which "at one time, and in one place, *two similar* phenomena cannot occur." This is an exhaustive definition of materiality. It is clear that under the conditions known to us, two similar phenomena, occurring simultaneously in one place, will compose one phenomenon. But this is obligatory for those conditions of existence which we know, i.e., for such matter as we perceive. For the universe it is absolutely not obligatory. We constantly observe the conditions of materiality in those cases in which we must create in our life *a sequence* of phenomena or are obliged to *select,* because our matter does not permit us to juxtapose in a definite interval of time more than a certain number of phenomena. The necessity for *selection* is perhaps the chief *visible* sign of materiality. Outside of matter, the necessity for selection is done away with, and if we imagine the life of a feeling being, independent of the conditions of materiality, such a being will be capable of possessing simultaneously such faculties as from our standpoint are incompatible, opposite, and eliminative of one another: the power of being in several places at the same time; to command different views; to perform opposite and mutually exclusive actions simultaneously.

In speaking of matter it is necessary always to remember that matter is not a substance, but a condition. Suppose for example, that a man is blind. It is impossible to regard this blindness as a substance; it is a condition of the existence of a given man. Matter is some sort of blindness.

Objective knowledge can grow infinitely, its progress depending on the perfection of its instruments and the refinement of its methods of observation and experiment. One thing only it cannot transcend — the limits of the three-dimensional sphere, i.e., the conditions of space and time, for the reason that objective knowledge is created under these conditions, and the conditions of the existence of the three-dimensional world are the conditions of its existence. Objective knowledge will always be subject to these conditions, for otherwise it would cease to exist. No apparatus, no instrument, will ever conquer these conditions, for should they conquer they would destroy themselves first of all. *Perpetual motion*, i.e., the violation of the fundamental laws of the three-dimensional world as we know it, would be the only victory over the three-dimensional world *in the three-dimensional world itself*.

But it is necessary to remember that objective knowledge does not study facts, but *only the perception of facts*.

In order that objective knowledge shall transcend the limits of the three-dimensional sphere, it is necessary that the conditions of perception shall change.

As long as this does not happen, our objective knowledge is confined within the limits *of an infinite three-dimensional sphere*. It can proceed infinitely upon the radii of that sphere, but it will never penetrate into that region *a section of which* constitutes our three-dimensional world. Moreover we know, from the preceding, that should our receptivity become more limited, then objective knowledge would be correspondingly limited also. It is impossible to convey to a dog the idea of the sphericality of the earth; to make it remember the weight of the sun and the distances between the planets is equally impossible. Its objective knowledge is vastly more *personal* than ours; and the cause of it lies in the dog's more limited psyche.

Thus we see that objective knowledge depends upon the properties of the psyche.

Indeed, between the objective knowledge of a savage and that of Herbert Spencer there is an enormous difference; but that of neither the one nor the other transcends the limit of the three-dimensional sphere, i.e., the limits of the "conditional," the unreal. In order to transcend the three-dimensional sphere it is necessary to expand or change the forms of receptivity.

Is the expansion of the limits of receptivity possible?

The study of complex forms of consciousness assures us that it is possible.

Plotinus, the famous Alexandrian philosopher (third century) affirmed that for perfect knowledge the subject and object must be united

— that the rational agent and the thing being comprehended must not be separate.

For that which *sees* is itself the thing, which IS SEEN. [*Select Works of Plotinus*. Bohn's Library, p. 271.]

Here it is indeed necessary to understand, "to see" other than in a literal sense. The "seeing" changes with the changes of the state of consciousness in which it is proceeding.

But what forms of consciousness exist?

Hindu philosophy makes the division into four states of consciousness: sleep, dream, waking, and the state of absolute consciousness — *turiya*.* (*The Ancient Wisdom*, Annie Besant.)

G. R. S. Mead, in the preface to Taylor's translation of Plotinus (*Bohn's Library*) correlates the terminology of Shankarâchârya — the leader of the *Advaita-Vedânta* school of ancient India — with that of Plotinus.

The first or spiritual state was ecstasy; from ecstasy it forgot itself into deep sleep; from profound sleep it awoke out of unconsciousness, but still within itself, into the internal world of dreams; from dreaming it passes finally into the thoroughly waking state, and the outer world of sense.

Ecstasy is the term used by Plotinus; it is entirely identical with the term *turiya* of Hindu psychology.

The consciousness, which is in a waking condition, is surrounded by what constitutes its sense-organs and receptive apparatus in the phenomenal world; it differentiates the "subjective" from the "objective," and differentiates its forms of perception from "reality." It recognizes the phenomenal objective world as reality, and dreams as unreality, and includes along with it, as being unreal, the entire subjective world. Its vague sensation of real things, lying beyond that which is apprehended by the organs of sense, i.e., sensations of noumena, consciousness identifies as it were with dreams — with the unreal, imaginary, abstract, subjective — and regards *phenomena* as the only reality.

Gradually convinced by reason of the unreality of phenomena, or inwardly sensing this unreality and the reality which lies behind, we free ourselves from the mirage of phenomena, we begin to understand that

* According to the interpretation of the Southern Hindu school of occultism, the four states of consciousness are understood in somewhat different order. The most remote from the True, the most illusory, is the waking state; the second — sleep — is already nearer to the True; the third — *deep sleep* without dreams — contact with the True; and the fourth, *sâmâdhi*, or ecstasy — union with the True.

all the phenomenal world is in substance subjective also, that the great realities lie deeper down. Then a complete change takes place in consciousness in all its concepts *about reality*. That which before was regarded as real becomes unreal, and that which was regarded as unreal becomes real.*

This transition into the absolute state of consciousness is "UNION WITH DIVINITY," "VISION OF GOD," EXPERIENCING THE "KINGDOM OF HEAVEN," "ENTERING NIRVANA." All these expressions of mystical religions represent the psychological fact of the expansion of consciousness, such an expansion that the consciousness absorbs itself in the *all*.

C. W. Leadbeater, in an essay, *Some Notes on the Higher Planes. Nirvana* (*The Theosophist*. July, 1910) writes:

Sir Edwin Arnold wrote of that beatific condition, that "the dewdrop slips into the shining sea."

Those who have passed through that most marvelous of experiences know that, paradoxical as it may seem, the sensation is exactly the reverse, and that a far closer description would be that THE OCEAN HAD SOMEHOW BEEN POURED INTO THE DROP!

The consciousness, wide as the sea, with "its centre everywhere and its circumference nowhere," is a great and glorious fact; but when a man attains it, it seems to him that his consciousness has widened to take in all that, not that he is merged into something else.

This pouring of the ocean into the drop occurs because the consciousness never loses itself, i.e., does not disappear, does not become extinguished. When it seems to us that consciousness is extinguished, in reality it is only changing its form, it ceases to be analogical to ours, and we lose the means of convincing ourselves of its existence.

We have no exact data at all to think that it is dissipated. In order to escape from the field possible to our observation, it is sufficient for consciousness TO CHANGE ONLY A LITTLE.

In the objective world, indeed, this "slipping of the dewdrop into the sea" leads to the annihilation of the drop, to the absorption of it by the sea. We have never observed another order of things in the objective world and therefore cannot imagine it. But in the *real*, i.e., the subjective world, of course another order must exist and operate. The DROP OF CONSCIOUSNESS merging with the SEA OF CONSCIOUSNESS *knows it, but does*

* The conceptions of the subjective and of the objective should undergo a change. The usual terminology will be incorrect for an exact understanding. Everything phenomenal will become subjective; and the truly objective will be that which under ordinary conditions is regarded as subjective or non-existent.

Plotinus on Knowledge

not itself cease to exist because of that. Therefore undoubtedly, the sea is absorbed by the drop.

In the *Letters to Flaccus* of Plotinus, we find a wonderful description of a psychology and theory of knowledge founded exactly upon the idea of the expansion of receptivity.

External objects present us only with appearances. Concerning them, therefore, we may be said to possess opinion rather than knowledge. The distinctions in the actual world of appearance are of import only to ordinary and practical men. Our question lies with the ideal reality that exists behind appearance. How does the mind perceive these ideas? Are they without us, and is the reason, like sensation, occupied with objects external to itself? What certainty would we then have — what assurance that our perception was infallible? The object perceived would be a something different from the mind perceiving it. We should have then an image instead of reality. It would be monstrous to believe for a moment that the mind was unable to perceive ideal truth as it is, and that we had not certainty and real knowledge concerning the world of intelligence. It follows, therefore, that this region of truth is not to be investigated as a thing external to us, and so only imperfectly known. It is within us. Here the objects we contemplate and that which contemplates are identical — both are thought. The subject cannot surely know an object different from itself. The world of ideas lies within our intelligence. Truth, therefore, is not the agreement of our apprehension of an external object with the object itself. It is the agreement of the mind with itself. Consciousness, therefore, is the sole basis of certainty. The mind is its own witness. Reason sees in itself that which is above itself and its source; and again, that which is below itself as still itself once more.

Knowledge has three degrees — opinion, science, illumination. The means or instrument of the first is sense; of the second dialectic; of the third intuition. To the last I subordinate reason. It is absolute knowledge founded on the identity of the mind knowing with the object known.

There is a raying out of all orders of existence, an external emanation from the ineffable One. There is again a returning impulse, drawing all upward and inward toward the centre from whence all came. . . . The wise man recognizes the idea of the good within him. This he develops by withdrawal into the holy place of his own soul. He who does not understand how the soul contains the beautiful within itself, seeks to realize beauty without by laborious production. His aim should rather be to concentrate and simplify, and so to expand his being; instead of going out into the manifold, to forsake it for the One, and to float upwards toward the divine fount of being whose stream flows within him.

You ask, how can we know the Infinite? I answer, not by reason. It is the office of reason to distinguish and define. The infinite, therefore, cannot be ranked among its objects. You can only apprehend the infinite by a faculty superior to reason, by entering into a state in which you are your finite self no longer — in which the divine essence is communicated to you. This is ecstasy. It is the liberation of your mind from its finite consciousness. Like can only apprehend like; when you thus cease to be finite, you become one with the infinite. In the reduction of your soul to its simplest self, its divine essence, you realize this union — this identity.

But this sublime condition is not of permanent duration. It is only now and then that we can enjoy this elevation above the limits of the body and the world. I myself have realized it but three times as yet, and Porphyry hitherto not once.

All that tends to purify and elevate the mind will assist you in this attainment, and facilitate the approach and the recurrence of these happy intervals. There are, then, different roads by which this end may be reached. The love of beauty which exalts the poet; that devotion to the One and that ascent of science which makes the ambition of the philosopher, and that love and those prayers by which some devout and ardent soul tends in its moral purity towards perfection — these are the great highways conducting to the height above the actual and the particular, where we stand in the immediate presence of the Infinite, who shines out as from the depths of the soul.

In another place in his works, Plotinus defines the ecstatic knowledge more exactly, presenting such properties of it as to reveal to us quite clearly that the infinite expansion of *subjective knowledge* is there meant.

When we see God [says Plotinus] we see him not by reason, but by something that is higher than reason. It is impossible however to say about him who sees that he sees, because he does not behold and discern *two different things* (the seer and the thing seen). He changes completely, ceases to be himself, preserves nothing of his I. Immersed in God, he constitutes one whole with Him; like the centre of a circle, which coincides with the centre of another circle.

CHAPTER XX

THERE is in existence an idea which a man should always call to mind when too much subjugated by the illusions of the reality of the *unreal*, visible world in which everything has a beginning and an end. It is the idea of infinity, the fact of infinity.

In the book *A New Era of Thought* — concerning which I have had already much to say — in the chapter "Space the Scientific Basis of Altruism and Religion," Hinton says:

. . . When we come upon infinity in any mode of our thought, it is a sign that that mode of thought is dealing with a higher reality than it is adapted for, and in struggling to represent it, can only do so by an infinite number of terms (of realities of a higher order).

Truly what is infinity, as the ordinary mind represents it to itself?

It is the only reality and at the same time it is the abyss, the bottomless pit into which the mind falls, after having risen to heights to which it is not native.

Let us imagine for a moment that a man begins to feel infinity in everything: every thought, every idea leads him to the realization of infinity.

This will inevitably happen to a man approaching an understanding of a higher order of reality.

But what will he feel under such circumstances?

He will sense a precipice, an abyss everywhere, no matter where he looks; and experience indeed an incredible horror, fear and sadness, until this fear and sadness shall transform themselves into the joy of the sensing of a new reality.

". . . An intolerable sadness is the very first experience of the Neo-phyte in occultism. . . ." says the author of *Light on the Path.*

We have already examined into the manner in which a two-dimensional being might approach to a comprehension of the third dimension. But we have never asked ourselves the question: what would it *feel*, beginning to sense the third dimension, beginning to be conscious of "a new world" environing it?

First of all, it would feel astonishment and fright — fright approaching horror; because in order to find the new world it must *lose* the old one.

Let us imagine the predicament of an animal in which flashes of *human* understanding have begun to appear.

What will it sense *first of all?* First of all, that its old world, *the world of the animal*, its comfortable, habitual world, the one in which it was born, to which it has become accustomed, and which it imagines to be the *only* real one, is crumbling away and falling all around it. Everything that before seemed real, becomes false, delusive, fantastic, unreal. The impression of the unreality of all its environment will be very strong.

Until such a being shall learn to comprehend the reality of another, higher order, until it shall understand that behind the crumbling old world one infinitely more beautiful and new is opening up, considerable time will necessarily pass. And during all this time, a being in whom this new consciousness is in process of unfoldment must pass from one abyss of despair to another, from one negation to another. It must repudiate *everything* around itself. Only by the repudiation of everything will the possibility of entering into a new life be realized.

With the beginning of the gradual loss of the old world, the logic of the two-dimensional being — or that which stood for it for logic — will suffer continual violation, and its strongest impression will be that there is *no logic at all*, that no laws of any sort even exist.

Formerly, when it was an animal, it reasoned:

This is this.	*This house is my own.*
That is that.	*That house is strange.*
This is not that.	*The strange house is not my own.*

The strange house and its own house the animal regards as *different objects*, having nothing in common. But now it will surprisedly understand that *the strange house* and *its own house* are EQUALLY *houses.*

How will it express this in its language of perceptions? Strictly speak-

Animal Logic

ing, it will not be able to express this at all, because it is impossible to express concepts in the language of an animal. The animal will simply mix up the sensations of the strange house and its own house. Confusedly, it will begin to feel some *new properties* in houses, and along with this it will feel less clearly those properties which made the strange house strange. Simultaneously with this, the animal will begin to sense *new* properties which it did not know before. As a result it will undoubtedly experience the necessity for a system of generalization of these new properties — the necessity for a new logic expressing the relations of the new order of things. But having no concepts it will not be in a position to construe the axioms of Aristotelian logic, and will express its impression of the new order in the form of the entirely absurd but more nearly true proposition:

This is that.

Or let us imagine that to the animal with the rudimentary logic expressing its *sensations,*

This is this.
That is that.
This is not that.

somebody tries to prove that two different objects, two houses — its *own* and *a strange one* — are similar, that they represent *one and the same thing,* that they are both *houses.* The animal will never credit this *similarity.* For it the two houses, its own, *where it is fed,* and the strange one, *where it is beaten* if it enters, will remain *entirely different.* There will be nothing in common in them for it, and the effort to prove to it the similarity of these two houses will lead to nothing *until it senses this itself.* Then, sensing confusedly the idea of the likeness of two different objects, and being without concepts, the animal will express this as something *illogical* from its own point of view. The idea, *this and that are similar objects,* the articulate two-dimensional being will translate into the language of its logic, in the shape of the formula: *this is that;* and of course will pronounce it an absurdity, and that the sensation of the new order of things leads to logical absurdities. But it will be unable to express that which it senses in any other way.

We are in exactly the same position — *when we dead awaken* — i.e., when we *men,* come to the realization of that other life, to the comprehension of higher things.

The same fright, the same *loss of the real*, the same impression of utter and never-ending illogicality, the same formula: "this is that," will afflict us.

In order to realize *the new world*, we must understand *the new logical order of things.*

Our usual logic assists us in the investigation of the relations of the phenomenal world only. Many attempts have been made to define *what logic is.* But logic is just as essentially undefinable as is mathematics.

What is mathematics? The science of magnitudes.

What is logic? The science of concepts.

But these are not definitions, they are only the *translation* of the name. Mathematics, or the science of magnitudes, is that system which studies the *quantitative* relations between things; logic, or the science of concepts, is that system which studies the *qualitative* (categorical) relations between things.

Logic has been built up quite in the same way as mathematics. As with logic, so also with mathematics (at least the generally known mathematics of "finite" and "constant" quantities), both were deduced by us from the observation of the phenomena of *our* world. Generalizing our observations, we gradually discovered those relations which we called the fundamental laws of the world.

In logic, these fundamental laws are included in the axioms of Aristotle and of Bacon.

A *is* A.
(*That which was* A *will be* A.)

A *is not* Not-A.
(*That which was* Not-A *will be* Not-A.)

Everything is either A *or* Not-A.
Everything will be either A *or* Not-A.

The logic of Aristotle and Bacon, developed and supplemented by their many followers, deals *with concepts only.*

Logos, the word, is the object of logic. An idea, in order to become the object of logical reasoning, in order to be subjected to the laws of logic, must be expressed in a word. That which cannot be expressed in a word cannot enter into a logical system. Moreover a word can enter into a logical system, can be subjected to logical laws, *only as a concept*.

At the same time we know very well that *not everything can be expressed in words*. In our life and in our feelings there is much that cannot be expressed in concepts. Thus it is clear that even at the present moment, at the present stage of our development, not everything can be entirely logical for us. There are many things which in their substance are *outside of logic* altogether. This includes the entire region of feelings, emotions, religion. All art is just one entire illogicality; and as we shall presently see, *mathematics*, the most exact of sciences, is entirely illogical.

If we compare the axioms of the logic of Aristotle and of Bacon with the axioms of mathematics as it is commonly known, we find between them complete similarity.

The axioms of logic,

A *is* A.
A *is not* Not-A.
Everything is either A *or* Not-A.

fully correspond to the fundamental axioms of mathematics, to the axioms of identity and difference.

Every magnitude is equal to itself.
The part is less than the whole.
Two magnitudes, equal separately to a third, are equal to each other, etc.

The similarity between the axioms of mathematics and those of logic extends very far, and this permits us to draw a conclusion about their similar origin.

The laws of mathematics and of logic are the laws of the reflection of the phenomenal world in our receptivity and in our reasoning faculty.

Just as the axioms of logic can deal with concepts only, and are related solely to them, so the axioms of mathematics apply to *finite* and *constant* magnitudes only, and are related solely to them.

THESE AXIOMS ARE UNTRUE IN RELATION TO INFINITE AND VARIABLE MAGNITUDES, just as the axioms of logic are untrue even in relation to emotions, to symbols, to the musicality and *the hidden meaning of words*, to say nothing of those ideas which cannot be expressed in words.

What does this mean?

Tertium Organum

It means that the axioms of logic and of mathematics are deduced by us from the observation of *phenomena*, i.e., of the phenomenal world, and represent in themselves a certain *conditional incorrectness*, which is necessary for the knowledge of the *unreal* "subjective" world — in the true meaning of that word.

As has been said before, we have in reality *two mathematics*. One, *the mathematics of finite and constant numbers*, represents a quite artificial construction for the solution of problems based on conditional data. The chief of these conditional data consists in the fact that in problems of *this mathematics* there is always taken *the t of the universe only*, i.e., one section only of the universe is taken, which section is never taken in conjunction with another one. This mathematics of finite and constant magnitudes studies *an artificial universe*, and is in itself something especially created on the basis of our observation of *phenomena*, and serves for the simplification of these observations. *Beyond phenomena* the mathematics of finite and constant numbers cannot go. It is dealing with an imaginary world, with imaginary magnitudes. The practical results of those applied sciences which are built upon mathematical science should not confuse the observer, because these are merely the solutions of problems in definite artificial conditions.

The other, *the mathematics of infinite and variable magnitudes*, represents something entirely real, built upon the reasonings in regard to *a real world*.

The first is related to the world of phenomena, which represents in itself nothing other than *our incorrect* apprehension and perception of the world.

The second is related to the world of noumena, which represents in itself *the world as it is*.

The first is unreal, it exists in *our consciousness, in our* imagination.

The second is real, it expresses the relations of a real world.

The mathematics of transfinite numbers, so called, may serve as an example of "real mathematics," violating the fundamental axioms of our mathematics (and logic).

By *transfinite numbers*, as their name implies, is meant numbers *beyond* infinity.

Infinity, as represented by the sign ∞ is the mathematical expression with which, as such, it is possible to perform all operations: divide, multiply, raise to powers. It is possible to raise infinity to the power of infinity — it will be ∞^∞. This magnitude is an infinite number of times greater than simple infinity. *And at the same time they are both equal*: $\infty = \infty^\infty$. And this is the most remarkable property of transfinite numbers. You may perform with them any operations whatsoever, *they will change in a corresponding manner, remaining at the same time equal*. This violates the fundamental laws of mathematics accepted for *finite* numbers. After a change, the finite number cannot be equal to itself. But here we see how, *changing*, the transfinite number remains equal to itself.

After all, transfinite numbers are entirely real. We can find examples corresponding to the expression ∞ and even ∞^∞ and ∞^{∞^∞} in our world.

Let us take a line — any segment of a line. We know that the number of points on this line is equal to infinity, for a point has no dimension. If our segment is equal to one inch, and beside it we shall imagine a segment a mile long, then in the little segment each point will correspond to a point in the large one. The number of points in a segment one inch long is infinite. The number of points in a segment one mile long is also infinite. We get $\infty = \infty$.

Let us now imagine a square, one side of which is a given segment, a. The number of *lines* in a square is infinite. The number of points in each line is infinite. Consequently, the number of points in a square is equal to infinity multiplied by itself an infinite number of times ∞^∞. This magnitude is undoubtedly infinitely greater than the first one: ∞, and at the same time they are equal, as all infinite magnitudes are equal, because, if there be an infinity, then it is one, and cannot change.

Upon the square a^2, let us construct a cube. This cube consists of an infinite number of squares, just as a square consists of an infinite number of lines, and a line of an infinite number of points. Consequently, the number of points in the cube, a^3 is equal to ∞^{∞^∞}, this expression is equal to the expression ∞^∞ and ∞, i.e., this means that an infinity continues to grow, *remaining at the same time unchanged*.

Thus in transfinite numbers, we see that two magnitudes equal separately to a third, can be not equal to each other. Generally speaking, we see that the fundamental axioms of our mathematics *do not work* there, are not there valid. We have therefore a full right to establish the law, that the fundamental axioms of mathematics enumerated above are not applicable to transfinite numbers, but are applicable and valid only for *finite* numbers.

We may also say that the fundamental axioms of our mathematics are valid for *constant* magnitudes only. Or in other words they demand *unity of time and unity of place.* That is, each magnitude is equal to itself at a *given* moment. But if we take a magnitude which varies, and take it in different moments, then it will not be equal to itself. Of course, we may say that changing, it becomes *another* magnitude, that it is a given magnitude only so long as it does not change. But this is precisely the thing that I am talking about.

The axioms of our usual mathematics are applicable to finite and *constant* magnitudes only.

Thus quite in opposition to the usual view, we must admit that the mathematics of finite and constant magnitudes is unreal, i.e., that it deals with the unreal relations of unreal magnitudes; while the mathematics of infinite and fluent magnitudes is real, i.e., that it deals with the real relations of real magnitudes.

Truly the greatest magnitudes of *the first mathematics* has no dimension whatever, it is equal to *zero*, or a point, in comparison with any magnitude of the second mathematics, ALL MAGNITUDES OF WHICH, DESPITE THEIR DIVERSITY, ARE EQUAL AMONG THEMSELVES.

Thus both here, as in logic, the axioms of the *new mathematics* appear as absurdities:

A magnitude can be not equal to itself.
A part can be equal to the whole, or it can be greater than the whole.
One of two equal magnitudes can be infinitely greater than another.
All DIFFERENT *magnitudes are equal among themselves.*

A complete analogy is observed between the axioms of mathematics and those of logic. The logical unit — a concept — possesses all the properties of a *finite* and constant magnitude. The fundamental axioms of mathematics and logic are essentially one and the same. They are correct under the same conditions, and under the same conditions they cease to be correct.

Without any exaggeration we may say that the fundamental axioms of mathematics and of logic are correct only just as long as mathematics and logic deal with magnitudes which are *artificial, conditional,* and which do not exist in nature.

Mathematics New and Old

The truth is that in nature there are no *finite*, constant magnitudes, just as also there are no *concepts*. The finite, constant magnitude, and the concept are conditional abstractions, not reality, but merely the sections of reality, so to speak.

How shall we reconcile the idea of the absence of constant magnitudes with the idea of *an immobile universe*? At first sight one appears to contradict the other. But in reality this contradiction does not exist. Not *this* universe is immobile, but the greater universe, the world of many dimensions, of which we know that perpetually moving section called the three-dimensional infinite sphere. Moreover, the very concepts of motion and immobility need revision, because, as we usually understand them with the aid of our reason, they do not correspond to reality.

Already we have analyzed in detail how the idea of motion follows from our time-sense, i.e., *from the imperfection of our space-sense.*

Were our space-sense more perfect in relation to any given object, say to the body of a given man, we could embrace all his life in time, from birth to death. Then within the limits of this embrace that life would be for us a constant magnitude. But now, at every given moment of it, it is for us not a constant but a variable magnitude. That which we call a body does not exist in reality. It is only the section of that four-dimensional body that we never see. We ought always to remember that our entire three-dimensional world does not exist in reality. It is a creation of our imperfect senses, the result of their imperfection. This is not *the world* but merely that which we see of the world. The three-dimensional world — this is the four-dimensional world observed through the narrow slit of our senses. Therefore all magnitudes which we regard as such in the three-dimensional world are not real magnitudes, but merely *artificially assumed.*

They do not exist really, in the same way as *the present* does not exist really. This has been dwelt upon before. By *the present* we designate the transition from the future into the past. But this transition has no extension. Therefore the present does not exist. Only the future and past exist.

Thus constant magnitudes in the three-dimensional world are only abstractions, just as *motion* in the three-dimensional world is, *in substance*, an abstraction. *In the three-dimensional world* there is no change, no motion. In order to think motion, we already need the four-dimensional world. The three-dimensional world does not exist in reality, or it exists only during one ideal moment. In the next ideal moment there already exists *another* three-dimensional world. Therefore the magnitude A in the following moment is already not A, but B, in the next C, and so forth to infinity. It is equal to itself in one ideal moment only. In other words, within the limits of each ideal moment the axioms of mathematics are true; for the comparison of two ideal moments they are merely conditional, as the logic of Bacon is conditional in comparison with the logic of Aristotle. *In time*, i.e., in relation to variable magnitudes, from the standpoint of the ideal moment, they are untrue.

The idea of constancy or variability emanates from the impotence of our limited reason to comprehend a thing otherwise than by its section. If we would comprehend a thing in four dimensions, let us say a human body from birth to death, then it will be the whole and *constant* body, the section of which we call *a-changing-in-time* human body. A moment of life, i.e., a body as we know it in the three-dimensional world, is a point on an infinite line. Could we comprehend this body as a whole, then we should know it as an *absolutely constant* magnitude, with all its multifariousness of forms, states and positions; but then to this constant magnitude the axioms of our mathematics and logic would be inapplicable, because it would be an *infinite* magnitude.

We cannot comprehend this infinite magnitude. We comprehend always its *sections only*. And our mathematics and logic are related to this imaginary section of the universe.

CHAPTER XXI

EVERYTHING that has been said about mathematical magnitudes is true also with regard to logical concepts. *Finite* mathematical magnitudes and *logical* concepts are subject to the same laws.

We have now established that the laws discovered by us in a space of three dimensions, and operating in that space, are inapplicable, incorrect and untrue in a space of a greater number of dimensions.

And as this is true of mathematics, so is it true of logic.

As soon as we begin to consider infinite and variable magnitudes instead of those which are finite and constant, we perceive that the fundamental axioms of our mathematics cannot be applied to the former class.

And as soon as we begin to think in other terms than those of concepts, we must be prepared to encounter an enormous number of absurdities *from the standpoint of existing logic.*

These absurdities seem to us such, because we approach the world of many dimensions with the logic of the three-dimensional world.

It has been proven already that to an animal, i.e., to a two-dimensional being, thinking not by concepts, but by perceptions, our logical ideas must seem absurd.

The *logical* relations in the world of many dimensions seem equally absurd to us. We have no reason whatsoever to hope that the relations of *the world of causes* can be logical from our point of view. On the contrary, it may be said that EVERYTHING LOGICAL is phenomenal. Nothing can be logical, from our standpoint, *there.* All that is *there* must seem to us *a logical absurdity,* nonsense. We must remember that it is impossible to penetrate there with *our logic.*

Tertium Organum

The relation of the general trend of the thought of humanity toward the "other world" has always been highly incorrect.

In "positivism" men have denied that other world altogether. This was because, not admitting the possibility of relations other than those formulated by Aristotle and Bacon, men denied the *very existence* of that which seemed absurd and impossible from the standpoint of those formulæ. Also, in spiritism they attempted to construct the noumenal world on the model of the phenomenal, that is, against reason, against nature, they wanted at all costs to prove that the other world is *logical from our standpoint*, that the same laws of causality operate just as in our world, and that the other world is nothing more than the extension of ours. The "other world" of spiritists or spiritualists in all existing descriptions of it is a naïve and barbaric concept of the unknown.

Positive philosophy perceived the absurdity of all dualistic theses, but having no power to expand the field of its activity, limited by logic and "the infinite sphere," it could think of nothing better than to DENY.

Mystical philosophy alone felt the possibility of relations other than those of the phenomenal world. But it was arrested by hazy and unclear sensations, finding it impossible to define and classify them.

Nevertheless, *science must come to mysticism*, because in mysticism there is a new method — and then to the study of different forms of consciousness, i.e., of forms of receptivity different from our own. Science should throw off almost everything old and should start afresh with a new theory of knowledge.

Science cannot deny the fact that mathematics grows, expands, and escapes from the limits of the visible and measurable world. Entire departments of mathematics take into consideration quantitative relations which did not and do not exist in the real world of positivism, i.e., relations which have no correspondence to any realities in the visible, three-dimensional world.

But there cannot be any mathematical relations to which the relation of some realities would not correspond. Therefore mathematics transcends the limits of our world, and penetrates into a world unknown. This is the *telescope*, by the aid of which we begin to investigate the *space of many dimensions* with its worlds. Mathematics goes ahead of our thought, ahead of our power of imagination and perception. *Even now* it is engaged in calculating relations which we cannot imagine or comprehend.

It is impossible to deny all this, even from the strictly "positivistic," i.e., *positive* standpoint. Thus science, having admitted the possibility

The Chains of Logic

of the expansion of mathematics beyond the limits of the sensuously perceived world — that is beyond the limits of a world *accessible* (though theoretically) to the organs of sense and their mechanical aids — must thereby recognize the expansion of the *real world* far beyond the limits of any "infinite sphere" or of our logic, i.e., must *recognize* the reality of "the world of many dimensions."

The recognition of the reality of the world of many dimensions is the *already accomplished* transition to, and understanding of, the world of the wondrous. And this transition to the wondrous is impossible without the recognition of the *reality* of new logical relations which are absurd and impossible from the standpoint of our logic.

What are the laws of our logic?

They are the laws of our receptivity of the three-dimensional *world*, or *the laws of our three-dimensional receptivity of the world*.

If we desire to escape from the three-dimensional world and go farther, we must first of all work out the fundamental logical principles which would permit us to observe the relations of things in a world of many dimensions — seeing in them a certain reasonableness, and not complete absurdity. If we enter there armed only with the principles of the logic of the three-dimensional world, these principles will drag us back, will not give us a chance to rise from the earth.

First of all we must throw off the chains of our logic. This is the first, the great, the chief liberation toward which humanity must strive. Man, throwing off the chains of "three-dimensional" logic, has already penetrated, in thought, into another world. And not only is this transition possible, but it is accomplished constantly. Although unhappily we are not entirely conscious of our rights in "another world," and often sacrifice these rights, regarding ourselves as limited to this *earthly* world, paths nevertheless exist. Poetry, mysticism, the idealistic philosophy of all ages and peoples, preserve the traces of such transitions. Following these traces, we ourselves can find the path. Ancient and modern thinkers have given us many keys with which we may open mysterious doors; many magical formulæ, before which these doors open of themselves. But we have not understood either the purpose of these keys or the meaning of the formulæ. We have also lost the understanding of magical ceremonies and rites of initiation into mysteries which had a single purpose: to help this transformation in the soul of man.

Therefore the doors remained closed, and we even denied that there was anything whatever behind them; or, suspecting the existence of another world, we regard it as similar to ours, and separate from ours, and tried to penetrate there unconscious of the fact that the chief obstacle in our path was our own division of the world into *this* world and *that*.

The world is one, only the ways of knowing it are different; and with imperfect methods of knowledge it is impossible to penetrate into that which is accessible to perfect methods only.

All attempts to penetrate mentally into that higher, noumenal world, or world of causes, by means of the logic of the phenomenal world, if they did not fail altogether, or did not lead to *castles in the air,* gave only one result: in becoming conscious of a new order of things, a man lost the sense of the reality of the old order. The visible world began to seem to him fantastic and unreal, everything all about him was disappearing, was vanishing like smoke, leaving a dreadful feeling of *illusion.* In everything he felt the abyss of infinity, and everything was plunging into the abyss.

This sense of the infinite is the first and most terrible trial before initiation. Nothing exists! A little miserable soul feels itself suspended in an infinite void. Then even this void disappears! Nothing exists. There is only infinity, a constant and continuous division and dissolution of everything. The mystical literature of all peoples abounds in references to this sensation of *darkness and emptiness.*

Such was that mysterious deity of the ancient Egyptians, about which there exists a story in the *Orpheus* myth, in which it is described as a *"Thrice-unknown darkness in contemplation of which all knowledge is resolved into ignorance."* *

This means that man must have felt horror transcending all limits as he approached the world of causes with the knowledge of the world of phenomena only, his instrument of logic having proved useless, because all the new eluded him. In *the new* as yet he sensed chaos only, *the old* had disappeared, gone away and become unreal. Horror and regret for the loss of the old mingled with horror of the new — unknown and *terrible by its infinitude.*

At this stage man experiences the same thing that an animal, becoming a man, would feel. Having looked into *a new world* for an instant, it is attracted by the life left behind. The world which it saw only for an instant seems but a dream, a vision, the creation of imagination, but the familiar old world, too, is never thereafter the same, it is too narrow, in it there is not sufficient room. The awakening consciousness can no longer live the free life of the beast. Already it knows something dif-

---

* "The Ancient Wisdom," by Annie Besant, Introd. p. 23, Theosophical Publishing Society, London.

The Sensation of Infinity

ferent, it hears some voices, even though *the body* holds it. And the animal does not know where or how it can escape from the body or from itself.

A man on the threshold of a new world experiences literally the same thing. He has heard celestial harmonies, and the wearisome songs of earth touch him no longer, nor do they move him — or if they touch and move him it is because they remind him of celestial harmonies, of the inaccessible, of the unknown. He has experienced the sensation of an unusual EXPANSION of consciousness, when everything was clear to him for a moment, and he cannot reconcile himself to the sluggish *earthly* work of the brain.

These moments of the "sensation of infinity" are accompanied by unusual emotions.

In theosophical literature, and in books on occultism, it is often asserted that on entering into the "astral" world, man begins to see new colors, colors which are not in the solar spectrum.* In this symbolism of the new colors of the "astral sphere" is conveyed the idea of those *new emotions* which man begins to feel along with the sensation of the expansion of consciousness — "of the sea pouring into the drop." This is the "strange bliss" of which mystics speak, the "heavenly light" which saints "see," the "new" sensations experienced by poets. Even conversational psychology identifies "ecstasy" with entirely unusual sensations, inaccessible and unknown to man in the life of every day.

This sensation of *light* and of unlimited joy is experienced at the moment of the expansion of consciousness (the unfoldment of *the mystical lotus* of the Hindu yogi), at the moment of the sensation of infinity, and it yields also the sensation of darkness and of unlimited horror.

What does this mean?

How shall we reconcile the sensation of light with the sensation of darkness, the sensation of joy with that of horror? Can these exist simultaneously? Do they occur simultaneously?

They do so occur, and must be exactly thus. Mystical literature gives us examples of it. The simultaneous sensations of light and darkness, joy and horror, symbolize as it were the strange duality and contradiction of human life. It may happen to a man of dual nature, who following one side of his nature has been led far into "spirit," and on the other side is deeply immersed in "matter," i.e., in illusion, in unreality — to one who believes too much in the reality of the unreal.

* Although it should be remembered that we see *only three* out of seven colors of the solar spectrum.

Generally speaking the sensation of light, of life, of consciousness penetrating all, of happiness, gives a *new* world. But the same world to the unprepared mind will give the sensation of infinite darkness and horror. In this case the sensation of horror will arise from *the loss of everything real*, from the disappearance of *this* world.

In order not to experience the horror of the new world, it is necessary to know it beforehand, either emotionally — by faith or love — or intellectually, by *reason*.

And in order not to experience horror from the loss of the old world, it is necessary to have renounced it *voluntarily* either through faith or reason.

One must renounce all the beautiful, bright world in which we are living; one must admit that it is ghostly, phantasmal, unreal, deceitful, illusory, *mayavic*. One must reconcile oneself to this unreality, not be afraid of it, but rejoice at it. One must give up everything. One must become POOR IN SPIRIT, i.e., make oneself *poor* by the effort of one's spirit.

This most profound philosophical truth is expressed in the beautiful evangelical symbol:

Blessed are the poor in spirit: for theirs is the kingdom of heaven.

These words become clear in the sense of a renouncement of the material world only. "Poor in spirit" does not mean poor materially, in the worldly meaning of the word, and still less does it signify *poverty of spirit*. Spiritual poverty is the renouncement of matter; such "poverty" is his when a man has no earth under his feet, no sky above his head.

Foxes have holes, and birds of the air have nests, but the Son of man hath not where to lay his head.

This is the poverty of the man who is *entirely* alone, because father, mother, other men, even the nearest *here on earth* he begins to regard differently, not as he regarded them before; and renounces them because he discerns the *true substances* that he is striving toward; just as, renouncing the phenomenal illusions of the world, he approaches the truly real.

The moment of transition — that terrible moment of *the loss of the old* and *the unfoldment of the new* — has been represented in innumerable allegories in ancient literature. To make this transition easy was the purpose of the *mysteries*. In India, in Egypt, in Greece, special preparatory rituals existed, sometimes merely symbolical, sometimes real, which actually brought a soul to the very portals of the new world, and opened these portals at the moment of *initiation*. But no outward rituals and ceremonies could take the place of self-initiation. The great work must have been going on *inside* the soul and mind of man.

But how can *logic* help a man to pass to the consciousness of a new and higher world?

We have seen that MATHEMATICS has already found the path into that higher order of things. Penetrating there, it first of all renounces its fundamental axioms of identity and difference.

In the world of infinite and fluent magnitudes, a magnitude may be *not equal to itself; a part may be equal to the whole; and of two equal magnitudes one may be infinitely greater than the other.*

All this sounds like an absurdity from the standpoint of the mathematics of finite and constant numbers. But the mathematics of finite and constant numbers is itself the calculation of relations between non-existent magnitudes, i.e., an absurdity. And therefore only that which from the standpoint of this mathematics seems an absurdity, can be the truth.

Logic now goes along the same path. It must renounce itself, come to perceive the necessity for its own annihilation — then out of it a new and higher logic can arise.

In his *Critique of Pure Reason* Kant proved the possibility of *transcendental logic.*

Before Bacon and earlier than Aristotle, in the ancient Hindu scriptures, the formulæ of this higher logic were given, opening the doors of mystery. But the meaning of these formulæ was rapidly lost. They were preserved in ancient books, but remained there as some strange mummeries of extinguished thought, the words without real content.

New thinkers again discovered these principles, and expressed them in new words, but again they remained incomprehensible, again they suffered transformation into some unnecessary ornamental form of words. *But the idea persisted.* A consciousness of the possibility of finding and establishing the laws of the higher world was never lost. Mystical philosophy never regarded the logic of Aristotle as all-embracing and all-powerful. It built its system *outside of logic* or above logic, unconsciously going along those paths of thought paved in remote antiquity.

The higher logic existed before *deductive* and *inductive* logic was formulated. This higher logic may be called *intuitive* logic — the logic of infinity, the logic of ecstasy.

Not only is this logic possible, but it *exists,* and has existed from time immemorial; it has been formulated many times; it has entered into philosophical systems as their key — but for some strange reason *has not been recognized as logic.*

It is possible to deduce the system of this logic from many *philosophical* systems. The most precise and complete formulation of the law of higher logic I find in the writing of Plotinus, in his *On Intelligible Beauty.* I shall quote this passage in the succeeding chapter.

I have called this system of higher logic *Tertium Organum* because *for us* it is *the third canon* — third instrument — *of thought* after those of Aristotle and Bacon. The first was the *Organon,* the second, *Novum Organum.* But *the third* existed earlier than the first.

Man, master of this instrument, of this key, may open the door of *the world of causes* without fear.

The axioms which *Tertium Organum* embraces cannot be formulated in our language. If we attempt to formulate them in spite of this, they will produce the impression of absurdities. Taking the axioms of Aristotle as a model, we may express the principal axiom of the new logic in our poor earthly language in the following manner:

A *is both* A *and Not-A.*

or

Everything is both A *and Not-A.*

or,

Everything is All.

But these axioms are in effect absolutely impossible. They are not *the axioms of higher logic,* they are merely *attempts* to express the axioms of this logic in concepts. In reality the ideas of higher logic are *inexpressible* in concepts. When we encounter such an inexpressibility it means that we have touched the world of causes.

The logical formula: A *is both* A *and Not-A,* corresponds to the mathematical formula: A *magnitude can be greater or less than itself.*

The absurdity of both these propositions shows that they cannot refer to our world. Of course *absurdity,* as such, is indeed not an index of the attributes of noumena, but the attributes of noumena will certainly be expressed in what are absurdities to us. To hope to find in the world of

The Higher Logic

causes anything logical from our standpoint is just as useless as to think that *the world of things* can exist in accordance with the laws of *a world of shadows* or stereometry according to the laws of planimetry.

To master the fundamental principles of *higher logic* means to master the fundamentals of the understanding of *a space of higher dimensions* or of the world of the wondrous.

In order to approach to a clear understanding of the relations of the multi-dimensional world we must free ourselves from all the "idols" of *our world,* as Bacon calls them, i.e., from all obstacles to *correct* receptivity and reasoning. Then we shall have taken the most important step toward an inner affinity with the world of the wondrous.

A two-dimensional being, in order to approach to an understanding of the three-dimensional world, already should have become *a three-dimensional being* before it can rid itself of its "idols," i.e., of its conventional — converted into axiomatic — ways of feeling and thinking, which create for it the illusion of two-dimensionality.

What is it exactly from which the two-dimensional being must liberate itself?

First of all — and most important — from the assurance that *that which it sees and senses really exists*; from this will come the consciousness of the incorrectness of its perception of the world, and then the idea that the *real, new* world must exist in quite other forms — new, incomparable, incommensurable with relation to the old ones. Then the two-dimensional being must overcome its sureness of the correctness of its *categories.* It must understand that things which seem to it different and separate from one another may be parts of some to it incomprehensible *whole,* or that they have much in common which it does not perceive; and that things which seem to it one and indivisible are in reality infinitely complex and multifarious.

The mental growth of the two-dimensional being must proceed along the path of the recognition of those common properties of objects, *unknown to it before,* which are the result of their similar origin or similar functions, incomprehensible from the point of view of a plane.

When once the two-dimensional being has admitted the possibility of the existence of hitherto unknown *common* properties of objects, which before seemed different, then it has already approached to our own understanding of the world. It has approached to our logic, has begun to understand *the collective name,* i.e., a word used *not as a proper noun,* but as an appellate noun — a word expressing a concept.

The "idols" of the two-dimensional being, hindering the development of its consciousness, are those *proper nouns*, which it has itself given to all the objects surrounding it. For such a being each object has its own proper noun, corresponding to its perception of the object; common names, corresponding to concepts, it knows not of. Only by getting rid of these *idols*, by understanding that the names of things can be not only proper, but common ones as well, will it be possible for it to advance farther, to develop mentally, to approach the human understanding of the world. Take the most simple sentence:

John and Peter are both men.

For the two-dimensional being this will be an absurdity, and it will represent the idea to itself after this fashion:

John and Peter are both Johns and Peters.

In other words, every one of our logical propositions will be an absurdity to it. Why this is so is clear. Such a thing has no concepts; *the proper nouns* which constitute the speech of such a being have no plurals. It is easy to understand that any plural of our speech will seem to it an absurdity.

Where are our "idols"? From what shall we liberate ourselves in order to pass to an understanding of the multi-dimensional world?

First of all we must get rid of our assurance that we see and sense that which exists in reality, and that the real world is like the world which we see — i.e., we must rid ourselves of the illusion of the material world. We must understand *mentally* all the illusoriness of the world perceived by us in space and time, and know that the *real* world cannot have anything in common with it; to understand that it is impossible to imagine the real world in terms of form; and finally we must perceive the conditionality of the axioms of our mathematics and logic, related as they are to the unreal phenomenal world.

In mathematics *the idea of infinity* will help us to do this. The unreality of *finite* magnitudes in comparison with infinite ones is obvious. In logic let us dwell upon *the idea of monism*, i.e., the fundamental unity of everything which exists, and consequently recognize the impossibility of constructing any axioms, which involve the idea of opposites — of theses and antitheses — upon which our logic is built.

The logic of Aristotle and of Bacon is at bottom *dualistic*. If we really deeply assimilate the idea of monism, we shall dethrone the "idol" of this logic.

The fundamental axioms of our logic reduce themselves to identity and contradiction, just as do the axioms of mathematics. At the bottom of them all lies the admission of our general axiom, namely, that every given *something* has *something* opposite to it; therefore every propo sition has its anti-proposition, every *thesis* has its *anti-thesis*. To the *existence* of any thing is opposed the *non-existence* of that thing. To the existence of the world is opposed the non-existence of the world. *Object* is opposed to *subject*; the objective world to the subjective; the I is opposed to the Not-I; to motion — immobility; to variability — constancy; to unity — heterogeneity; to truth — falsehood; to good — evil. And in conclusion, to every A in general is opposed *Not-A*.

The recognition of the reality of these divisions is necessary for the acceptance of the fundamental axioms of the logic of Aristotle and Bacon, i.e., the absolute and incontestable recognition of the *duality of the world* — of dualism. The recognition of the *unreality* of these divisions and that of the unity of all opposites is necessary for the comprehension of *higher logic*.

At the very beginning of this book the existence of THE WORLD and of THE PSYCHE was admitted, i.e., the reality of the dual division of everything existent, because all other opposites are derived from this opposition.

Duality is the condition of *our* knowledge of the phenomenal (three-dimensional) world; this is the *instrument* of our knowledge of phenomena. But when we come to the knowledge of the noumenal world (or the world of many dimensions), this duality begins to hinder us, appears as an obstacle to knowledge.

Dualism is the chief "idol"; let us free ourselves from it.

The two-dimensional being, in order to comprehend the relations of things in three dimensions and our logic, must renounce its "idol" — the absolute singularity of objects which permits it to call them solely by their proper names.

We, in order to comprehend the world of many dimensions, must renounce *the idol of duality*.

But the application of *monism* to practical thought meets the insurmountable obstacle of our language. Our language is incapable of expressing *the unity of opposites*, just as it cannot express *spatially* the relation of cause to effect. Therefore we must reconcile ourselves to the fact that all attempts to express *super-logical* relations in our language will seem absurdities, and really can only *give hints* at that which we wish to express.

Thus the formula,

A *is both* A *and Not-A,*

or,

Everything is both A and Not-A,

representing the principal axioms of higher logic, expressed in our language of concepts, sounds absurd from the standpoint of our usual logic, *and is not essentially true.*

Let us therefore reconcile ourselves to the fact that it is *impossible* to express super-logical relations in our language as it is at present constituted.

The formula, "A *is both* A *and Not-A*" is untrue because in the world of causes there exists no opposition between "A" and "Not-A." But we cannot express their real relation. It would be more correct to say:

A *is all*.

But this also would be untrue, because "A" is not only *all*, but also *an arbitrary part* of all, and at the same time a *given* part.

This is exactly the thing which our language cannot express. It is to this that we must accustom our thought, and train it along these lines.

We must train our thought to the idea that separateness and inclusiveness are not opposed in the real world, but exist together and simultaneously without contradicting one another. Let us understand that in the real world one and the same thing can be both a part and the whole, i.e., that the whole, without changing, can be its own part; understand that there are no opposites in general, that *everything* is a certain *image of all*.

And then, beginning to understand all this, we shall grasp the separate ideas concerning the essentials of the "noumenal world," or *the world of many dimensions* in which we really live.

In such case the *higher logic*, even with its imperfect formulæ, as they appear in our rough language of concepts, represents in spite of this

Properties of the World of Causes

a powerful instrument of knowledge of the world, our only means of preservation from deceptions.

The application of this instrument of thought gives the key to the mysteries of nature, to *the world as it is*.

Let us endeavor to enumerate those properties of THE WORLD OF CAUSES which result from all the foregoing.

It is first of all necessary to reiterate that it is impossible to express in words the properties of the world of causes. Every thought *expressed* about them in our ordinary language will be *false*. That is, we may say in relation of the "real" world that *"every spoken thought is a lie."* It is possible to speak about it only conditionally, by hints, by symbols. And if one *interprets literally anything said about it,* nothing but absurdity results. Generally speaking, *everything said in words* regarding the world of causes is likely to seem absurd, and *is in reality its mutilation.* The truth it is impossible to express; it is possible only to give a hint at it, to give an impulse to thought. But everyone must discover the truth for himself. "Another's truth" is worse than a lie, because it is *two lies*. This explains why truth very often can be expressed only by means of paradox, or even in the form of a lie. Because, in order to speak of truth without a lie, we should know some other language — ours is unsuitable.

What then are we able to say about the world of many dimensions, about the world of noumena, or world of causes?

1. In that world "TIME" must exist spatially, i.e. *temporal* events must exist and not happen — exist before and after their manifestation, and be located in one section, as it were. Effects must exist simultaneously with causes. That which we name *the law of causality* cannot exist there, because time is a necessary condition for it. There cannot be anything which is measured by years, days, hours — there cannot be before, now, after. *Moments* of different epochs, divided by great intervals of time, exist simultaneously, and may touch one another. Along with this, all the *possibilities* of a given moment, even those opposite to one another, and all their results up to infinity, must be *actualized* simultaneously with a given moment, but the length of a moment can be different on different planes.

2. There is nothing measurable by our measures, nothing *commensurable* with our objects, nothing *greater* or *less* than our objects. There is nothing situated on the right or left side, above or below one of our objects. There can be nothing *similar* to our objects, lines or figures

and at the same time exist. Different *points* in our space, divided for us by enormous distances, may meet there. "Distance" or "proximity" are there defined by inner "affinity" or "remoteness," by sympathy or antipathy, i.e., by properties which seem to us to be subjective.

3. There is neither matter nor motion. There is nothing that could possibly be weighed or photographed, or expressed in the formulæ of physical energy. There is nothing which has *form, color* or *odor* — nothing possessing the properties of physical bodies. Nevertheless, the properties of the world of causes, granted an understanding of certain laws, can be considered in enumerated categories.

4. There is nothing dead or unconscious. Everything lives, everything breathes, thinks, feels; everything is conscious, and everything speaks.

5. In that world the axioms of our mathematics cannot be applied, because there is nothing *finite*. Everything there is infinite and, from our standpoint, *variable*.

6. The laws of our logic cannot act there. From the standpoint of our logic, that world is *illogical*. This is the realm the laws of which are expressed in *Tertium Organum*.

7. The *separateness* of our world does not exist there. *Everything is the whole*. And each particle of dust, without mentioning of course every life and every conscious being, lives a life which is *one with the whole* and includes *the whole* within itself.

8. In that world the *duality* of our world cannot exist. There *being* is not opposed to *non-being*. *Life* is not opposed to *death*. On the contrary, the one includes the other within itself. The unity and multiplicity of the I; the I and the Not-I; motion and immobility; union and separateness; good and evil; truth and falsehood — all these divisions are impossible there. *Everything subjective is objective, and everything objective is subjective*. That world is the world of the *unity of opposites*.

9. The sensation of the *reality* of that world must be accompanied by the sensation of the *unreality* of this one. At the same time the difference between real and unreal cannot exist there, just as the difference between subjective and objective cannot exist.

10. *That world* and *our world* are not two different worlds. The world is one. That which we call our world is merely *our incorrect perception of the world*: the world seen by us through a narrow slit. *That world* begins to be sensed by us as *the wondrous*, i.e., as something opposite to the reality *of this world*, and at the same time *this*, our earthly world, begins to seem unreal. *The sense of the wondrous* is the key to that world.

11. But everything that can be said about it will not define our rela-

The World of Causes and the All

tion to that world until we come to understand that even comprehending it we will not be able to grasp it as a whole, i.e., in all its variety of relations, but can think of it only in this or that aspect.

12. Everything that is said about the world of causes refers also to *the All*. But between our world and *the All* there may be many transitions.

CHAPTER XXII

To trace historically the process of the development of those ideas and systems founded upon higher logic or proceeding from it, would indeed be a matter of great interest and importance. But this would be difficult and almost impossible of accomplishment because we lack definite knowledge of the time and origin, the means of transmitting, and the sequence of ideas in ancient philosophical systems and religious teachings. There are innumerable guesses and speculations concerning the manner of this succession. Many of these guesses and speculations are accepted as unquestioned until new ones appear which controvert them. The opinions of different investigators in regard to these questions are very divergent, and the truth is often difficult to determine — it would be more accurate to say "impossible" if conclusions had to be based upon the material accessible to logical investigation.

I shall not dwell at all on the question of the *succession of ideas,* either from the historical or any other point of view.

The proposed outline of systems which refer to the world of noumena is not intended to be complete. This is not "the history of thought," but merely examples of movements of thought which have led to similar conclusions.

Philosophy in India

In the book *Theosophy* (or *Psychological Religion*) the noted scholar Max Müller gives an interesting analysis of mystical religions and mystical philosophical systems. He dwells much on India and her teachings.

That which we can study nowhere but in India is the all-absorbing influence which religion and philosophy may exercise on the human mind. So far as we can judge a large class of people in India, not only the priestly class, but the nobility also, not men only but women, never looked upon their life on earth as something real. What was real to them was the invisible, the life to come. What formed the theme of their conversations, what formed the subject of their meditations, was the real that alone lent some kind of reality to this unreal phenomenal world. Whoever was supposed to have caught a new ray of truth was visited by young and old, was honored by princes and by kings, was looked upon indeed as holding a position far above that of kings and princes. This is the side of life of ancient India which deserves our study, because there has been nothing like it in the whole world, not even in Greece or Palestine.

I know quite well, [says Müller] that there never can be a whole nation of philosophers or metaphysical dreamers . . . and we must never forget that all through history, it is the few, not the many, who impress their character on a nation, and have a right to represent it as a whole. What do we know of Greece at the time of the Ionian and Eleatic philosophers, except the utterances of Seven Sages? What do we know of the Jews at the time of Moses, except the traditions preserved in the Laws and the Prophets? It is the prophets, the poets, the lawgivers and teachers, however small their number, who speak in the name of the people, and who alone stand out to represent the nondescript multitude behind them, to speak their thoughts and to express their sentiments.

Real Indian philosophy, even in that embryonic form in which we find it in the *Upanishads*, stands completely by itself. And if we ask what was the highest purpose of the teachings of the *Upanishads* we can state it in three words, as it has been stated by the greatest *Vedânta* * teachers themselves, namely *Tat twam asi*. This means *Thou art That*. *That* stands for that which is known to us under different names in different systems of ancient and modern philosophy. It is Zeus or the *Eis Theos* or *To On* in Greece; it is what Plato meant by the *Eternal Idea*, what Agnostics call the *Unknowable*, what I call the *Infinite in Nature*. This is what in India is called *Brahman*, the being behind all beings, the power that emits the universe, sustains it and draws it back again to itself. The *Thou* is what I called the *Infinite in man*, the Soul, the Self, the being behind every human Ego, free from all bodily fetters, free from passions, free from all attachments (*Atman*). The expression: *Thou art*

---

* *Vedânta* is *the end of the Vedas*, the abridgment and commentaries on the Vedas. *P. Ouspensky.*

Tertium Organum

That — means: *thy soul is the Brahman;* or in other words, the subject and the object of all being and of all knowing are one and the same.

This is the gist of what I call *Psychological Religion* or *Theosophy*, the highest summit of thought which the human mind has reached, which has found different expressions in different religions and philosophies, but nowhere such a clear and powerful realization as in the ancient *Upanishads* of India.

For as long as the individual soul does not free itself from Nescience, or a belief in duality, it takes something else for itself. True knowledge of the Self or true self-knowledge, expresses itself in the words, *"Thou art That"* or *"I am Brahman,"* the nature of Brahman being unchangeable eternal cognition. Until that stage has been reached, the individual soul is fettered by the body, by the organs of sense, nay even by the mind and its various functions.

The Soul (The Self) says the Vedânta philosopher, cannot be different from the *Brahman,* because *Brahman* comprehends *all* reality and nothing that really is can therefore be different from *Brahman.* Secondly, the individual self cannot be conceived as a modification of *Brahman,* because *Brahman* by itself cannot be changed, whether by itself, because it is one and perfect in itself, or by anything outside of it (because there exists nothing outside of it). Here we see [says Müller], the Vedântist moving on exactly the same stratum of thought in which Eleatic philosophers moved in Greece. "If there is one Infinite," they said, "there cannot be another, for the other would limit the one, and thus render it finite, so, as applied to God, the Eleatics argued: "If God is to be the mightiest and the best, he must be one, for if there were two or more, he would not be the mightiest and best." The Eleatics continued their monistic argument by showing that this One Infinite Being cannot be divided, so that anything could be called a portion of it, because there is no power that could separate anything from it. Nay, it cannot even have parts, for, as it has no beginning and no end, it can have no parts, for a part has a beginning and an end.

These Eleatic ideas — namely that there is and there can be only One Absolute Being, infinite, unchangeable, without a second, without parts and passions — are the same ideas which underlie the *Upanishads* and have been fully worked out in the *Vedânta-Sutras.*

In most of the religions of the ancient world [says Müller] the relation between the soul and God has been represented as a return of the soul to God. A yearning for God, a kind of divine home-sickness, finds expression in most religions, but the road that is to lead us home, and the reception which the soul may expect in the Father's house have been represented in very different ways in different religions.

Eleatic Monism

According to some religious teachers, a return of the soul to God is possible after death only. . . .

According to other religious teachers, the final beatitude of the soul can be achieved in this life. . . . That beatitude requires knowledge only, knowledge of the necessary unity of what is divine in man with what is divine in God. The Brahmins call it self-knowledge, that is to say, the knowledge that our true self, if it is anything, can only be that Self which is All in All, and beside which there is nothing else. Sometimes this conception of the intimate relation between the human and the divine natures comes suddenly, as the result of an unexplained intuition or self-recollection. Sometimes, however, it seems as if the force of logic had driven the human mind to the same result. If God had once been recognized as the Infinite in nature and the soul as the Infinite in man, it seemed to follow that there could not be two Infinites. The Eleatics had clearly passed through a similar phase of thought in their own philosophy. It there is an Infinite, they said, it is one, for if there were two they could not be Infinite, but would be finite one toward the other. But that which exists is infinite, and there cannot be more such. Therefore that which exists is one.

Nothing can be more definite than this Eleatic Monism, and with it the admission of a soul, the Infinite in man, as different from God, the Infinite in nature, would have been inconceivable.

In India it was so expressed that *Brahman* and *Atman* (the spirit) were in their nature one.

The early Christians also, at least those who had been brought up in the schools of Neo-platonist philosophy, had a clear perception that if the soul is infinite and immortal in its nature, it cannot be anything beside God, but that it must be of God and in God. St. Paul gave but his own bold expression to the same faith or knowledge, when he uttered the words which have startled so many theologians: *In Him we live and move and have our being.* If anyone else had uttered these words they would at once have been condemned as pantheism. No doubt they are pantheism, and yet they express the very key-note of Christianity. The divine sonship of man is only a metaphorical expression but it was meant originally to embody the same idea. . . . And when the question was asked how the consciousness of this divine sonship could ever have been lost, the answer given by Christianity was, by *sin*, the answer given by the *Upanishads* was, by *avidya*, nescience. This marks the similarity, and at the same time the characteristic difference between these two religions. The question how *nescience* laid hold on the human soul, and made it imagine that it could live or move or have its true being anywhere but in *Brahman*, remains as unanswerable in Hindu philosophy as in Christianity the question how sin first came into the world.

Both philosophies, that of the East and that of the West [says Müller] start from a common point, namely from the conviction that our ordinary knowledge is uncertain, if not altogether wrong. This revolt of the human mind against itself is the first step in all philosophy.

In our own philosophical language we may put the question thus: how did the real become phenomenal, and how can the phenomenal become real again? Or, in other words, how was the infinite changed into the finite, how was the eternal changed into the temporal, and how can the temporal regain its eternal nature? Or, to put it into more familiar language, how was this world created, and how can it be uncreated again?

Nescience or *avidya* is regarded as the cause of the phenomenal semblance.

In the *Upanishads* the meaning of *Brahman* changes. Sometimes it is almost an objective God, existing separately from the world. But then we see *Brahman* as the essence of all things . . . and the soul, knowing that it is no longer separated from that essence, learns the highest lesson of the whole *Vedânta* doctrine: *Tat twam asi; "Thou art That,"* that is to say, "Thou who for a time didst seem to be something by thyself, art that, art really nothing apart from the divine essence." To know *Brahman* is to be Brahman. . . .

Almost in the same words as the Eleatic philosophers and the German mystics of the fourteenth century, the Vedântists argue that it would be self-contradictory to admit that there could be anything besides the Infinite or *Brahman*, which is All in All, and that therefore the soul also cannot be anything different from it, can never claim a separate and independent existence.

Brahman has to be conceived as perfect, and therefore unchangeable, the soul cannot be conceived as a real modification or deterioration of Brahman.

And as *Brahman* has neither beginning nor end, neither can it have any parts; therefore the soul cannot be a part of *Brahman*, but the whole of *Brahman* must be present in every individual soul. This is the same as the teaching of Plotinus, who held with equal consistency, that the True Being is totally present in every part of the Universe.

The Vedânta-philosophy rests on the foundation thesis that the soul or the Absolute Being or *Brahman*, are one in their essence. . . .

The fundamental principle of the Vedânta-philosophy is that in reality there exists and there can exist nothing but *Brahman*, that *Brahman* is everything. Idealistic philosophy has swept away this world-old prejudice more thoroughly in India than anywhere else.

The nescience (which creates the separation between the individual soul and Brahman) can be removed by science or knowledge only. And this knowledge or *vidya* is imparted by the *Vedânta*, which shows that all our ordinary knowledge is simply the result of ignorance or nescience, is uncertain, deceitful, and perishable, or as we should say, is phenomenal, relative, and conditioned. The true knowledge or complete insight cannot be gained by sensuous perception nor by inference. According to the orthodox Vedântist, *Sruti* alone, or what is called revelation, can impart that knowledge and remove that nescience which is innate in human nature.

Of the Higher *Brahman* nothing can be predicated but that it is, and that through our nescience, it appears to be this or that.

When a great Indian sage was asked to describe *Brahman*, he was simply silent — that was his answer.

When it is said that *Brahman* is, that means at the same time that Brahman is not; that is to say, that *Brahman* is nothing of what is supposed to exist in our sensuous perceptions.

Whatever we may think of this philosophy, we cannot deny its metaphysical boldness and its logical consistency. If *Brahman* is all in all, the One without a second, nothing can be said to exist that is not *Brahman*. There is no room for anything outside the infinite and the Universal, nor is there room for two infinites, for the infinite in nature and the infinite in man. There is and there can be one infinite, one *Brahman* only. This is the beginning and the end of the Vedânta.

As the shortest summary of the ideas of the Vedânta two verses of *Sankara*, the commentator and interpreter of *Vedânta* are often quoted:

> *Brahma is true, the world is false.*
> *The soul is Brahma and is nothing else.*

This is really a very perfect summary. What truly and really exists is Brahman, the One Absolute Being; the world is false, or rather is not what it seems to be; that is, everything which is present to us by means of sense is phenomenal and relative, and can be nothing else. The soul again, or rather every man's soul, though it may seem to be this or that, is in reality nothing but *Brahma*.

In relation to the question of the origin of the world two famous commentators of the *Vedânta*, *Sankara and Râmânuga* differ. *Râmânuga* holds to the theory of evolution, *Sankara* — to the theory of illusion.

It is very important to observe that the Vedântist does not go so far as certain Buddhist philosophers who look upon the phenomenal world as simply *nothing*. No, their world is real, only it is not what it seems to be. *Sankara* claims for the phenomenal world a reality sufficient for all practical purposes, sufficient to determine our practical life, our moral obligations.

There *is* a veil. But the Vedânta-philosophy teaches us that the eternal light behind it can always be perceived more or less clearly through philosophical knowledge. It can be perceived, because in reality it is always there.

It may seem strange to find the results of the philosophy of Kant and his followers thus anticipated under varying expressions in the *Upanishads* and in the Vedânta-philosophy of ancient India.

In the chapters about the *Logos* and about *Christian Theosophy* Max
Müller says that religion is the bridge between the *Visible* and the *Invisible*, between *Finite* and *Infinite*.

It may be truly said that the founders of the religions of the world have
all been bridge-builders. As soon as the existence of a Beyond, of a Heaven
above the earth, of Powers above us and beneath us has been recognized, a
great gulf seemed to be fixed.

Among contemporary thinkers the noted psychologist, Prof. William
James, approached nearer than all others to the ideas of Max Müller's
theosophy.

In the last chapter of his book, *The Varieties of Religious Experience*, Prof. James says:

The warring gods and formulas of the various religions do indeed cancel
each other, but there is a certain uniform deliverance in which religions all
appear to meet — this is *the liberation of the soul.* . . . Man becomes conscious that if his higher part is conterminous and continuous with a MORE of
the same quality, which is operative in the universe outside of him, and which
he can keep in working touch with, and in a fashion get on board of, he can
save himself when all his lower being has gone to pieces in the wreck.

What is the objective "Truth" of content of religious experiences? Is
such a "more" merely our own notion, or does it really exist? If so, in what
shape does it exist? And in what form should we conceive of that "union"
with it of which religious geniuses are so convinced?

It is in answering these questions that the various theologies perform their
theoretic work, and that their divergencies most come to light. They all agree
that the "more" really exists; though some of them hold it to exist in the
shape of a personal God or gods while others are satisfied to conceive it as
a stream of ideal tendency. . . . It is when they treat of the experience of
"union" with it that their speculative differences appear most clearly. Over
this point pantheism and theism, nature and second birth, works and grace
and Karma, immortality and reincarnation, rationalism and mysticism, carry
on inveterate disputes.

At the end of my lecture on Philosophy I held out the notion that an
impartial science of religions might sift out from the midst of their discrepancies a common body of doctrine which she might also formulate on terms
to which physical science need not object. This, I said, she might adopt as
her own reconciling hypothesis, and recommend it for general belief.

Let me then propose as an hypothesis that whatever it may be on its
farther side, the "more" with which in religious experience we feel ourselves

What is Mysticism?

connected is on its *hither* side the subconscious continuation of our conscious life.

The conscious person is continuous with a wider self. . . .

The further limits of our being plunge, it seems to me, into an altogether other dimension of existence from the sensible and merely "understandable" world.

Name it the mystical region, or the super-natural region. . . . We belong to it, in a more intimate sense than that in which we belong to the visible world, for we belong in the most intimate sense wherever our ideals belong. . . . The communion with this invisible world is a real process with real results. . . .

. . . Personal religious experience has its roots and centre in mystical states of consciousness.

But what, after all, is mysticism?

Returning to the terminology established in the foregoing chapters, we may say that "mystical states of consciousness" are closely bound up with knowledge received under conditions of expanded receptivity.

Until quite recently psychology did not recognize the reality of the mystical experience and regarded all mystical states as *pathological ones* — unhealthy conditions of the normal consciousness. Even now, many positivist-psychologists hold to this opinion, embracing in one common classification real mystical states, pseudo-mystical perversions of the usual state, purely psychopathic states and more or less conscious deceit.

This of course can be of no assistance to a correct understanding of the question. Before going further let us therefore establish certain criteria for the identification of real mystical states:

Prof. James enumerates the following: ineffability, noetic quality, transiency, passivity. But some of these characteristics belong also to *simple emotional states*, and he fails to define exactly how mystical states can be distinguished from emotional ones of analogous character.

Considering mystical states as "knowledge by expanded consciousness," it is possible to give quite definite criteria for their discernment and their differentiation from the generality of psychic experiences.

1. Mystical states give *knowledge* WHICH NOTHING ELSE CAN GIVE.
2. Mystical states give knowledge of the *real world* with all its signs and characteristics.
3. The mystical states of men of different ages and different peoples

exhibit an astonishing similarity, sometimes amounting to complete identity.

4. The results of the mystical experience are *entirely illogical* from our ordinary point of view. They are *super-logical*, i.e., *Tertium Organum*, WHICH IS THE KEY TO MYSTICAL EXPERIENCE, is applicable to them in all its entirety.

The last-named criterion is especially important — the *illogicality* of the data of mystical experience forced science to repudiate them. Now we have established that illogicality (from our standpoint) is the necessary condition of the knowledge of truth or of the real world. This does not mean that everything that is illogical is true and real, but it means absolutely, that everything true and real is *illogical* from our standpoint.

We have established the fact that it is impossible to approach the truth with our logic, and we have also established the possibility of penetrating into these heretofore inaccessible regions by means of *the new canon of thought*.

The consciousness of the necessity for such an instrument of thought undoubtedly existed from far back. For what, in substance, does the formula *Tat twam asi* represent if not THE FUNDAMENTAL AXIOM OF HIGHER LOGIC?

Thou art That means: *thou art both thou and not thou,* and corresponds to the super-logical formula, A *is both* A *and* Not-A.

If we examine ancient writings from this standpoint, then we shall understand that their authors were searching for *a new logic*, and were not satisfied with the logic of the things of the phenomenal world. The seeming *illogicality* of ancient philosophical systems, which portrayed an *ideal* world, as it were, instead of an existing one, will then become comprehensible, for in these portrayals of an ideal world, systems of *higher logic* often lie concealed.

One of such *misunderstood* attempts to construe a system of higher logic, to give a precise instrument of thought, penetrating beyond the limits of the visible world, is the treatise by Plotinus *On Intelligible Beauty.*

Describing HEAVEN and THE GODS, Plotinus says:

All the gods are venerable and beautiful, and their beauty is immense. What else however is it but intellect through which they are such? And because intellect energizes in them in so great a degree as to render them visible (by its light)? For it is not because their bodies are beautiful. For these gods that have bodies do not through this derive their subsistence as gods; but these also are gods through intellect. For they are not at one time wise, and at another destitute of wisdom; but they are always wise, in an impassive, stable and pure intellect. They likewise know all things, not human concerns (precedaneously) but their own, which are divine, and such as intellect sees. . . . For all things there are heaven, and there the earth is heaven, as also are the sea, animals, plants, and men. The gods likewise that it contains do not think men undeserving of their regard, nor anything else that is there (because everything there is divine). And they occupy and pervade without ceasing the whole of that (blissful) region. For the life which is there is unattended with labor, and truth (as Plato says in the "Phædrus") is their generator, and nutriment, their essence and nurse. They likewise see all things, not those with which generation, but those with which essence is present. And they perceive themselves in others. For all things there are diaphanous; and nothing is dark and resisting, but everything is apparent to everyone internally and throughout. For light everywhere meets with light; *since everything contains all things in itself and again sees all things in another. So that all things are everywhere, and all is all. Each thing likewise is everything.* And the splendor there is infinite. For everything there is great, since even that which is small is great. *The sun too which is there is all the stars; and again each star is the sun and all the stars. . . . In each however, a different property predominates, but at the same time all things are visible in each.* Motion likewise there is pure; for the motion is not confounded by a mover different from it. Permanency also suffers no change of its nature, because it is not mingled with the unstable. And the beautiful there is beautiful, because it does not subsist in beauty (as in a subject). Each thing too is there established, not as in a foreign land, but the seat of each thing is that which each thing is. . . . Nor is the thing itself different from the place in which it subsists. For the subject of it is intellect, and it is itself intellect . . . *There each part always proceeds from the whole, and is at the same time each part and the whole. For it appears indeed as a part; but by him whose sight is acute, it will be seen as a whole.* . . . There is likewise no weariness of the vision which is there, nor any plenitude of perception which can bring intuition to an end. For neither was there any vacuity, which when filled might cause the visive energy to cease; nor is this one thing, but that another, so as to occasion a part of one thing is not to be amicable with that of another.

And the knowledge which is possible there is insatiable. . . . For by seeing itself more abundantly it perceives both itself and the objects of its perception to be infinite, it follows its own nature (in unceasing contemplation). The life there is wisdom; a wisdom not obtained by a reasoning process, because the whole of it always was, and is not in any respect deficient, so as to be in want of investigation. But it is the first wisdom, and is not derived from another.*

Closely akin to Plotinus is Jacob Boehme, who was a common shoe-maker in the German town of Goerlitz (end of the XVI and the beginning of the XVII century), and has left a whole series of remarkable writings in which he describes revelations vouchsafed him in moments of illumination.

His first "illumination" occurred in 1600 A.D., when he was twenty-five years old.†

Sitting one day in his room, *his eyes fell upon a burnished pewter dish, which reflected the sunshine with such marvelous splendor that he fell into an inward ecstasy,* and it seemed to him as if he could now look into the principles and deepest foundations of things. He believed that it was only a fancy, and in order to banish it from his mind he went out upon the green. But here he remarked that he gazed into the very heart of things, the very herbs and grass, and that actual nature harmonized with what he had inwardly seen. He said nothing of this to anyone, but praised and thanked God in silence.

Of the first illumination Boehme's biographer says: "He learned to know the innermost foundation of nature, and acquire the capacity to see henceforth with the eyes of the soul into the heart of all things, a faculty which remained with him even in his normal condition."

About the year 1600, in the twenty-fifth year of his age, he was again surrounded by the divine light and replenished with the heavenly knowledge; insomuch as going abroad in the fields to a green before Neys Gate, at Goerlitz, he there sat down and, viewing the herbs and grass of the field in his inward light, he saw into their essences, use and properties, which were discovered to him by their lineaments, figures and signatures. In like manner he beheld the whole creation, and from that foundation he afterwards wrote his book, *"De Signatura Rerum."* In the unfolding of those mysteries before his understanding he had a great measure of joy, yet returned home and took care of his family and lived in great peace and silence, scarce intimating to any these wonderful things that had befallen him, and in the year 1610, being again taken into this light, lest the mysteries revealed to him should

* Abridged quotation from "Select Works of Plotinus," transl. by Thomas Taylor. Bohn's Library, pp. lxxiii and lxxiv.

† All the ensuing quotations are from the books of Prof. William James, and of Dr. R. M. Bucke.

pass through him as a stream, and rather for a memorial than intending any publication, he wrote his first book, called "Aurora, or the Morning Redness."

The first illumination, in 1600, was not complete. Ten years later (1610) he had another remarkable inward experience. What he had previously seen only chaotically, fragmentarily, and in isolated glimpses, he now beheld as a coherent whole and in more definite outlines.

When his third illumination took place, that which in former visions had appeared to him chaotic and multifarious was now recognized by him as a unity, *like a harp of many strings, of which each string is a separate instrument, while the whole is only one harp.**

He now recognized the divine order of nature, and how from the trunk of the tree of life spring different branches, bearing manifold leaves and flowers and fruits, and he became impressed with the necessity of writing down what he saw and preserved the record.

He himself speaks of this final and complete illumination as follows:

The gate was opened to me that in one quarter of an hour I saw and knew more than if I had been many years at a university, at which I exceedingly admired and thereupon turned my praise to God for it. For I saw and knew the beings of all beings, the byss and abyss and the eternal generation of the Holy Trinity, the descent and original of the world and of all creatures through divine wisdom. I knew and saw in myself all the three worlds, namely, (1) the divine (angelical and paradisical) (2) and the dark (the original of the nature to the fire) and (3) then the external and visible world (being a procreation or external birth from both the internal and spiritual worlds). And I saw and knew the whole working essence in the evil and the good and the original and the existence of each of them; and likewise how the fruitful — bearing — womb of eternity brought forth. So that I did not only greatly wonder at it but did also exceedingly rejoice.

Describing "illuminations" Boehme writes, in one of his books:

Suddenly . . . my spirit did break through . . . even into the innermost birth of Geniture of the Deity, and there I was embraced with love, as a bridegroom embraces his dearly beloved bride. But the greatness of the triumphing that was in the spirit I cannot express either in speaking or writing; neither can it be compared to anything, but that wherein the life is generated in the midst of death, and it is like the resurrection from the dead. In this light my spirit suddenly saw through all, and in and by all creatures, even

---

* See quotation from Van Manen's book, Chap. xi, pp. 118–20.

Tertium Organum

in herbs and grass, it knew God, who he is, and how he is, and what his work is; and suddenly in that light my will was set on, by a mighty impulse, to describe the being of God. But because I could not presently apprehend the deepest births of God in their being and comprehend them in my reason, there passed almost twelve years before the exact understanding thereof was given me. And it was with me as with a young tree which is planted on the ground, and at first is young and tender, and flourishing to the eye, especially if it comes on lustily in its growing. But it does not bear fruit presently; and, though it blossoms, they fall off; also many a cold wind, frost and snow, puff upon it, before it comes to any growth and bearing of fruit.

Boehme's books are full of wonderment before these mysteries with which he was confronted.

I was as simple concerning the hidden mysteries as the meanest of all; but *my vision of the wonders of God* taught me, so that I must write of his wonders; though indeed my purpose is to write this for a memorandum for myself. . . .

Not I, the I that I am, know these things: but God knows them in me.

If you will behold your own self and the outer world, and what is taking place thereon, you will find that you, with regard to your external being, are that external world.

The *Dialogues* between *Disciple* and *Master* are remarkable (Disciple and Master should be understood to refer to the lower and the higher consciousness of man).

The Disciple said to his Master:

How may I come to the supersensual life, that I may see God and hear him speak?

His *Master* said:

When thou canst throw thyself but for a moment into that where no creature dwelleth, then thou hearest what God speaketh.

Disciple — Is that near at hand or far off?

Master — It is in thee. And if thou canst for a while but cease from all thy thinking and willing, then thou shalt hear the unspeakable words of God.

Disciple — How can I hear him speak, when I stand still from thinking and willing?

Master — When thou standest still from the thinking of self, and the willing of self; "When both thy intellect and will are quiet, and passive to the impressions of the Eternal Word and Spirit; And when thy soul is winged up, and above that which is temporal, the outward senses, and the imagina-

Disciple and Master

tion being locked up by holy abstraction," then the Eternal hearing, seeing, and speaking, will be revealed in thee; and so God "heareth and seeth through thee," being now the organ of his spirit; and so God speaketh in thee, and whispereth to thy spirit, and thy spirit heareth his voice. Blessed art thou therefore if that thou canst stand still from self-thinking and self-willing, and canst stop the wheel of imagination and senses; forasmuch as hereby thou mayest arrive at length to see the great salvation of God, being made capable of all manner of Divine sensations and heavenly communications. Since it is naught indeed but thine own hearing and willing that do wonder thee, so that thou dost not see and hear God.

Disciple — Loving Master, I can no more endure anything should divert me, how shall I find the nearest way to him?

Master — Where the way is hardest there walk thou, and take up what the world rejecteth; and what the world doth, that do not thou. Walk contrary to the world in all things. And then thou comest the nearest way to him.

Disciple — . . . Oh how may I arrive at the unity of will, and how come into the unity of vision?

Master — . . . Mark now what I say: The Right Eye looketh in thee into Eternity. The Left Eye looketh backward in thee into time. If now thou sufferest thyself to be always looking into nature, and the things of time, it will be impossible for thee ever to arrive at the unity, which thou wishest for. Remember this; and be upon thy watch. Give not thy mind leave to enter in, nor to fill itself with, that which is without thee; neither look thou backward upon thyself . . . Let not thy Left Eye deceive thee, by making continually one representation after another, and stirring up thereby an earnest longing in the self-propriety; but let thy Right Eye command back this Left . . . And only bringing the Eye of Time into the Eye of Eternity . . . and descending through the Light of God into the Light of Nature . . . shalt thou arrive at the Unity of Vision or Uniformity of Will.

In another dialogue the Disciple and the Master converse about heaven and hell.

The *Disciple* asked his Master:
Whither go the souls when they leave these mortal bodies?
His *Master* answered:
The soul needeth no going forth anywhere.
Disciple — Does it not enter into heaven or hell?
Master — No, there is no such kind of entering. . . . The soul hath heaven and hell in itself . . . and whether of the two states — either heaven or hell — shall be manifested in the soul, in that it standeth.

The quotations given here are sufficient to indicate the character of the writings of an unlearned *shoemaker* from a little provincial town in Germany of the XVI–XVII centuries. Boehme is remarkable for the bright intellectuality of his comprehensions, although there is in them a strong moral element also.

In the book above mentioned (*The Varieties of Religious Experience*) Prof. James dwells with great attention on Christian Mysticism, which afforded him much material for establishing the fact of the cognitive aspect of mysticism.

I borrow from him the following description of the mystical experiences of certain Christian saints.

St. Ignatius confessed one day to Father Laynez that a single hour of meditation at Manfesa had taught him more truths about heavenly things than all the teachings of all the doctors put together could have taught him. . . . One day in orison, on the steps of the choir of the Dominican Church, he saw in a distinct manner the plan of divine wisdom in the creation of the world. On another occasion, during a procession, his spirit was ravished on God, and it was given him to contemplate, in a form and images fitted to the weak understanding of a dweller on earth, the deep mystery of the holy Trinity. This last vision flooded his heart with such sweetness, that mere memory of it in after times made him shed abundant tears.

"One day, being in orison," Saint Teresa writes, "it was granted me to perceive in one instant how all things are seen and contained in God. I did not perceive them in their proper form, and nevertheless the view I had of them was of a sovereign clearness and has remained vividly impressed upon my soul. It is one of the most signal of all the graces which the Lord has granted me. . . . The view was so subtle and delicate that the understanding cannot grasp it."

She goes on to tell [Prof. James writes] how it was as if the Deity was an enormous and sovereignly limpid diamond, in which all our actions were contained in such a way that their full sinfulness appeared evident as never before.

"Our Lord made me comprehend," she writes, "in what way it is that one God can be in three Persons. He made me see it so clearly that I remained as extremely surprised as I was comforted . . . and now, when I think of the holy Trinity, or hear it spoken of, I understand how the three adorable Persons form only one God and I experience an unspeakable happiness."

Christian Mysticism

Christian mysticism, as Prof. James shows, is very near to the *Ve-dánta* and the *Upanishads*. That fountain-head of Christian mysticism, Dionysius the Areopagite, tells about the absolute truth in *negative formulæ only*.

"The cause of all things is neither soul nor intellect; nor has it imagination, opinion, or reason, or intelligence; nor is it reason or intelligence; nor is it spoken or thought. It is neither number, nor order, nor magnitude, nor littlement, nor equality, nor inequality, nor similarity, nor dissimilarity. It neither stands, nor moves, nor rests. . . . It is neither essence, nor eternity, nor time. Even intellectual contact does not belong to it. It is neither science nor truth. It is not even royalty or wisdom; not one; not unity; not divinity or goodness nor even spirit as we know it."

The writings of the mystics of the Greek Orthodox Church are collected in the books *The Love of the Good*, comprising five large and formidable volumes. I selected several examples of profound and fine mysticism from the book, *Superconsciousness and the Paths to its Attainment*, by M. V. Lodizhensky (in Russian), who studied these books and found therein remarkable examples of philosophical thought.

Imagine a circle, says *Avva Dorotheus* (VII century), and in the middle of it a centre; and from this centre forthgoing radii-rays. The farther these radii go from the centre, the more divergent and remote from one another they become; conversely, the nearer they approach to the centre, the more they come together among themselves. Now suppose that this circle is the world: the very middle of it, God; and the straight lines (radii) going from the centre to the circumference, or from the circumference to the centre, are the paths of life of men. And in this case also, to the extent that the saints approach the middle of the circle, desiring to approach God, do they, by so doing, come nearer to God and to one another. . . . Reason similarly with regard to their withdrawing from God . . . they withdraw also from one another, and by so much as they withdraw from one another do they withdraw from God. Such is the attribute of love: to the extent that we are distant from God and do not love Him, each of us is far from his neighbor also. If we love God, then to the extent that we approach to Him through love of Him, do we unite in love with our neighbors; and the closer our union with them, the closer is our union with God also.*

(*Superconsciousness*, p. 266)

* The author of "Superconsciousness," M. V. Lodizhensky, told me that in the summer of 1910 he was in "Yasnaya Poliana," the residence of L. Tolstoy, and he conversed with him about the mystics and "The Love of the Good." Tolstoy was at

Hear now, says St. Isaac of Syria (VI century), how man becomes refined, acquires spirituality, and becomes like the invisible forces. . . . When the vision soars above things earthly, and above all troubles over earthly doings, and begins to experience revelations concerning that which is within, hidden from sight, and when it will turn its gaze upward, and experiences faith in the guidance of future ages, and the ardent desire for promised things, when it will search for hidden mysteries, then faith itself consumes this knowledge and so transforms and regenerates it that it becomes entirely spiritual. Then may the vision soar on pinions into regions incorporeal, may touch the depths of an inaccessible sea, participating in the mind Divine, and the miraculous acts of guidance in the hearts of thinking and feeling beings, discovering spiritual mysteries which become then comprehensible by the refined and simple mind. Then the inner senses are awakened to spirituality after the manner that they will be in the life immortal and incorruptible, for even here this redemption of the mind is a true symbol of the general redemption.

(*Superconsciousness, p.* 370)

When the grace of the Holy Spirit, says Maxim Kapsokalivit, descends on anyone, there is shown to him nothing of the sensuous world, but that which he never saw or never imagined. Then the understanding of such a man receives from the Holy Spirit the highest and hidden mysteries which according to the divine Paul, neither the human eye can understand nor the human reason comprehend unaided. (I Corinthians ii, 9.) And that thou mayest understand how our reason sees them, try to apprehend that which I shall say to thee. Wax, when it is placed far from fire, is solid, and it is possible to take it and hold it, but as soon as it is thrown in fire it immediately melts, takes fire, burns, blazes and ends thus in the midst of flames. So also is human reason when it is alone by itself, ununited with God; then it comprehends in the usual way and according to its power all things surrounding it; but as it approaches the fire of Divinity and of the Holy Ghost, then is it entirely enveloped by that Divine fire, and immersed in Divine meditation, and then in that fire of Divinity it is impossible for it to think about its own affairs and about that which it desires.

(*Superconsciousness, p.* 370)

first very skeptical about them, but when Mr. Lodizhensky read to him the quotation, given here, about the circle, Tolstoy became very enthusiastic, and ran into another room and got a letter in which a triangle was drawn. It appeared that he had independently almost grasped the thought of Avva Dorotheus, and had written to some one that God was the apex of a triangle: men the points within the angles; approaching to one another they approach to God, approaching God, they do the same toward one another. Several days afterward Tolstoy rode over to Mr. Lodizhensky's, near Tula, and read different parts of "The Love of the Good," much regretting that he had not known the books before. — *P. D. Ouspensky.*

Mystic Testimonies

St. Basil the Great says about the revelation of God: Absolutely unutterable and indescribable are the lightning-like splendors of Divine beauty; neither can speech express nor hearing apprehend. Shall we name the brilliance of the morning star, the brightness of the moon, the radiance of the sun — the glory of all these is unworthy of being compared with the true light, standing farther from it than does the gloomiest night and the most terrible darkness from midday brightness. This beauty, invisible to bodily eyes, comprehensible to soul and mind only, if it illumines some of the saints leaves in them an unbearable wound through their desire that this vision of Divine beauty should extend over an eternity of life; disturbed by this earthly life, they loathe it as though it were a prison.

(Superconsciousness, p. 372)

St. Theognis says: A strange word will I say to thee. There is some hidden mystery which proceeds between God and the soul. This is experienced by those who achieve the highest heights of perfect purity of love and faith, when man, changing completely unites with God, as His own, through ceaseless prayer and contemplation.

(Superconsciousness, p. 381)

Certain parts of the writings of Clement of Alexandria (second century) are remarkably interesting.

It appears to us that painting appears to take in the whole field of view in the scenes represented. But it gives a false description of the view, according to the rules of the art, employing the signs that result from the incidents of the lines of vision. By this means, the higher and the lower points in the view, and those between, are preserved; and some objects seem to appear in the foreground, and others in the background, and others to appear in some other way, on the smooth and level surface. So also philosophers copy the truth, after the manner of painting.*

Clement of Alexandria here reveals one very important aspect of *truth*, namely, its *inexpressibility in words* and the entire conditionality of all philosophical systems and formulations. Dialectically truth is represented only in perspective — i.e., in an *inevitably* deformed shape — such is his idea.

What time and labor would be saved, and from what enormous and unnecessary suffering would humanity save itself, could it but understand this one simple thing: that *truth cannot be expressed in our language.*

* "The Ante-Nicene Fathers," Vol. II, pp. 463, 464, Buffalo, The Christian Literature Publishing Co., 1885.

Tertium Organum

Then would men cease to think that they possessed truth, would cease to force others to accept *their truth* at any cost, would see that others may approach truth from *another direction*, exactly as they themselves approach it, by a way of their own. How many arguments, how many religious struggles, how much of violence toward the thoughts of others would be rendered unnecessary and impossible if men would only understand that *nobody* possesses truth, but all are seeking for it, each in his own way.

The ideas of Clement of Alexandria about God are highly interesting, and closely approximate to those of the Vedânta, and particularly to the ideas of the Chinese philosophers.

The discourse respecting God is the most difficult to handle. For since the first principle of everything is difficult to find out, the absolutely first and the oldest principle, which is the cause of all other things being and having been, is difficult to exhibit. For how can that be expressed which is neither genus, nor difference, nor species, nor individual, nor number; nay more, is neither an event, nor that to which an event happens? No one can rightly express this wholly. For on account of his greatness he is ranked as the All and is the Father of the universe. Nor are any parts to be predicated of them. For the one is indivisible, wherefore also it is infinite, not considered with reference to its being without dimensions, and not having a limit. And therefore it is without form and name. And if we name it, we do not do so properly, terming it either the one, or the good, or mind, or Absolute Being, or Father, or God, or Creator, or Lord. We speak not as supplying His Name; but for want, we use good names, in order that the mind may have these as points of support, so as not to err in other respects.*

Among Chinese mystical philosophers our attention is arrested by Lao-Tzŭ (VI cent. B.C.), and *Chuang-Tzŭ* (IV cent. B.C.) by the cleanliness of thought and the unusual simplicity with which they express the most profound doctrines of idealism.

The Sayings of Lao-Tzŭ

The Tao which can be expressed in words is not the eternal Tao; the name which can be uttered is not its eternal name.†

Tao eludes the sense of sight, and is therefore called colorless. It eludes the sense of hearing, and is therefore called soundless. It eludes the sense of

* Ibid. p. 493.
† Abridged quotation from "The Sayings of Lao Tzŭ," Wisdom of the East Series.

touch, and is therefore called incorporeal. These three qualities cannot be apprehended, and hence they may be blended into unity.

Ceaseless in action, it cannot be named, but returns again to nothingness. We may call it the form of the formless, the image of the imageless, the fleeting and the indeterminable.

There is something chaotic, yet complete, which existed before heaven and earth. Oh, how still it is, and formless, standing alone without changing, reaching everywhere, without suffering harm!

Its name I know not. To designate it I call it Tao. Endeavoring to describe it, I call it Great.

Being Great, it passes on; passing on, it becomes remote; having become remote it returns.

The law of Tao is its own spontaneity.

Tao in its unchanging aspect has no name.

The mightiest manifestations of active force flow from Tao.

Tao as it exists in the world is like great rivers and seas which receive the streams from the valleys.

All-pervading is the Great Tao. It can be at once on the right hand and on the left.

Tao is a great square with no angles, a great sound which cannot be heard, a great image with no form.

Tao produced Unity; Unity produced Duality; Duality produced Trinity; and Trinity produced all existing objects.

He who acts in accordance with Tao, becomes one with Tao.

All the world says that my Tao is great, but unlike other teachings. It is just because it is great that it appears unlike other teachings. If it had this likeness, long ago would its smallness have been known.

The sage attends to the inner and not to the outer; he puts away the objective and holds to the subjective.

The sage occupies himself with inaction, and conveys instructions without words.

Who is there that can make muddy water clear? But if allowed to remain still it will gradually become clear of itself. Who is there that can secure a state of absolute repose? But let time go on, and the state of repose will gradually arise.

Tao is eternally inactive, and yet it leaves nothing undone.

The pursuit of book-learning brings about daily increase (i.e., the increase of knowledge). The practice of Tao brings about daily loss (i.e., the loss of ignorance). Repeat the loss again and again, and you arrive at inaction. Practice inaction, and there is nothing which cannot be done.

Practice inaction, occupy yourself with doing nothing.

Leave all things to take their natural course, and do not interfere.

All things in Nature work silently.

Tertium Organum

Among mankind, the recognition of beauty as such implies the idea of ugliness, and the recognition of good implies the idea of evil.

Cast off your holiness, rid yourself of sagacity, and the people will benefit a hundredfold.

Those who know do not speak; those who speak do not know.

He who acts, destroys; he who grasps, loses. Therefore the sage does not act, and so he does not destroy; he does not grasp, and so he does not lose.

The soft overcomes the hard; the weak overcomes the strong. There is no one in the world but knows this truth, and no one who can put it into practice.

A Meditation of Chuang-Tzŭ

You cannot speak of ocean to a well-frog — the creature of a narrower sphere. You cannot speak of ice to a summer insect — the creature of a season. You cannot speak of Tao to a pedagogue, his scope is too restricted.

But now that you have emerged from your narrow sphere and have seen the great ocean, you know your own significance, and I can speak to you of great principles. . . .

Dimensions are limitless; time is endless. Conditions are not invariable; terms are not final.

There is nothing which is not objective; there is nothing which is not subjective. But it is impossible to start from the objective. Only from subjective knowledge is it possible to proceed to objective knowledge.

When subjective and objective are both without their correlates, that is the very axis of Tao.

Tao has its laws and its evidences. It is devoid both of action and of form. It may be obtained but cannot be seen.

Spiritual beings draw their spirituality from Tao.

To Tao no point in time is long ago.

Tao cannot be existent. If it were existent, it could not be non-existent. The very name of Tao is only adapted for convenience' sake. Predestination and chance are limited to material existences. How can they bear upon the infinite?

Tao is something beyond material existences. It cannot be conveyed either by words or by silence. In that state which is neither speech nor silence, its transcendental nature may be apprehended.*

In contemporary Theosophical literature, two little books stand out: *The Voice of the Silence* by H. P. Blavatsky, and *Light on the Path* by Mabel Collins. In both of them there is much of real mystical sentiment.

* "Musings of a Chinese Mystic," Wisdom of the East Series.

Modern Theosophy

The Voice of the Silence

He who would hear the voice of the silence, the soundless sound, and comprehend it, he has to learn the nature of the perfect inward concentration of the mind, accompanied by complete abstraction from everything pertaining to the external Universe, or the world of senses.

Having become indifferent to objects of perception, the pupil must seek out the Rajah of the senses, the Thought-Producer, him who awakes illusions.

The mind is the great slayer of the real.

Let the Disciple slay the Slayer.

For —

When to himself his form appears unreal, as do on waking all the forms he sees in dreams;

When he ceases to hear the many, he may discern the ONE — the inner sound which kills the outer.

Then only, not till then, shall he forsake the region of ASAT, the false, to come into the realm of SAT, the true.

Before the soul can see, the harmony within must be attained, and fleshly eyes be rendered blind to illusion.

Before the soul can hear, the image (man) has to become as deaf to warnings as to whispers, to cries of bellowing elephants as to the silvery buzzing of the golden firefly.

.   .   .   .

And then to the inner ear will speak —

THE VOICE OF THE SILENCE

And say:

— If thy Soul smiles while bathing in the sunlight of thy life; if thy soul sings within her chrysalis of flesh and matter; if thy soul weeps inside her castle of illusion; if thy soul struggles to break the silver thread that binds her to the MASTER, know, O Disciple, thy soul is of the earth.

.   .   .   .

Give up thy life, if thou wouldst live.

Learn to discern the real from the false, the ever-fleeting from the everlasting. Learn above all to separate head-learning from soul-wisdom, the "Eye" from the "Heart" doctrine.

.   .   .   .

Light on the Path, like The Voice of the Silence, is full of symbols, hints and hidden meanings. This is a little book which makes demands upon the reader. Its meaning is elusive, and it requires to be read in a fitting state of spirit. Light on the Path prepares the "disciple" to meet the "Master," i.e., the ordinary consciousness for communion with the higher consciousness. According to the author of *Light on the Path*, the term "THE MASTERS" is a symbolical expression for the "Divine Life." *

Light on the Path

Before the eyes can see they must be incapable of tears. Before the ear can hear it must have lost its sensitiveness. Before the voice can speak in the presence of the Masters it must have lost the power to wound. Before the soul can stand in the presence of the Masters its feet must be washed in the blood of the heart.

. . . .

Kill out all sense of separateness.
Desire only that which is within you.
Desire only that which is beyond you.
Desire only that which is unattainable.
For within you is the light of the world. . . . If you are unable to perceive it within you, it is useless to look for it elsewhere. . . . it is unattainable, because it forever recedes. You will enter the light, but you will never touch the Flame. . . .
Seek out the way.
Look for the flower to bloom in the silence that follows the storm: not till then. . . .
And on the deep silence the mysterious event will occur which will prove that the way has been found. Call it by what name you will, it speaks in a voice that speaks where there is none to speak — it is a messenger that comes, a messenger without form or substance; or it is the flower of the soul that has opened. It cannot be described by any metaphor.

. . . .

To hear the voice of the silence is to understand that from within comes the only true guidance. . . . For when the disciple is ready, the Master is ready also.
Hold fast to that which is neither substance nor existence.
Listen only to the voice which is soundless.
Look only on that which is invisible. . . .

Prof. James calls attention in his book to the unusually vivid emotionality of mystic experiences, and to the quite unusual sensations felt by mystics.

The deliciousness of some of these states seems to be beyond anything known in ordinary consciousness. It evidently involves organic sensi-

---

* "Light on the Path," p. 92, London, Theosophical Publishing Co.

bilities, for it is spoken of as something too extreme to be borne, and as verging on bodily pain. But it is too subtle and piercing a delight for ordinary words to denote. God's touches, the wounds of his spear, references to ebriety and to mystical union have to figure in the phraseology by which it is shadowed forth.

The joy of communion with God, described by *St. Simeon the New Theologian* * (X century) may serve as an example of such an experience.

I am wounded by the arrow of His love (writes St. Simeon). He is Himself inside of me, in my heart; he embraces me, kisses me, fills me with light. . . . A new flower grows in me, new because it is joyous. . . . This flower is of an unutterable form, is seen when it grows merely, then suddenly disappears . . . it is of indescribable appearance; attracts my mind to itself, causes forgetfulness of everything to do with fear, and then flies suddenly away. Then does the tree of fear remain again lacking fruit; I moan in sorrow and pray to thee, my Christ; again I see the flower amid the branches, I chain my attention to it alone, and see not the tree alone, but the brilliant flower attracting me to itself irresistibly; this flower grows in the end into the fruit of love. . . . Incomprehensible is it how from fear grows love.

Mysticism penetrates into all religions.

In India, [Prof. James says] training in mystical insight has been known from time immemorial under the name of yoga. Yoga means the experimental union of the individual with the divine. It is based on persevering exercise; and the diet, posture, breathing, intellectual concentration, and moral discipline vary slightly in the different systems which teach it. The yogi, or disciple, who has by these means overcome the obscurations of his lower nature sufficiently, enters into the condition termed *samadhi*, "and he comes face to face with facts which no instinct or reason can ever know."
. . . When a man comes out of *samadhi* Vedântists assure us that he remains "enlightened, a sage, a prophet, a saint, his whole character changed, his life changed, illumined."

The Buddhists use the word *samadhi* as well as the Hindus; but *dhyana* is their special word for the higher states of contemplation.

Higher stages still of contemplation are mentioned — a region where there exists nothing, and where the meditator says: "There exists absolutely nothing," and stops. Then he reaches another region, he says: "There are neither ideas nor absence of ideas," and stops again. Then another region where, "having reached the end of both idea and perception, he stops finally." This

* Paul Anikieff, "Mysticism of St. Simeon the New Theologian," St. Petersburg, 1906.

would seem to be, not yet *Nirvana*, but as close an approach to it as this life affords.*

In Mohammedanism there is much of mysticism also. The most characteristic expression of Moslem mysticism is Persian *Sufism*. This is at the same time a religious sect and a philosophical school of high idealistic character, which struggled against materialism and against the narrow fanaticism and the literal understanding of the Koran. The Sufis interpreted the Koran mystically. Sufism — this is the philosophical free-thinking of Mohammedanism, united with an entirely original symbolical and brightly sensuous poetry which has always a hidden mystical character. The blossoming of Sufism occurred in the early centuries of the second millennium of the Christian era.

Sufism remained for a long time incomprehensible to European thought. From the point of view of Christian theology and Christian morality the mixing up of sensuousness and religious ecstasy is incomprehensible, but in the Orient the two coexisted with perfect harmony. In the Christian world "the flesh" has always been regarded as inimical to "the spirit." In the Moslem world the fleshly and sensuous was accepted as a symbol of spiritual things. The expression of philosophical and religious truths "in the language of love" was a widely disseminated custom throughout the Orient. These things are "Oriental flowers of eloquence." All allegories, all metaphors were taken from "love." "Mohammed fell in love with God," the Arabs say, desiring to convey the brightness of the religious ardor of Mohammed. *"Select for thyself a new wife every spring of the new year, because last year's calendar is no good"* — says the Persian poet and philosopher *Sa'di*. And in such curious form *Sa'di* expresses the thought that Ibsen puts in the mouth of Dr. Stockman: *"Truths are not as many believe like long-living Methuselahs. Under normal conditions a truth may exist about seventeen or eighteen years, rarely longer."*

The poetry of the Sufis will become clearer to us if we always keep in mind this general sensuous character of the literary language of the Orient, the heritage of profound antiquity. A classic example of this ancient literature is the *Song of Songs*.

Many parts of the Bible and all ancient myths and stories are distinguished by a sensuousness of form strange to us.

"The Persian mystical poetical Sufis wrote about the love of God in

* Prof. W. James, "The Varieties of Religious Experience," pp. 400, 401

expressions applicable to their beautiful women," says the translator of *Jami* and other poets, Davis — "because, as they explained this, nobody can write in heavenly language and be understood." (*Persian Mystics.*)

"The idea of Sufism," Max Müller says, "*is a loving union of the soul with God.*" "The Sufi holds that there is nothing in human language that can express the love between the soul and God so well as the love between man and woman and that if he is to speak of the union between the two at all, he can only do so in the symbolic language of earthly love." When we read some of the Sufi enraptured poetry, we must remember that the Sufi poets use a number of expressions which have a recognized meaning in their language. Their *sleep* means meditation; *perfume* — hope of divine favor; *kisses* and *embraces* — the raptures of piety; *wine* means spiritual knowledge, etc.

The flowers which a lover of God had gathered in his rose-garden, and which he wished to give to his friends, so overpowered his mind by their fragrance that they fell out of his lap and withered, *Sa'di* says. A poet desires to express by this, that the glory of ecstatic visions pales and fades away when it has to be put into human language. — (Max Müller — *Theosophy.*)

Generally speaking, never and nowhere has poetry been so blended with mysticism as in Sufism. The Sufi poets frequently lived the strange lives of hermits, anchorites and wanderers, at the same time singing of love, the beauty of women, the aroma of roses and wine.

Jêlal eddîn describes as follows the communion of the soul with God:

A loved one said to her lover to try him early one morning: "O such a one, son of such a one, I marvel whether you hold me more dear, or yourself; tell me truly, O ardent lover!" He answered: "I am so entirely absorbed in you, that I am full of you from head to foot. Of my own existence nothing but the man remains, in my being is nothing beside you, O object of my desire. Therefore I am thus lost in you. As a stone which has been changed into a pure ruby, is filled with the bright light of the sun." — (Max Müller.)

In two well-known poems of *Jami* (XV century), *Salaman and Abasl* and *Yusuf and Zulaikha*, the "ascending of the soul," its purification and its union with God, is represented in the most passionate forms.

Prof. James pays great attention in his book to *mystical states under narcosis*.

"This is a realm that public opinion and ethical philosophy have long since branded as pathological, though private practice and certain lyric strains of poetry seem still to bear witness of its ideality.

"Nitrous oxide and ether, especially nitrous oxide, when sufficiently diluted with air, stimulates the mystical consciousness in an extraordinary degree. Depth beyond depth of truth seems revealed to the inhaler. This truth fades out, however, or escapes, at the moment of coming to; and if any words remain over in which it seemed to clothe itself, they prove to be the veriest nonsense. Nevertheless, the sense of a profound meaning having been there persists; and I know more than one person who is persuaded that in the nitrous oxide trance we have a genuine metaphysical revelation.

"Some years ago I myself made some observations on this aspect of nitrous oxide intoxication, and reported them in print. One conclusion was forced upon my mind at that time, and my impression of its truth has ever since remained unshaken. It is that our normal waking consciousness, rational consciousness as we call it, is but one special type of consciousness, whilst all about it, parted from it by the filmiest of screens, there are potential forms of consciousness entirely different. We may go through life without suspecting their existence, but apply the requisite stimulus and at a touch they are there in all their completeness, definite types of mentality which probably somewhere have their field of application and adaptation. No account of the universe in its totality can be final which leaves these other forms of consciousness quite disregarded. At any rate, they forbid a premature closing of our accounts with reality.

"The whole drift of my education goes to persuade me that the world of our present consciousness is only one out of many worlds of consciousness that exist, and that those other worlds must contain experiences which have a meaning for our life also.

"Looking back on my experiences, they all converge toward a kind of insight to which I cannot help ascribing some metaphysical significance. The keynote of it is invariably a reconciliation. It is as if the opposites of the world, whose contradictions and conflict make all our difficulties and troubles, were melted into unity. Not only do they, as contrasted species, belong to one and the same genus, but *one of the species* — the nobler and the better one — *is itself the genus, so soaks up and absorbs its opposite into itself*. This is a dark saying, I know, when thus expressed in terms of common logic, but I cannot wholly escape from its authority. I feel as if it must mean something, something like what the Hegelian philosophy means, if one could only lay hold of it more clearly. Those

Anaesthetic Revelation

who have ears to hear let them hear; to me the loving sense of its reality only comes in the artificial mystic state of mind.

"What reader of Hegel can doubt that sense of a perfected being with all its otherness soaked up in itself, which dominates his whole philosophy, must have come from the prominence in his consciousness of mystical moods like this, in most persons kept subliminal? The notion is thoroughly characteristic of the mystical level, and the *Aufgabe* (the problem) of making it articulate was surely set to Hegel's intellect by mystical feeling.

"I have friends who believe in the anæsthetic revelation. For them too it is a monistic insight, in which the *other* in its various forms appears absorbed into the One.*

"Into this pervading genus," writes one of them, "we pass, forgetting and forgotten, and thenceforth each is all, in God. There is no higher, no deeper, no other, than the life in which we are founded. The one remains, the many change and pass; and each and every one of us is the One that remains. . . . This is the ultimatum. . . . As sure as being — whence is all our care — so sure is content, beyond duplexity, antithesis, or trouble, where I have triumphed in a solitude that God is not above." — (B. P. Blood: *The Anæsthetic Revelation and the Gist of Philosophy*, Amsterdam, N. Y., 1874.)

Xenos Clark, a philosopher who died young (at Amherst in the '80's) was also impressed by the revelation.

"In the first place," he once wrote to me, "Mr. Blood and I agree that the revelation is, if anything, non-emotional. It is, as Mr. Blood says, the one sole and sufficient insight why or not why, but how, the present is pushed on by the past, and sucked forward by the vacuity of the future. . . . It is an *initiation of the past*. The real secret would be the formulæ by which the 'now' keeps exfoliating out of itself, yet never escapes. We simply fill the hole with the dirt we dug out. Ordinary philosophy is like a hound hunting its own tail. The more he hunts the farther he has to go, and his nose never catches up with his heels, because it is forever ahead of them. So the present is already a foregone conclusion, and I am ever too late to understand it. *But at the moment of recovery from anæsthesis, then, before starting on life, I catch, so to speak, a glimpse of my heels, a glimpse of the eternal process just in the act of starting.* The truth is that we travel on a journey that was accomplished before we set out; and the real end of philosophy is accomplished, not when we arrive at, but when we remain in, our destination (being already there) — which may occur vicariously in this life when we cease our intellectual questioning. That is why there is a smile upon the face of revelation, as we view it. It tells us that we are forever half a second too late — that's all."

"You could kiss your own lips, and have all the fun to yourself," it says, "if you only knew the trick. It would be perfectly easy if they would just stay there till you got around to them. Why don't you manage it somehow?"

In his latest pamphlet Mr. Blood describes the value of the anæsthetic revelation for life as follows:

"The Anæsthetic Revelation is the initiation of man into the mystery of the open secret of Being, revealed as the inevitable vortex of continuity. Inevitable is the word. Its motive is inherent — it is what has to be. It is not for any love or hate, nor for joy or sorrow, nor good nor ill. End, beginning, or purpose, it knows not of.

"It affords no particular of the multiplicity and variety of things; but it fills the appreciation of the historical and the sacred with a secular and intimately personal illumination of the nature and motive of existence. . . .

"Although it is at first startling in its solemnity, it becomes directly such a matter of course — so old-fashioned, and so akin to proverbs, that it inspires exultation rather than fear, and the sense of safety, as identified with the aboriginal and the universal. But no words may express the surpassing certainty of the patient that he is realizing the primordial Adamic surprise of life.

"Repetition of the experience finds it ever the same, and as if it could not possibly be otherwise. The subject resumes his normal consciousness only to partially and fitfully remember its occurrence, and to try to formulate its baffling import — with this consolatory after-thought: that he has known the oldest truth, and that he has done with human theories as to the origin, meaning, or destiny of the race. He is beyond instruction in 'spiritual things.'

"The lesson is one of central safety; the kingdom is within. All days are judgment days: but there can be no climacteric purpose of eternity, nor any scheme of the whole. The astronomer abridges the row of bewildering figures by increasing his unit of measurement: so may we reduce the distracting multiplicity of things to the unity for which each of us stands.

"This has been my moral sustenance since I have known of it. In my first printed mention of it I declared: The world is no more the alien terror that was taught me. Spurning the cloud-grimed and still sultry battlements whence so lately Jehovan thunders boomed, my gray gull lifts her wings against the nightfall, and takes the dim leagues with a fearless eye. And now, after twenty-seven years of this experience, the wing is grayer, but the eye is fearless still, while I renew and doubly emphasize that declaration. I know — as having known — the meaning of existence: the sane center of the universe — at once the wonder and the assurance of the soul — for which the speech of reason has as yet no name but the Anæsthetic Revelations."

I subjoin, Prof. James says, another interesting anæsthetic revelation. This is what the subject, a gifted woman, writes about her experience, when she was taking ether for a surgical operation.

Experience under Ether

"I wondered if I was in a prison being tortured, and why I remembered, having heard it said that people 'learn through suffering,' and in view of what I was seeing, the inadequacy of this saying struck me so much that I said, aloud, 'to suffer is to learn.' With that I became unconscious again, and my last dream immediately preceded my real coming to. It only lasted a few seconds and was most vivid and real to me, though it may not be clear in words.

"A great Being or Power was traveling through the sky, his foot was on a kind of lightning as a wheel is on a rail, it was his pathway. The lightning was made of innumerable spirits close to one another, and I was one of them. He moved in a straight line, and each part of the streak or flash came into its short conscious existence only that he might travel. I seemed to be directly under the foot of God, and I thought he was grinding his own life up out of my pain. Then I saw that what he had been trying with all his might to do was to *change his course, to bend* the line of lightning to which he was tied, in the direction in which he wanted to go. I felt my flexibility and helplessness, and I knew that he would succeed. He bended me, turning his corner by means of my hurt, hurting me more than I had ever been hurt in my life, and at the acutest point of this, as he passed, I SAW.

"I understood for a moment things that I have now forgotten, things that no one could remember while retaining sanity. The angle was an obtuse angle, and I remember thinking as I woke that had he made it a right or acute angle, I should have both suffered and 'seen' still more, and should probably have died.

"He went on and I came to. In that moment the whole of my life passed before me, including each little meaningless piece of distress, and I understood them. This is what it had all meant, *this* was the piece of work it had all been contributing to do.

"I did not see God's purpose. I only saw his intentness and his entire relentlessness toward his means. He thought no more of me than a man thinks of hurting a cartridge when he is firing. And yet, on waking, my first feeling was, and it came with tears, 'Domine non sum digna,' for I had been lifted into a position for which I was too small. I realized that in that half hour under ether I had served God more distinctly and purely than I had ever done in my life before, or than I am capable of desiring to do. I was the means of his achieving and revealing something, I know not what or to whom, and that to the exact extent of my capacity for suffering.

"While regaining consciousness I wondered why, since I had gone so deep, I had seen nothing of what saints call the *love* of God, nothing but his relentlessness. And then I heard an answer, which I could only just catch, saying, 'Knowledge and Love are One, and the measure is suffering' — I give the words as they came to me. With that I came finally to into what seemed a dream world compared with the reality of what I was leaving. . . ."

273

Tertium Organum

I. S. Symonds, whom Prof. James mentions, tells of an interesting mystical experience with chloroform:

"After the choking and stifling had passed away, I seemed at first in a state of utter blankness, then came flashes of intense light, alternating with blackness, and with a keen vision of what was going on in the room around me, but no sensation of touch. I thought that I was near death; when suddenly, my soul became aware of God, who was manifestly dealing with me, handling me, so to speak, in an intense personal present reality. I felt him streaming in like light upon me. I cannot describe the ecstasy I felt. Then as I gradually awoke from the influence of the anæsthetic, the old sense of my relation to the world began to return, and the new sense of my relation to God began to fade. I suddenly leapt to my feet on the chair where I was sitting, and shrieked out, 'It is too horrible, it is too horrible, it is too horrible,' meaning that I could not bear this disillusionment. At last I awoke . . . calling to the two surgeons (who were frightened) 'why did you not kill me? Why would you not let me die?' "

Anæsthetic states are very similar to those strange moments experienced by epileptics during their fits of illness. An artistic description of epileptic states we find in Dostoyevsky's, *The Idiot*.

He remembered among other things that he always had one minute just before the epileptic fit (if it came on while he was awake) when suddenly in the midst of sadness, spiritual darkness and oppression, there seemed at moments a flash of light on his brain and with extraordinary impetus all his vital forces suddenly began working at their highest tension. The sense of life, the consciousness of self, were multiplied ten times at these moments which passed like a flash of lightning. His mind and his heart were flooded with extraordinary light; all his uneasiness, all his doubts, all his anxieties were relieved at once; they were all merged in a lofty calm, full of serene, harmonious joy and hope.

Thinking of that moment later, when he was all right again, he often said to himself that all these gleams and flashes of the highest sensation of life and self-consciousness, and therefore also of the highest form of existence, were nothing but disease, the interruption of the normal condition. . . . And yet he came at last to an extremely paradoxical conclusion. What if it is disease? he decided, if the result, if the minute of sensation, remembered and analyzed afterwards in health, turns out to be the acme of harmony and beauty, and gives a feeling, unknown and undivined till then, of completeness, of proportion, of reconciliation, and of ecstatic devotional merging in the highest synthesis of life?

These vague expressions seemed to him very comprehensible, though too weak. That it was "beauty and worship," that it really was the "highest synthesis of life" he could not doubt, and could not admit the possibility of doubt. . . . He was quite capable of judging of that when the attack was over. These moments were only an extraordinary quickening of self-consciousness — if the condition was to be expressed in one word — and at the same time of the direct sensation of existence in the most intense degree. Since at that second, that is at the very last conscious moment before the fit, he had time to say to himself clearly and consciously, "Yet for this moment one might give one's whole life!" then without doubt that moment was really worth the whole of life. . . . For the very thing had happened; he actually had said to himself at that second, that, for the infinite happiness he had fel' in it, that second really might well be worth the whole of life.

"At that moment," as he told Rogozhin one day in Moscow . . . "at that moment I seemed somehow to understand the extraordinary saying that *there shall be time no longer*. Probably," he added, smiling, "this is the very second which was not long enough for the water to be spilt out of Mohammed's pitcher, though the epileptic prophet had time to gaze at all the habitations of Allah."*

Narcosis or epilepsy are not at all necessary conditions to induce mystical states in ordinary men.

"Certain aspects of nature appear to have the peculiar power of awakening such mystical moods," says James.

It would be more correct to say that *in all conditions* of encompassing nature this power lies concealed. The change of the seasons — the first snow, the awakening of spring, the summer days, rainy and warm, the aroma of autumn — awakes in us strange "moods" which we ourselves do not understand. Sometimes these moods intensify, and become the sensation of a complete oneness with nature. In the life of every man there are moments which act upon him more powerfully than others. Upon one a *thunderstorm* acts mystically, upon another, *sunrise*, a third *the sea, the forest, rocks, fire*. The voice of sex embraces much of that same mystical sense of *nature*.

In the sex impulse man puts himself in the most personal relation with nature. The comparison of the sensation of woman experienced by man, or *vice versa*, with the feeling for nature is met with very often. And *it is really the same sensation* as is given by forest, prairie, sea, mountains, only in this case it is even more intense, awakens more inner voices, forces the sounding of more inner strings.

* "The Idiot," by Fyodor Dostoyevsky, transl. of Constance Garnett, New York The Macmillan Co.

Animals often give the mystical sensation of nature to men. Almost everyone has his favorite animal, with which he has some inner affinity. In these animals, or through them, men sense nature intimately and personally.

In Hindu occultism there is the belief that every man has his corresponding animal, through which it is possible to act upon him magically, through which he himself can act upon others, and into which he can transform himself or be by others transformed.

Each Hindu deity has his own particular animal.

Brahma has a goose; *Vishnu* an eagle; *Shiva* a bull; *Indra* an elephant; *Kali* (*Durga*) a tiger; *Rama* a buffalo; *Ganesha* a rat; *Agni* a ram; *Kartikkeya* (or *Subrananyia*) a peacock, and *Kama* (the god of love) a parrot.

The same thing is true of Greece: all the deities of Olympus had their animals.

In the religion of Egypt sacred animals played an enormous part, and in Egypt the *cat*, the most magical of all animals, was held as sacred.

The sense of nature sometimes unfolds something infinitely new and profound in things which seemed to have been known a long time and in themselves contained nothing mystical.

The consciousness of God's nearness came to me sometimes [quotes Prof. James] . . . *a presence*, I might say . . . something in myself made me feel a part of something bigger than I, that was controlling. I felt myself one with the grass, the trees, birds, insects, everything in Nature. I exulted in the mere fact of existence, of being a part of it all — the drizzling rain, the shadow of the clouds, the tree-trunks, and so on.

In my own note book of 1908 I found a description of the same experienced state of consciousness.

It was in the sea of Marmora, on a rainy day of winter, the far-off high and rocky shores were of a pronounced violet color of every shade, including the most tender, fading into gray and blending with the gray sky. The sea was the color of lead mixed with silver. I remember all these colors. The steamer was going north. I remained at the rail, looking at the waves. The white crests of waves were running toward us. A wave would run at the ship, raised as if desiring to hurl its crest upon it, rushing up with a howl. The steamer heeled, shuddered, and slowly straightened back; then from afar a new wave came running. I watched this play of the waves with the ship, and felt them draw me to themselves. It was not at all that desire to jump down which one feels in mountains but something infinitely more subtle. The waves were drawing my soul to themselves. And suddenly I felt that it went to them. It lasted an instant, perhaps less than an instant, but I entered into the waves and with them rushed with a howl at the ship. And in that instant *I became all*. The waves — they were myself: the far violet mountains, the wind, the clouds hurrying from the north, the great steamship, heeling and rushing irresistibly forward — all were myself. I sensed the enormous heavy body — *my body* — all its motions, shudderings, waverings and vibrations, fire, pressure of steam and weight of engines were *inside of me*, the unmerciful and unyielding propelling screw which pushed and pushed me forward, never for a moment releasing *me*, the rudder which determined all my motion — all this was myself: also two sailors . . . and the black snake of smoke coming in clouds out of the funnel . . . all.

It was an instant of unusual freedom, joy and expansion. A second — and the spell of charm disappeared. It passed like a dream when one tries to remember it. But the sensation was so powerful, so bright, and so unusual that I was afraid to move and waited for it to recur. But it did not return, and a moment later I could not say that it had been — could not say whether it was a reality or merely the *thought* that, looking at the waves, it might be so.

Two years afterwards the yellowish waves of the Finnish gulf and a green sky gave me a taste of the same sensation, but this time it was dissipated almost before it appeared.

The examples given in this chapter do not by any means exhaust the mystical experience of humanity.

But what do we infer from them?

First of all, *unity of experience*. In mystical sensations all men feel definitely something in common, having a similar meaning and connection one with another. The mystics of many ages and many peoples speak the same language and use the same words. This is the first and most important thing that speaks for the reality of the mystical experience. Next is the complete harmony of data regarding such experience with the theoretically deduced *conditions of the world causes*; the sensation of the *unity of all*, so characteristic of mysticism; a new sensation of time, the sense of infinity; joy or horror; knowledge of the whole in the part; infinite life and infinite consciousness. All these are real *sensed* facts in the mystical experience. And these facts are *theoretically correct*. They are such as they should be according to the conclusions of THE MATHEMATICS OF THE INFINITE AND OF THE HIGHER LOGIC. This is all that is possible to say about them.

CHAPTER XXIII

VERY many men believe that the fundamental problems of life are absolutely unsolvable, that humanity will never know why it is striving, or for what it is striving, for what it suffers, or whither it is bound. It is regarded as almost indecent even to raise these questions. It is decreed that we live "so" — that we "simply live" thinking of nothing or thinking only on that which yields a solution — on the surface at least. Men have despaired of finding answers to fundamental questions and so have left them alone.

Yet at the same time men are not in the least aware of *what really* created in them such a sense of insolubility and despair. Whence comes this feeling *that it is better not to think about many things?*

In reality we feel this despair only when we begin to regard man as something "finite," finished; when we see nothing beyond man, and think that we already know everything about him. In such form the problem is truly a desperate one. A cold wind blows on us from all those social theories promising incalculable welfare on earth, leaving a sense of dissatisfaction and chill even when we believe their promises.

Why? What is all this for? Well, everybody will be well fed and well taken care of — Splendid! *But after that, what?*

Let us suppose — although it is difficult, almost impossible to imagine — that materialistic culture, of itself, has led men to a fortunate state of existence. On earth, then, there exists an unadulterated civilization and culture. *But after that, what?*

After that, many resounding phrases of "incredible horizons" opening before *science.* "Communication with the planet Mars," "The chemi-

278

Positivism a Dusty Answer

cal synthesis of protoplasm," "The utilization of the rotation of the earth around the sun," "Energy imprisoned in an atom," "Vaccine for all diseases," "*Life to the length of a hundred years*" — or even to one hundred and fifty! After that perhaps, "The artificial creation of men" — but beyond this imagination fails.

It is possible to dig through the earth, but that would be entirely useless.

Here indeed we encounter that feeling of the insolubility of the main questions concerning the aims of existence, and that feeling of despair on account of our lack of understanding.

Truly, suppose that we have dug completely through the earth — what then? Shall we dig in another direction? But it is all very wearisome after all. Nevertheless the various positivistic social theories, "historical materialism," and so forth, promise nothing better, and can promise nothing. To get any answer at all to such tormenting questions we must turn in quite another direction: to the psychological method of study of man and of humanity. And here we see with amazement, that the psychological method gives an entirely satisfactory answer to those fundamental questions which seem to us quite insoluble, and around about which we fruitlessly wander equipped with the defective instrument of the positivistic method.

The psychological method gives a direct answer at least to the question of the immediate purpose of our existence. For some strange reason men do not care to accept this answer; and they desire at all costs to receive an answer in some form that they like, refusing to recognize anything that is different from that form. They require the solution of the destiny of man as they fancy him, and they do not want to recognize that *man* can and must become entirely different. In him there are not as yet manifest those faculties which will create his future. Man must not and cannot remain such as he is now. To think of the future of this man is just as absurd as to think of the future of a child as if it were always going to remain a child. The analogy is not quite complete, for the reason that probably only a small part of humanity is capable of growth, but nevertheless this comparison paints a true picture of our usual attitude toward this question. And the fate of that greater part of humanity which will prove incapable of growth, depends not upon itself, but upon that minority which will progress. Only inner growth, the unfoldment of new forces, will give to man a correct understanding of himself, his ways, his future, and give him power to organize life on earth. At the present time the general concept "man" is too undifferentiated and includes within himself *entirely different categories*, those capable of development and those incapable. In men capable of development, new faculties are stirring into life, though not as yet manifest, because for their manifestation they require a special culture, a special education. *The new conception of humanity disposes of the idea of equality*, which after all does not exist, and it tries to establish the signs and facts of the differences between men, because humanity will need soon to divide the "progressing" from the "incapable of progress" — *the wheat from the tares*, for the tares are growing too fast, and choke the growth of the wheat.

This is the key to the understanding of our life, and this key was found long ago!

The enigma was solved long ago. But different thinkers, living in different epochs, finding the solution, expressed it differently, and often, not knowing one another, trod the same path amid enormous difficulties, unaware of their predecessors and contemporaries who had gone and were going along the selfsame path.

In the world's literature there exist books, usually little known, which accidentally or by design may happen to be assembled on one shelf in one library. These, taken together, will yield so clear and complete a picture of human existence, its path and its goal, that there will be no further doubts about the destiny of humanity (though only its minor part), but a destiny of *quite a different sort* from those hard labors of digging through the globe, which positive philosophy, "historical materialism" and "socialism" have in store for humankind.

And if it seems to us that we do not as yet know our destiny, if we still doubt, and do not dare to part with the hopeless "positivistic" view of life, it is primarily because men of different categories, having quite different futures, are commingled into one in our perception; and secondarily because the necessary ideas by means of which we might understand the true relation of forces have not won for themselves their rightful place in official science — do not represent any *recognized* division or branch of science; it is rarely possible to find them all in one book and it is even rarely possible to find books expressing these ideas assembled together.

We do not understand many things because we too easily and too arbitrarily specialize. Philosophy, religion, psychology, mathematics, the natural sciences, sociology, the history of culture, art — each has its own separate literature. There is no complete whole at all. Even the little *bridges* between these separate literatures are built very badly and unsuccessfully, while they are often altogether absent. And this formation of special literatures is the chief evil and the chief obstacle to a correct understanding of things. Each "literature" elaborates its own terminology, its own language, which is incomprehensible to the students of other literatures, and *does not coincide* with other languages; by this it defines its own limits the more sharply, divides itself from others, and makes these limits impassable.

But there are movements of thought which strive not in words, but in action, to fight this specialization.

Books are appearing which it is impossible to refer to any accepted library classification, which it is impossible to "enroll" in any faculty. These books are the forerunners of a new literature which will break down all fences built in the region of thought, and will clearly show to those who desire to know, where they are going and where they can go.

The names of the authors of these books yield the most unexpected combinations. I shall not now mention the names of these authors, or the titles of these books, but shall dwell only upon the writings of Edward Carpenter and Dr. R. M. Bucke.

Edward Carpenter, directly and without any allegories and symbols, formulated the thought that the existing consciousness by which contemporary man lives, is merely the transitory form of another higher consciousness, which *even now* is manifesting in certain men, after appropriate preparation and training.

This higher consciousness Edward Carpenter names *cosmic consciousness*.

Carpenter traveled in the Orient, visited India and Ceylon, and there he found men, yogis and ascetics, striving to achieve *cosmic consciousness*, and he holds the opinion that the path to cosmic consciousness is already found in the Orient.

In the book, *From Adam's Peak to Elephanta*, he says:

The West seeks the individual consciousness — the enriched mind, ready perceptions and memories, individual hopes and fears, ambitions, loves, conquests — the self, the local self, in all its phases and forms — and sorely doubts whether such a thing as an universal consciousness exists. The East seeks the universal consciousness, and in these cases where its quest succeeds individual self and life thin away to a mere film, and are only the shadows cast by the glory revealed beyond.

The individual consciousness takes the form of *Thought*, which is fluid and mobile like quicksilver, perpetually in a state of change and unrest, fraught with pain and effort; the other consciousness is *not* in the form of thought. It touches, sees, hears, and is those things which it perceives, without motion, without change, without effort, without distinction of subject and object, but with a vast and incredible joy.

The individual consciousness is specially related to the body. The organs of the body are in some degree its organs. But the *whole* body is only as one organ of the cosmic consciousness. To attain this latter one must have the power of knowing one's self separate from the body — of passing into a state of *ecstasy*, in fact. Without this the cosmic consciousness cannot be experienced.

All the subsequent writings of Carpenter, and especially his book of free verse, *Towards Democracy*, deal with the psychology of ecstatic experiences and portray the path whereby man goes toward this *principal aim of his existence*, i.e., to a new consciousness.

Only the attainment of this principal aim will illumine for man the past and the future; it will be a seership, an awakening — without this, with only the ordinary sleepy, "individual" consciousness, man is blind, and cannot hope to know anything that he cannot feel with his stick.

Dr. Bucke, in his book, *Cosmic Consciousness*, gives the psychological view of this awakening of the new consciousness.

I shall give, in abbreviated form, several quotations from his book.

I

What is Cosmic Consciousness?

Cosmic Consciousness is a higher form of consciousness than that possessed by the ordinary man. This last is called Self Consciousness and is that faculty upon which rests all of our life (both subjective and objective) which is not common to us and the higher animals, except that small part of it which is derived from the few individuals who have had the higher consciousness above named. To make the matter clear it must be understood that there are three forms or grades of consciousness. (1) *Simple Consciousness*, which is possessed by, say, the upper half of the animal kingdom. (2) *Self Consciousness* possessed by man in addition to the simple consciousness, which is similar in man and in animals.* (3) *Cosmic Consciousness*. By means of simple consciousness a dog or a horse is just as conscious of the things about him as a man is; he is also conscious of his own limbs and body and knows that these are a part of himself. By virtue of self-consciousness man is not only conscious of trees, rocks, water, his own limbs and body, but he becomes conscious of himself as a distinct entity apart from all the rest of the universe.

It is as good as certain that no animal can realize himself in that way.

* This division constitutes Dr. Bucke's principal error. Human consciousness, i.e., the consciousness of the enormous majority of men, is "simple consciousness"; "self-consciousness," like "cosmic consciousness," exists only in a flash.

Cosmic Consciousness

Further, by means of self-consciousness, man becomes capable of treating his own mental states as objects of consciousness. The animal is, as it were, immersed in his consciousness as a fish in the sea; he cannot, even in imagination, get outside of it for one moment so as to realize it. But man by virtue of self-consciousness can step aside, as it were, from himself and think: " Yes, that thought that I had about that matter is true; I know it is true and I know that I know it is true." There is no evidence that any animal can think, but if they could we should soon know it. Between two creatures living together, as dogs or horses and men, and each self-conscious, it would be the simplest matter in the world to open up communication. We do, by watching the dog's acts, enter into his mind pretty freely. If he were self-conscious, we must have learned it long ago. We have not learned it and it is as good as certain that no dog, horse, elephant or ape ever was self-conscious. Another thing: on man's self-consciousness is built everything in and about us distinctly human. Language is the objective of which self-consciousness is the subjective. Self-consciousness and language (two in one for they are two halves of the same thing) are the sine qua non of human social life, of manners, of institutions, of industries of all kinds, of all arts useful and fine. If any animal possessed self-consciousness it would build a superstructure of language. . . . But no animal has done this, therefore, we infer that no animal has self-consciousness. The possession of self-consciousness and language (its other self) by man creates an enormous gap between him and the highest creature possessing simple consciousness merely.

Cosmic Consciousness is a third form, which is as far above Self Consciousness as is that above Simple Consciousness. The prime characteristic of Cosmic Consciousness is, as its name implies, a consciousness of the cosmos, that is, of the life and order of the universe. Along with the consciousness of the cosmos there occurs an intellectual enlightenment or illumination which alone would place the individual on a new plane of existence — would make him almost a member of a new species. To this is added a state of moral exaltation, an indescribable feeling of elevation, elation and joyousness, and a quickening of the moral sense, which is fully as striking and more important both to the individual and to the race than is the enhanced intellectual power. With these come what may be called a sense of immortality, a consciousness of eternal life, not a conviction that he shall have this, but the consciousness that he has it already.

Only a personal experience of it, or a prolonged study of men who have passed into the new life, will enable us to realize what this actually is. The writer expects his work to be useful in two ways: first, in broadening the general view of human life by comprehending in our mental vision this important phase of it, then by enabling us to realize, in some measure, the true status of certain men who, down to the present, are either exalted to the ranks of gods or are adjudged insane. The writer takes the view that our descendants will sooner or later reach, as a race, the condition of cosmic consciousness, just as long ago, our ancestors passed from simple to self-consciousness. He believes that this step in evolution is even now being made, since it is clear to him both that men with the faculty in question are becoming more and more common and also that as a race we are approaching nearer and nearer to that stage of the self-conscious mind from which the transition to the cosmic conscious is effected. He knows that intelligent contact with cosmic conscious minds assists self-conscious individuals in the ascent to the higher plane.

II

The immediate future of our race [the writer thinks] is indescribably hopeful. There are at the present moment impending over us three revolutions, the least of which would dwarf the ordinary historic upheaval called by that name into absolute insignificance.* They are: (1) the material, economic and social revolution which will depend upon and result from the establishment of aerial navigation. (2) The economic and social revolution which will abolish individual ownership and rid the earth at once of two immense evils — riches and poverty. And (3) the psychical revolution of which there is here question.

Either of the first two would (and will) radically change the conditions of, and greatly uplift, human life; but the third will do more for humanity than both of the former, were their importance multiplied by hundreds or even thousands.

The three operating (as they will) together will literally create a new heaven and a new earth. Old things will be done away and all will become new.

Before aerial navigation national boundaries, tariffs and perhaps distinctions of language will fade out. Great cities will no longer have reason for being and will melt away. The men who now dwell in cities will inhabit in summer the mountains and the seashores; building often in airy and beautiful spots, now almost or quite inaccessible, commanding the most extensive and magnificent views. In the winter they will probably dwell in communities of moderate size. As herding together, as now, in great cities, so the isolation of the worker of the soil will become a thing of the past. Space will be practically annihilated, there will be no crowding together and no enforced solitude.

Before socialism crushing toil, cruel anxiety, insulting and demoralizing riches, poverty and its ills will become subjects for historical novels.*

In contact with the flux of cosmic consciousness all religions known and named today will be melted down. The human soul will be revolutionized. Religion will absolutely dominate the race. It will not depend on traditions.

* See the comment 1, pp. 292–3.   * See the comment 2, pp. 293–4.

It will not be believed and disbelieved. It will be part of life, not belonging to certain hours, times, occasions. It will not be in sacred books, nor in the mouths of priests. It will not dwell in churches and meetings and forms and days. Its life will not be in prayers, hymns nor discourses. It will not depend on special revelations, on the words of gods who came down to teach, nor on any bible or bibles. It will have no mission to save men from their sins or to secure their entrance to heaven. It will not teach a future immortality nor future glories, for immortality and all glory will exist in the here and now. The evidence of immortality will live in every heart as sight in every eye. Doubt of God and of eternal life will be as impossible as is now doubt of existence; the evidence of each will be the same. Religion will govern every minute of every day of all life. Churches, priests, forms, creeds, prayers, all agents, all intermediaries between the individual man and God will be permanently replaced by direct unmistakable intercourse. Sin will no longer exist nor will salvation be desired. Men will not worry about death or a future, about the kingdom of heaven, about what may come with and after the cessation of the life of the present body. Each soul will feel and know itself to be immortal, will feel and know that the entire universe with all its good and with all its beauty is for it and belongs to it forever. The world peopled by men possessing cosmic consciousness will be as far removed from the world of today as this is from the world as it was before the advent of self-consciousness.

III

There is a tradition, probably very old, to the effect that the first man was innocent and happy until he ate of the fruit of the tree of the knowledge of good and evil. That having eaten thereof he became aware that he was naked and was ashamed. Further, that there sin was born into the world, the miserable sense whereof replaced man's former feeling of innocency; that then and not till then man began to labor and to cover his body. Stranger than all, the story runs, that along with this change or immediately following upon it there came into man's mind the remarkable conviction which has never since left it, but which has been kept alive by its own inherent vitality and by the teaching of all true seers, prophets and poets that man will be saved by the rising up within him of a Savior — the Christ.

Man's progenitor was a creature with simple consciousness merely. He was (as are today the animals) incapable of sin and equally incapable of shame (at least in the human sense). He had no feeling or knowledge of good and evil. He as yet knew nothing of what we call work and had never labored. From this state he fell (or rose) into self-consciousness, his eyes were opened, he knew he was naked, he felt shame, acquired the sense of sin (became in fact what is called a sinner) and learned to do certain things in order to encompass certain ends — that is, he learned to labor.

Tertium Organum

For weary aeons this condition has lasted — the sense of sin still haunts his pathway — by the sweat of his brow he still eats bread — he is still ashamed. Where is the deliverer, the Saviour? Who or what?

The Savior of man is Cosmic Consciousness — in Paul's language, the Christ. The cosmic sense (in whatever mind it appears) crushes the serpent's head — destroys sin, shame, the sense of good and evil, as contrasted one with the other, and will annihilate labor, though not human activity.

IV

A personal exposition of the writer's own experience of cosmic consciousness may help the reader to understand the meaning of the following facts:

In childhood he was subject at times to a sort of ecstasy of curiosity and hope. As on one special occasion when about ten years old he earnestly longed to die that the secrets of the beyond, if there were any beyond, might be revealed to him. . . .

At the age of thirty he fell in with "Leaves of Grass," and at once saw that it contained, in greater measure than any book so far found, what he had so long been looking for. He read the "Leaves" eagerly, even passionately, but for several years derived little from them. At last light broke and there was revealed to him (as far perhaps as such things can be revealed) at least some of the meanings. Then occurred that to which the foregoing is the preface.

It was in the early spring, at the beginning of his thirty-sixth year. He and two friends had spent the evening reading Wordsworth, Shelley, Keats, Browning, and especially Whitman. They parted at midnight and he had a long drive in a hansom (it was in an English city). His mind, deeply under the influence of the ideas, images and emotions called up by the reading and talk of the evening, was calm and peaceful. He was in a state of quiet, almost passive enjoyment. All at once, without warning of any kind, he found himself wrapped around as it were by a flame-colored cloud. For an instant he thought of fire, some sudden conflagration in the great city; the next he knew the light was within himself. Directly afterwards came upon him a sense of exultation, of immense joyousness accompanied or immediately followed by an intellectual illumination quite impossible to describe. Into his brain streamed one momentary lightning-flash of the Brahmic splendor which has ever since lightened his life; upon his heart fell one drop of Brahmic Bliss, leaving thenceforward for always an after taste of heaven. Among other things he did not come to believe, he saw and knew that the cosmos is not dead matter but a living Presence, that the soul of man is immortal, that the universe is so built and ordered that without peradventure all things work together for the good of each and all, that the foundation principle of the world is what we call love and that the happiness of everyone in the long run is absolutely certain. He claims he learned more within the few seconds during

which the illumination lasted than in previous months or even years of study and that he learned much that no study could ever have taught.

The illumination itself continued not more than a few moments, but its effects proved ineffaceable; it was impossible for him ever to forget what he at that time saw and knew; neither did he, nor could he, ever doubt the truth of what was then presented to his mind. There was no return that night or at any other time of the experience.

The supreme occurrence of that night was his real and sole initiation to the new and higher order of ideas. But it was only an initiation. He saw the light but had no more idea whence it came and what it meant than had the first creature that saw the light of the sun. Years afterwards he met a man who had had a large experience in the higher life. His conversations with this man threw a flood of light upon the meaning of what he had himself experienced.

Looking round then upon the world of man, he saw the significance of the subjective light in the case of Paul and in that of Mohammed. The secret of Whitman's transcendent greatness was revealed to him. Personal intercourse and conversations with men,* who had similar experiences assisted greatly in the broadening and clearing up of his speculations.

After spending much time and labor in thinking he came to the conclusion that there exists a family sprung from, living among, but scarcely forming a part of ordinary humanity, whose members are spread abroad throughout the advanced races of mankind and throughout the last forty centuries of the world's history.

The trait that distinguishes these people from other men is this: Their spiritual eyes have been opened and they *have seen*. The better known members of this group who, if they were collected together, could be accommodated all at one time in a modern drawing-room, have created all the great modern religions, beginning with Taoism and Buddhism, and speaking generally, have created, through religion and literature, modern civilization. Not that they have contributed any large numerical proportion of the books which have been written, but that they have produced the few books which have inspired the larger number of all that have been written in modern times. These men dominate the last twenty-five, especially the last five centuries as stars of the first magnitude dominate the midnight sky.

V

It remains to say a few words upon the psychological origin of what is called in this book Cosmic Consciousness.

Although in the birth of Cosmic Consciousness the moral nature plays an important part, it will be better for many reasons to confine our attention at present to the evolution of the intellect. In this evolution there are

* Among whom was Edward Carpenter.

four distinct steps. The first of them was taken when upon the primary quality of excitability sensation was established. At this point began the acquisition and more or less perfect registration of sense impressions — that is, of percepts. A percept is of course a sense impression. If we could go back far enough we should find among our ancestors a creature whose whole intellect was made up simply of these percepts. But this creature had in it what may be called an eligibility of growth, and what happened with it was something like this: Individually and from generation to generation it accumulated these percepts, the constant repetition of which, calling for further and further registration, led, in the struggle for existence and under the law of natural selection, to an accumulation of cells in the central sense ganglia; at last a condition was reached in which it became possible for our ancestor to combine groups of these percepts into what we today call a recept. This process is very similar to that of composite photography. Similar percepts (as of a tree) are registered one over the other until they are generalized into the percept of a tree.

Now the work of accumulation begins again on a higher plane: the sensory organs keep steadily at work manufacturing percepts; the receptual centers keep steadily at work manufacturing more and yet more recepts from the old and the new percepts; the capacity of the central ganglia is constantly taxed to do necessary registration of percepts, the necessary elaboration of these into recepts; then as the ganglia by use and selection are improved they constantly manufacture from percepts and from the initial simple recepts, more and more complex, that is, higher and higher recepts.

At last, after many thousands of generations have lived and died, comes a time when the mind has reached the highest possible point of purely receptual intelligence; the accumulation of percepts and of recepts has gone on until no greater stores of impressions can be laid up and no further elaboration of these can be accomplished on the plane of receptual intelligence. Then another break is made and the higher recepts are replaced by concepts. The relation of a concept to a recept is somewhat similar to the relation of algebra to arithmetic. A recept is a composite image of hundreds, perhaps thousands of percepts; it is itself an image abstracted from many images; but a concept is that same composite image — that same recept — named, ticketed, and, as it were, dismissed. A concept is in fact neither more nor less than a *named recept* — the name that is, the sign (as in algebra), standing henceforth for the thing itself, that is, for the recept.

Now it is clear as day to any one who will give the least thought to the subject, that the revolution by which concepts are substituted for recepts increases the efficiency of the brain for thought as much as the introduction of machinery increases the capacity of the race for work — as much as the use of algebra increases the power of the mind in mathematical calculations. To

The Supra-Conceptual Mind

replace a great cumbersome recept by a simple sign was almost like replacing actual goods — as wheat, fabrics and hardware — by entries in the ledger.

But, as hinted above, in order that a recept may be replaced by a concept it must be named, or, in other words, marked with a sign which stands for it — just as a check stands for a piece of goods; in other words, the race that is in possession of concepts is also, and necessarily, in possession of language. Further, it should be noted, as the possession of concepts implies the possession of language, so the possession of concepts and language (which are in reality two aspects of the same thing) implies the possession of self-consciousness. All this means that there is a moment in the evolution of mind when the receptual intellect, capable of simple consciousness only, becomes almost or quite instantaneously a conceptual intellect in possession of language and self-consciousness.

Our intellect, then, today is made up of a very complex mixture of percepts, recepts and concepts.

The next chapter in the story is the accumulation of concepts. This is a double process, each individual accumulates a larger and larger number while the individual concepts are becoming constantly more and more complex.

Is there to be any limit to this growth of concepts in number and complexity? Whoever will seriously consider that question will see that there must be a limit. No such process could go on to infinity.

We have seen that the expansion of the perceptual mind had a necessary limit: that its continued life led inevitably up to and into the receptual mind; that the receptual mind by its own growth was inevitably led up to and into the conceptual mind. A priori considerations make it certain that a corresponding outlet will be found for the conceptual mind.

But we do not need to depend upon abstract reasoning to demonstrate the necsssary existence of the supra-conceptual mind, since it exists and can be studied with no more difficulty than other natural phenomena. The supra-conceptual intellect, the elements of which instead of being concepts are intuitions, is already (in small numbers it is true) an established fact, and the form of consciousness that belongs to that intellect may be called and has been called — Cosmic Consciousness.

The basic fact in cosmic consciousness is implied in its name — that fact is consciousness of the cosmos — this is what is called in the East the "Brahmic Splendor," which is in Dante's phrase capable of trans-humanizing a man into a god. Whitman, who has an immense deal to say about it, speaks of it in one place as "ineffable light — light rare, untellable, lighting the very light — beyond all signs, description, languages." This consciousness shows the cosmos to consist not of dead matter governed by unconscious, rigid, and unintending law; it shows it on the contrary as entirely immaterial, entirely spiritual and entirely alive; it shows that death is an absurdity, that everyone and everything has eternal life; it shows that the universe is God and that God is the Universe. . . . A great deal of this is of course, from the point of view of self-consciousness, absurd; it is nevertheless undoubtedly true. Now all this does not mean that when a man has cosmic consciousness he knows everything about the universe. We all know that when at three years of age we acquired self-consciousness, we did not at once know all about ourselves. . . . So neither does a man know all about the cosmos merely because he becomes conscious of it. . . .

If it has taken the race several thousand years to learn a smattering of the science of humanity since its acquisition of self-consciousness, so it may take it millions of years to acquire cosmic consciousness.

As on self-consciousness is based the human world as we see it with all its works and ways, so on cosmic consciousness is based the higher religions and the higher philosophies and what comes from them, and on it will be based, when it becomes more general, a new world of which it would be idle to try to speak today.

The philosophy of the birth of cosmic consciousness in the individual is very similar to that of the birth of self-consciousness. The mind becomes overcrowded (as it were) with concepts and these are constantly becoming larger, more numerous and more and more complex; some day (the conditions being all favorable) the fusion, or what might be called the chemical union, of several of them and of certain moral elements takes place; the result is an intuition and the establishment of the intuitional mind, or, in other words, cosmic consciousness.*

The scheme by which the mind is built up is uniform from beginning to end: a recept is made of many percepts; a concept of many or several recepts and percepts, and an intuition is made of many concepts, recepts and percepts together with other elements belonging to and drawn from the moral nature. The cosmic vision or the cosmic intuition, from which what may be called the new mind takes its name, is thus seen to be simply the complex and union of all prior thought and experience — just as self-consciousness is the complex and union of all thought and experience prior to it.

Cosmic consciousness, like other forms of consciousness, is capable of growth, it may have different forms, different degrees.

It must not be supposed that because a man has cosmic consciousness he is therefore omniscient or infallible. Men of cosmic consciousness have reached a higher level; but on that level there can be different degrees of consciousness. And it must be still more evident that, however godlike the faculty may be, those who first acquire it, living in diverse ages and countries, passing their life in different surroundings, brought up to view life from totally different

* See the comment 3, p. 294.

Mind and Language

points of view, must necessarily interpret somewhat differently those things which they see in the new world which they enter.

Language corresponds to the intellect and is therefore capable of expressing it perfectly and directly; on the other hand, the functions of the moral nature are not connected with language and are only capable of indirect and imperfect expression by its agency. Perhaps music, which certainly has its roots in the moral nature, is, as at present existing, the beginning of a language which will tally and express emotions as words tally and express ideas. . . .

Language is the exact tally of the intellect; for every concept there is a word or words and for every word there is a concept. . . . No word can come into being except as the expression of a concept, neither can a new concept be formed without the formation (at the same time) of the new word which is its expression. But as a matter of fact ninety-nine out of every hundred of our sense impressions and emotions have never been represented in the intellect by concepts and therefore remain unexpressed and inexpressible except by roundabout description and suggestion.

As the correspondence of words and concepts is not casual or temporary but resides in the nature of these and continues during all time and under all circumstances absolutely constant, so changes in one of the factors must correspond with changes in the other. So evolution of intellect must be accompanied by evolution of language. An evolution of language will be evidence of evolution of intellect.

It seems that in every, or nearly every man who enters into cosmic consciousness apprehension is at first more or less excited, the person doubting whether the new sense may not be a symptom or form of insanity. Mohammed was greatly alarmed. The Apostle Paul was alarmed in the same manner.

The first thing each person asks himself upon experiencing the new sense is: Does what I see and feel represent reality or am I suffering from a delusion? The fact that the new experience seems even more real than the old teachings of consciousness does not at first fully reassure him, because he knows the force of delusions.

Simultaneously or instantly following the above sense and emotional experiences there comes to the person an intellectual illumination quite impossible to describe. Like a flash there is presented to his consciousness a clear conception (a vision) in outline of the meaning and drift of the universe. He does not come to believe merely; but he sees and knows that the cosmos, which to the self-conscious mind seems made up of dead matter, is in fact far otherwise – is in very truth a living presence. He sees that instead of men being, as it were, patches of life scattered through an infinite sea of non-living substance, they are in reality specks of relative death in an infinite ocean of life. He sees that the life which is in man is eternal, as all life is eternal, that the soul of man is as immortal as God is. . . .

A man learns infinitely much of the new. Especially does he obtain such a conception of THE WHOLE — or at least of an immense WHOLE — as dwarfs all conception, imagination or speculation, such a conception as makes the old attempts to mentally grasp the universe and its meaning petty and even ridiculous.

This expansion of the intellect enormously increases the capacity both for learning and initiating.

The history of the development and appearance of cosmic consciousness *in humanity* is the same as that of the development of all the various psychic faculties. These faculties appear first in certain exceptional individuals, then become more frequent, thereafter become susceptible of development in all, and at last begin to belong to all men from their birth. Rare, exceptional, unique abilities appear in man in mature age, sometimes even in senility. Becoming more common they manifest as "talents" in younger men. And then they appear as "abilities" even in children. At last they become the common property of all from their birth, and their absence is regarded as a monstrosity.

Such is the faculty of *speech* (i.e., the faculty of making concepts). Probably in a distant past, at the beginning of the appearance of self-consciousness, this faculty was the gift of a few exceptional individuals and it began then to appear perhaps in senility. After that it began to appear more frequently and to manifest itself earlier. Probably there was a period when *speech* was not a gift of all men just as are not now artistic talents, the musical sense, the sense of color and form. Gradually it became *possible* for all and then inevitable and necessary, if some physical defect did not prevent its manifestation.

COMMENTS ON THE QUOTATIONS FROM DR. BUCKE'S BOOK

1. Though I am quoting Dr. Bucke's opinion regarding three coming revolutions, let me note that I do not at all share his optimism regarding social life, which, as follows from what he says, can and must change by reason of material causes (the conquest of the air and social revolution). The only possible ground for favorable changes in the outer life (provided such changes are generally possible) can only be changes in the inner life — i.e., those changes which Dr. Bucke calls the psychical revolu-

tion. This is the only thing that can create a better future for men. All cultural conquests in the realm of the material are double-edged, may equally serve for good or for evil. A change of consciousness can alone be a guarantee of the surcease of wilful misuses of the powers given by culture, and only thus will culture cease to be a "growth of barbarity." Democratic organization and the nominal rule of the majority guarantee nothing: on the contrary, even now, where they are realized — though only in name — they create without delay, and promise in future to create on a larger scale, violence toward the minority, the limitation of the individual, and the curtailment of freedom.

2. Dr. Bucke says that once human consciousness is attained, then further evolution is inevitable. In this affirmation Dr. Bucke makes a mistake common to all men who dogmatize about evolution. Having painted a very true picture of the consecutive gradations of the forms of consciousness observed by us — of animal-vegetable, of animal, and of man — Dr. Bucke considers this gradation exclusively in the light of the evolution of one form from another, not at all admitting the possibility of other points of view: for example, the fact that each of the existing forms is a link of *separate* evolutionary chains, i.e., that the evolutions of animal-vegetables, of animals and of men are different, go by different routes, and do not impinge upon one another. And this standpoint is entirely justifiable when we take into consideration the fact that we *never know* transitional forms. Moreover Dr. Bucke makes an entirely arbitrary conclusion concerning the *inevitability* of the further evolution of man, because unconscious evolution (i.e., unconscious for the individual directed by the consciousness of the species) in the vegetable and animal kingdoms is impossible with the appearance of reasoning in man. It is necessary to recognize that the mind of a man depends upon itself to a considerably greater degree than the mind of an animal. The mind of a man has far more power over itself; it can assist in its own evolution, and can also *impede* it. We are confronted with the general question: can unconscious evolution proceed with the appearance of reasoning? It is far more correct to suppose that the appearance of reasoning annihilates the possibility of unconscious evolution. Power over evolution passes from the group-soul (or from nature) to the individual itself. Further evolution, if it take place, cannot be an elemental and unconscious affair, but will result solely from conscious *efforts toward growth.** This is the most interesting point in the whole process, but Dr. Bucke fails to bring it out. *Man*, not striving toward evolution, not conscious of its possibility, not

* See p. 292. Quotation from Mabel Collins' book.

helping it, will not evolve. And the individual who is not evolving does not remain in a static condition, but goes down, *degenerates* (i.e, some of his elements begin their own evolution, inimical to the whole). This is the general law. And if we take into consideration what an infinitesimal percentage of men think and are capable of thinking of their evolution (or their striving toward higher things) then we shall see that to talk about the inevitability of this *evolution is at least naive*.

3. Speaking of the formation of a higher faculty of knowledge and reason, Dr. Bucke fails to take into consideration one very important circumstance. He himself previously remarks that the blending of concepts with emotional elements proceeds in the mind, and *as a result of this a* new understanding appears, and then cosmic consciousness. Thus it follows from his own words that cosmic consciousness is not simply a blending of concepts with emotional elements, or ideas with feelings, but is *the result* of this blending. Dr. Bucke however does not dwell on this with sufficient attention. Moreover he further regards the fundamental element of cosmic consciousness as the blending of sensations, perceptions and concepts with elements properly belonging to the emotional nature. This is a mistake, because one element of cosmic consciousness is not simply *the blending* of thought and feeling, but *the result* of this blending, or in other words: thought and feeling *plus something else*, plus something else that is absent either in the intellect or in the emotional nature.

But Dr. Bucke regards this new faculty of understanding and reasoning as a product of *the evolution of existing faculties* and this vitiates all his deductions. Let us imagine that some scientist from another planet, not suspecting the existence of *man*, studies the horse, and its "evolution" from colt to saddle-horse, and regards as its highest evolution the horse with the horseman in the saddle. From our standpoint it is clearly impossible to regard a man sitting in the horse's saddle as a fact of *horse* evolution, but from the point of view of the scientist who knows nothing about man, this will be only logical. Dr. Bucke finds himself in exactly this position when he regards that which transcends the region of humanity altogether as a fact of human evolution. Man possessing cosmic consciousness, or approaching cosmic consciousness is not merely man, but man with something higher added. Dr. Bucke, like Edward Carpenter in many cases also, is handicapped by the desire not to go too strongly counter to accepted views (although that is inevitable); by the desire to reconcile those views with the "new thought," to flatten out contradictions, to reduce everything to one thing, which is of course impossible

— as is the reconciliation of correct and incorrect, true and false views upon one and the same thing.

The greater part of Dr. Bucke's book consists of examples and quotations from the teachings and writings of men of "cosmic consciousness" in the history of the world. He draws parallels between these teachings, and establishes the *unity* of the forms of transition into the new state of consciousness in men of different centuries and of different peoples, and the unity of their sensations of the world and of the self, testifying more than anything else to the genuineness and reality of their experiences.

The founders of world-religions, prophets, philosophers, poets — these are men of "cosmic consciousness" according to Dr. Bucke's book. He does not pretend to present a full list of them, and it is of course possible to add many names to his list.*

But after all, various little imperfections of Dr. Bucke's book are not important, nor additions which might possibly be made. What is important is the general conclusion to which Dr. Bucke comes — the possibility and the immanence of the NEW CONSCIOUSNESS.

All this announces to us the nearness of the NEW HUMANITY. We are building without taking into consideration the fact that a NEW MASTER must come who may not at all like everything that we have built. Our "social sciences," sociology, and so forth, have in view only man, while as I have several times shown before, the concept "man" is a complex one, and includes in itself different categories of men going along different paths. The future belongs *not to man, but to superman,* who is already born, and lives among us.

A higher race is rapidly emerging among humanity, and it is emerging by reason of its quite remarkable understanding of the world and life.

It will be truly a HIGHER RACE — and there will be no possibility of any falsification, any substitution, or any usurpation at all. It will be

---

* Dr. Bucke makes a very important error concerning self-consciousness. In his opinion "simple consciousness" characterizes an animal and "self-consciousness" characterizes a man. But as a matter of fact a prolonged self-consciousness *during* sensation, feeling or thinking is a very rare phenomenon in man, usually that which is called self-consciousness is simply thought and it goes *post factum*. True self-consciousness exists in man only potentially, and, if it manifests itself, it does so only by moments. These moments of self-consciousness should not be identified with prolonged self-consciousness. Prolonged self-consciousness is already "a new consciousness," and there is the possibility of moments of cosmic consciousness, which in the course of further development may, in turn, become prolonged.

impossible for anything to be *bought*, or *appropriated* to oneself by deceit or by might. Not only will this race be, but it already is.

The men approaching the transition into a new race begin already to know one another: already are established pass-words and countersigns. And perhaps those social and political questions so sharply put forward in our time may be solved on quite another plane and by quite a different method than we think — may be solved by the entrance into the arena of a new race CONSCIOUS OF ITSELF which will judge the old races.

In my remarks I called attention to certain imperfections in Dr. Bucke's book arising chiefly from a strange indecisiveness of his, from his timidity in asserting the dominant significance of *the new consciousness*. This results from the desire of Dr. Bucke to establish the future of humanity from a positivistic standpoint upon social and political revolutions. But we may regard this view as having lost all validity. The bankruptcy of materialism, i.e., "logical" systems, when it comes to organizing life on earth is now evident in the bloody epoch which we are undergoing, even to those men who but yesterday were prating of "culture" and "civilization." It became clearer and clearer that the changes in the outer life of the majority, when these changes come, will do so *as a result* of inner changes in a few.

We may say further with regard to Dr. Bucke's entire book, that touching the idea *of the natural growth* of consciousness, he does not notice that these faculties do not unfold themselves perforce: conscious work on them is necessary. And he does not dwell at all on conscious efforts in this direction, on the idea of the *culture* of cosmic consciousness. Meanwhile there exists a whole series of psychological teachings (occultism, yoga, etc.) and a large literature having in view a systematic culture of the higher consciousness. Dr. Bucke does not remark this, and insists upon the idea of natural growth, although he himself several times touches upon the culture of consciousness. In one portion of his book he speaks very contemptuously regarding the use of narcotics for the creation of ecstatic states, not taking into consideration the fact that narcotics cannot *give* anything which man does not possess (this is the explanation of the different action of narcotics on different men), but can only in certain cases unfold that which is already in the soul of man. This entirely alters the point of view upon narcotics, as Prof. William James has shown in his book, *The Varieties of Religious Experience*.

In general, allured by the evolutionary point of view, and looking at *the future,* Dr. Bucke, like many others, does not pay sufficient attention to *the present.* That new consciousness which men may discover or unfold *in themselves now* is indeed far more important than that which may or may not appear in *other men* millenniums hence.

Regarding from different standpoints the complex forms of the manifestation of spirit, and analyzing the views and opinions of various authors, we are always confronted with what seem to be consecutive phases or consecutive stages of this unfoldment. And we find such phases or stages to be four in number. Further consideration of the living world known to us, from the lower animal organisms up to the highly developed body of man, reveals the simultaneous existence of all four forms of consciousness to which all other aspects of the inner life correspond: the sense of space and time, the form of activity, etc. Still further consideration of *man of the higher type* reveals the presence of all the four forms of consciousness which are in living nature, with forms corresponding to them.

Forms of Consciousness	Living World	Man of Higher Type
Latent Consciousness, similar to our instincts and subconscious feelings.	Cells, groups of cells, plants, lower animals, and organs and parts of body of higher animals and of man.	Cells, groups of cells, tissues and organs of the body.
Simple Consciousness and flashes of thought.	Animals possessing complex organisms. Absence of consciousness of death.	Body, instincts, desires, voices of the body, emotions.
Reasoning. Moments of self-consciousness and flashes of cosmic consciousness.	Man. Consciousness of death or fantastic theories of immortality.	Simple emotions, logical reason, mind.
Self-consciousness and beginning of cosmic consciousness.	Man of higher type. Beginning of immortality.	Higher emotions, higher intellect, intuition, mystical wisdom.

The simultaneous coexistence of all four forms of consciousness at once, both in nature and in the higher type of man, makes the exclusively evolutionary standpoint seem forced and artificial. The evolutionary standpoint is often made the means of escape from difficult problems, and from hard thinking.

Some people apply the evolutionary theory where there is no necessity for it whatever. In many cases this is a compromise of thought. Not understanding the existing variety of forms, and not possessing the skill to think of all this *as a unity*, men have recourse to the evolutionary idea, and regard this great variety of forms as an ascending ladder — not because this conforms to facts, but from a desire to systematize the observed facts at all costs, though on entirely artificial foundations. It appears to men that having built a system they already know something, whereas in reality the absence of a system is often much nearer to real knowledge than an artificial system.

"Evolutionists," being incapable of understanding the whole, without representing it to themselves as a chain, one link of which is connected with another, are like the blind men in the Oriental fable, who feel of an elephant in different places, and one affirms that the elephant is like pillars, another that it is like a thick rope, and so forth. The evolutionists, however, add to this that the trunk of the elephant must *evolve* from the feet, the ears from the trunk, and so on. But we after all know that this is an *elephant*, i.e., a single being, unknown to men who are blind. Such a being is the living world. And with regard to the forms of consciousness, it is far more correct to consider them not as consecutive phases or steps of evolution which are separate from one another, but as different sides or parts of one whole which we do not know.

In "man" this unity is apparent. All forms of consciousness in him can exist simultaneously; the life of cells and organs, with their consciousness; the life of the entire body, taken as a whole; the life of the emotions and of the logical reason, and the life of the higher understanding and feeling.

The higher form of consciousness is not necessary *for life*; it is possible to live without it. But without it the organization and orderliness of life is impossible. Long under the domination of materialism and positive thinking, forgetting and perverting religious ideas, men thought that it was possible to live by the merely logical mind alone. But now, little by little, it is becoming quite evident to those who have eyes, that merely by the exercise of logical reason men will not be able to organize their life on earth, and if they do not finally exterminate themselves, as some tribes and peoples are doing, in any case they will create (and have already created) impossible conditions of life in which everything gained will be lost — i.e., everything that was given them in the past by men of self-consciousness and cosmic consciousness.

The living world of nature (including man) is analogous to man; and it is more correct and more convenient to regard the different forms of consciousness in different divisions and strata of living nature as belonging to one organism and performing different, but related functions, than as separate, and evolving from one another. Then the necessity disappears for all this naïve theorizing on the subject of evolution. We do not regard the organs and members of the body of man as evolved one from another *in a given individual* and we should not be guilty of the same error with relation to the organs and members of the body of living nature.

I do not deny the law of evolution, but the application of it to the explanation of many phenomena of life is in great need of correction.

Firstly, if we accept the idea of one common evolution, after all it is necessary to remember that the types which develop slower, the remnants of evolution, may not continue to follow after, and at a slow pace, *the same* evolution, but may begin an evolution of their own, developing in many cases exactly those properties on account of which they were thrown out from basic evolution.

Secondly, though we accept the law of evolution, there is no necessity to regard all existing forms as having been developed one from another (like man from the ape, for example). In such cases it is more correct to regard them all as the *highest types* in *their own* evolution. The absence of intermediate forms makes this view much more probable than that which is usually accepted, and which gives such rich material for discussions about the obligatory and inevitable perfection of all — "perfection" from our standpoint.

The views propounded here are indeed more difficult than the usual evolutionary point of view, just as the conception of the living world as an *entire* organism is more difficult; but this difficulty must be surmounted. I have said already that the real world must be illogical from the usual points of view, and by no means can it be made simple and comprehensible to one and all. The theory of evolution is in need of many corrections, additions, and much development. If we consider the existing forms on any given plane, it will be quite impossible to declare that all these forms evolved from the simplest forms on this plane. Some undoubtedly evolved from the lowest ones; others resulted from the process of degeneration of the higher ones; a third class developed from the remnants of some evolved form — while a fourth class resulted as a consequence of the incursion into the given plane of the properties and characteristics of some higher plane. It is certainly impossible to regard these complex forms as developed by an evolutionary process upon the given plane.

The below classification will show more clearly this correlation of forms of manifestation of consciousness, or of different states of consciousness.

First form. A sense of one-dimensional space in relation to the outer world. Everything transpires on a line, as it were. Sensations are not differentiated. Consciousness is immersed in itself, in its work of nutrition, digestion and assimilation of food, etc. This is the state of the cell, the group of cells, of tissues and organs of the body of an animal, of plants and lower organisms. In a man this is the "instinctive mind."

Second form. A sense of two-dimensional space. This is the state of the animal. That which is for us the third dimension, for it is motion. It already senses, feels, but does not think. Everything that it sees appears to it as genuinely real. Emotional life and flashes of thought in a man.

Third form. A sense of three-dimensional space. Logical thinking. Philosophical division into I and Not-I. Dogmatic religions or dualistic spiritism. Codified morality. Division into spirit and matter. Positivistic science. The idea of evolution. A mechanical universe. The understanding of cosmic ideas as metaphors. Imperialism, "historical materialism," socialism, etc. Subjection of the personality to society and law. Automatism. Death as the extinction of the personality. Intellect and flashes of self-consciousness.

Fourth form. Beginning of the understanding of four-dimensional space. A new concept of time. The possibility of more prolonged self-consciousness. Flashes of cosmic consciousness. The idea and sometimes the sensation of a living universe. A striving toward the wondrous. Sensation of infinity. Beginning of self-conscious will and moments of cosmic consciousness. Possibility of personal immortality.

Thus the third form includes that "man" whom science studies. But the fourth form is characteristic of the man who is beginning to pass out of the field of observation of positivism and logical understanding.

The table at the end of the book is a summing up of the contents of the entire book, and shows more in detail the correlation of the observed forms of consciousness in the living world and in "man."

EVOLUTION OR CULTURE?

The most interesting and important questions arising with regard to cosmic consciousness may be summed up as follows: 1. — Is the manifestation of cosmic consciousness a problem of the distant future, and of other generations — i.e., must cosmic consciousness appear as the result of an evolutionary process, after centuries and millenniums, and will it then become a common property or a property of the majority? And 2. — Can cosmic consciousness make its appearance *now* in contemporary man, i.e., at least as the result of a certain education and self-development which will aid the unfolding in him of dominant forces and capabilities, i.e., as the result of a certain *culture?*

It seems to me that with regard to this, the following ideas are tenable:

The possibility of the appearance or development of cosmic consciousness belongs to the few.

But even in the case of those men in whom cosmic consciousness may appear, certain quite definite inner and outer conditions are requisite for its manifestation — a certain *culture,* the education of those elements congenial to cosmic consciousness, and the elimination of those hostile to it.

The distinguishing signs of those men in whom cosmic consciousness is likely to manifest are not studied at all.

The first of these signs is the constant or frequent sensation that the world is not at all as it appears; that what is most important in it is not at all what is considered most important. The quest of the wondrous, sensed as the only real and true, results from this impression of the unreality of the world and everything related thereto.

High mental culture, high intellectual attainments, are not necessary conditions at all. The example of many *saints,* who were not intellectual, but who undoubtedly attained cosmic consciousness, shows that cosmic consciousness may develop in purely emotional soil, i.e., in the given case as a result of religious emotion. Cosmic consciousness is also possible of attainment through the emotion attendant upon creation — in painters, musicians and poets. Art in its highest manifestations is a path to cosmic consciousness.

But equally in all cases the unfoldment of cosmic consciousness demands a certain *culture*, a correspondent life. From all the examples cited by Dr. Bucke, and all others that one might add, it would not be possible to select a single case in which cosmic consciousness unfolded in conditions of inner life adverse to it, i.e., in moments of absorption by the *outer* life, with its struggles, its emotions and interests.

For the manifestation of cosmic consciousness it is necessary that the center of gravity of *everything* shall lie for man in the inner world, in self-consciousness, and not in the outer world at all.

If we assume that Dr. Bucke himself had been surrounded by entirely different conditions than those in which he found himself at the moment of experiencing cosmic consciousness, then in all probability his illumination would not have come at all.

He spent the evening reading poetry in the company of men of high intellectual and emotional development, and was returning home full of the thoughts and emotions of the evening.

But if instead of this he had spent the evening playing cards in the society of men whose interests were common and whose conversation was vulgar, or at a political meeting, or had he worked a night shift in a factory at a turning-lathe or written a newspaper editorial in which he himself did not believe and nobody else would believe — then we may declare with certainty that no cosmic consciousness would have appeared in him at all. For it undoubtedly demands a great freedom, and concentration on the inner world.

This conclusion in regard to the necessity for special culture and definitely favorable inner and outer conditions does not necessarily mean that cosmic consciousness is likely to manifest *in every man* who is put in these conditions. There are men, probably an enormous majority of contemporary humanity, in whom exists no such possibility at all. And in those who do not possess it in some sort already, it cannot be created by any culture whatever, in the same way that no kind or amount of culture will make an animal speak the language of man. The possibility of the manifestation of cosmic consciousness cannot be inoculated artificially. A man is either born with or without it. This possibility can be throttled or developed, but it cannot be created.

Not all can learn to discern the real from the false; but he who can will not receive this gift of discernment free. This is a thing of great labor, a thing of great work, which demands boldness of thought and boldness of feeling.

CONCLUSION

In conclusion I wish to speak of those wonderful words, full of profound mystery from the *Apocalypse* and the apostle Paul's *Epistle to the Ephesians,* which are placed as the epigraph of this book.

The Apocalyptic angel swears that THERE SHALL BE TIME NO LONGER. We know not what the author of the Apocalypse wanted to convey, but we do know those STATES OF SPIRIT when time disappears. We know that in this very thing, *in the change of the time-sense,* the beginning of the fourth form of consciousness is expressed, the beginning of the transition to COSMIC CONSCIOUSNESS.

In this and in phrases similar to it, the profound philosophical content of the evangelical teaching sometimes flashes forth. And the understanding of the fact that the MYSTERY OF TIME is the first mystery to be revealed is the first step toward the development of cosmic consciousness along the intellectual path.

But what did the Apocalyptic sentence mean? Did it mean precisely what we are now able to construe in it — or was it simply a bit of verbal art, a rhetorical figure of speech, the accidental harping of a string which has continued to sound up to our own time, through centuries and millenniums, with such a wonderfully powerful, true and beautiful tone of thought? We know not now, nor shall we ever, but the words are full of splendor, and we may accept them as a symbol of remote and inaccessible truth.

The apostle Paul's words are even more strange, even more startling by reason of their *mathematical* exactness. (A friend showed me these words in A. Dobroluboff's *From the Book Invisible,* who saw in them a direct reference to "the fourth measure of space.")

Truly, what does this mean?

. . . That ye, being rooted and grounded in *love,* may be able to comprehend with all *saints* what is the BREADTH and LENGTH and DEPTH and HEIGHT.

First of all, what does the *comprehension of breadth and length and depth and height* mean? What is it but the *comprehension of space?* And we now know that the comprehension of the mysteries of space is the beginning of the higher comprehension.

The apostle says that "being rooted and grounded in *love,* with all *saints*" they may comprehend *what space is.*

Here arises the question: why must *love* give comprehension? That *love* leads to *sanctity* — this is easily understood. Love in the sense that the apostle Paul understands it (Chapter XIII of the *First Epistle to the Corinthians*) is the highest of all emotions, the *synthesis*, the blending of all highest emotions. Incontestably, this leads to *sanctity*. *Sanctity*: that is the state of the spirit liberated from the *duality* of man, from his eternal disharmony of soul and body. In the language of the apostle Paul *sanctity* meant even a little less than in our contemporary language. He called all members of his church *saints*; sanctity meant to him righteousness, morality, religiosity. We say that all this is merely *the path to sanctity*. Sanctity is something more — something *attained*. But it is after all immaterial how we shall understand his words — in his meaning or in ours — *sanctity* is a superhuman quality. In the region of morality it corresponds to *genius* in the region of mind. *Love is the path to sainthood.*

But with sanctity the apostle Paul unites KNOWLEDGE. Saints *comprehend* what is the breadth and length and depth and height; and he says that all — through love — may *comprehend* this with them. But may comprehend what, exactly? COMPREHEND SPACE. Because "breadth and length and depth and height" translated into our language of shorter definitions actually means *space*.

This last is the most strange.

How could the apostle Paul possibly KNOW that sanctity gives a new understanding of *space*? We *know that it must give it*, but FROM WHAT could he know that?

None of his contemporaries ever united sanctity with the idea of the comprehension of space; and in general there was no discussion at all about "space" at that time, at least among the Greeks and Romans. Only now, *after Kant*, and after we have had access to the treasures of thought of the Orient, do we understand that the transition into a new phase of consciousness is impossible without the expansion of the space-sense.

But we wonder if this is what the apostle Paul wanted to say — that strange man: Roman official, persecutor of the first Christianity who became its preacher, philosopher, mystic; the man who "saw God," the bold reformer and moralist of his time, who fought for "the spirit" against "the letter" and was of course not responsible for the fact that he himself was understood by others not in "the spirit," but in "the letter." Is it *this* that he wanted to say? We do not know.

But let us look at these words of the *Apocalypse* and the *Epistles* from the standpoint of our usual "positivistic thinking," which sometimes condescendingly agrees to admit the "metaphorical meaning" of mysticism. What shall we see?

WE SHALL SEE NOTHING!

Positivism an Arrest of Thought

The flash of *mystery*, which appeared just for an instant, will immediately disappear. The words will be without any content, nothing in them will attract our wearied attention, which will merely glide over them as it glides over everything. We will indifferently turn the page and indifferently close the book.

An interesting metaphor, yes: But nothing else!

And we fail to observe that we rob ourselves, deprive life of all beauty, all mystery, all content; and wonder afterwards why everything is so uninteresting and detestable to us, why we do not desire to live, and why we do not understand anything around us; we wonder why brute force wins, or deceit and falsification, though to these things we have nothing to oppose.

THE METHOD IS NO GOOD.

In its time "positivism" appeared as something refreshing, sober, healthful and *progressive*, which explored new avenues of thought.

After the sentimental speculations of naïve dualism "positivism" was indeed a great step forward. Positivism became a symbol of the *progress* of thought.

But we see now that it inevitably leads to *materialism*. And in this form it arrests thought. From revolutionary, persecuted, anarchistic, freethinking, positivism became the basis of official science. It is decked-out in full dress. It is given medals. There are academies and universities dedicated to its service. It is recognized; it teaches; it tyrannizes over thought.

But having attained to well-being and prosperity, positivism immediately opposed obstacles to the forward march of thought.

A Chinese wall of "positivistic" sciences and methods is built up around free investigation. Everything rising above this wall is condemned as *unscientific*.

And seen in this way positivism, which before was a symbol of progress, now appears as *conservative, reactionary*.

The existing order is already established in the world of thought, and to fight against it is declared to be a crime.

With astonishing rapidity those principles which only yesterday expressed the highest radicalism in the region of thought have become the basis of opportunism in the region of ideas and serve as blind alleys, stopping the progress of thought. In our eyes this occurred with the idea of evolution, on which it is now possible to build up anything, and with the help of which it is possible to tear down anything.

But thought, which is free, cannot be bound by any limits.

The true motion which lies at the foundation of everything, is *the motion of thought. True energy is the energy of consciousness*. And *truth* itself is motion, and can never lead to arrestment, to the cessation of search.

ALL THAT ARRESTS THE MOTION OF THOUGHT — IS FALSE.

Therefore the true and real progress of thought is only in the broadest striving toward knowledge, that does not recognize the possibility of arrestment in any *found* forms of knowledge at all. The meaning of life is in eternal search. *And only in that search* can we find something truly new.

TABLE OF THE FOUR FORMS OF THE MANIFESTATION OF CONSCIOUSNESS

	1ST FORM	2ND FORM	3RD FORM	4TH FORM
THE SENSE OF SPACE AND TIME	The sense of one-dimensional space. The world on the line. The line as space, everything else as time. Everything except things lying on this line is in motion.	The sense of two-dimensional space. The world on the plane. The plane as space, everything else as time. Angles and curves as motions.	The sense of three-dimensional space. The world in an infinite sphere. The *sphere* as space. Everything else as time. Phenomena as motions. A becoming and changing universe.	The sense of four-dimensional space. Spatial sensation of time.
PSYCHOLOGY	Appearance of the first sensation. Sensation a unit. Its division into two. The gradual evolution of sensations and the accumulation of remembrances concerning them.	Perception. The expression of sensations by cries, sounds, motions. The absence of words and speech. Were there speech it would consist of substantives only.	Concept. Words. Judgment. Syllogism. Reasoning. Speech. Written language. Allegory. Emotions.	Self-consciousness. New sensations. Higher emotions. Expansion of concepts. Direct knowledge. Symbolism. Cosmic consciousness.
LOGIC	The absence of thinking, or 'a *confused* thinking of the 2nd form.	This is this. That is that. This is not that. The beginnings of logic. The logic of the uniqueness of each separate thing.	A is A. A is not Not-A. Everything is either A or Not-A. Dualistic logic. A logic of antitheses. Syllogism.	A is both A and Not-A. *Tat twam asi. Thou art that.* "Tertium Organum." Logic of the unity of all.

MATHEMATICS	The absence of numeration, or a *confused* numeration of the 2nd form.	The comparison of *separate* visible objects or *separate* perceptions. The direct sensation of quantity. *Computation* within the limits of this sensation.	Every magnitude is equal to itself. The part is less than the whole, etc. Finite and constant numbers. The geometry of Euclid.	A magnitude can be not equal to itself. The part can be equal to the whole, etc. Metageometry. Mathematics of variable and infinite magnitudes.
FORMS OF ACTIONS	Reflex, unconscious, responsive action to external irritation.	Instinct. "Emotional" and expedient action without consciousness of results. Seeming consciousness. Inability to manipulate a lever.	The consciousness of the purpose of actions performed. The *possibility* of a consciousness of actions. The cause of actions in the outer world in impressions received from the outer world. The impossibility of independent actions without impulses coming from the outside.	The starting of conscious actions. The starting of actions with the understanding of their cosmical meaning and purposes. The commencement of independent actions *proceeding from oneself*. MAGIC.
MORALS	Unconscious actions (like the actions of a man asleep).	The beginnings of the maternal, family, and tribal instincts. Laws of the life of the *species* as a condition of evolution. The unconscious submission to the "group soul" of the species manifesting through instincts.	Logical and conventional division into good and evil. The submission to the group consciousness of the family, of the clan, of the tribe, of the nation, of humanity, of the class, of the party, of a custom, of a fashion, etc.	The return to the law inside oneself. *A new conscience.* Emancipation from submission to the group-consciousness. The realization of oneself as an independent unit.

	1ST FORM	2ND FORM	3RD FORM	4TH FORM
FORMS OF CONSCIOUSNESS	Potential consciousness. Consciousness in a latent state—asleep. Consciousness as in sleep without dreams.	Simple consciousness. "It pains me," but the impossibility of saying, "I am conscious that it pains me." The reflected state of consciousness. Vision as in dreams. The passive state of consciousness.	The ability to think of one's states of consciousness. The division of I and Not-I. Active consciousness. *The moment when further evolution can be conscious only.*	The commencement of self-consciousness. Ecstatic states. Transitions to cosmic consciousness.
FORMS OF KNOWLEDGE	Unconscious receptivity of the environment, and unconscious reaction to it. "ADAPTABILITY."	The beginnings of attention. Observation. The accumulation of instincts. The recognition of everything *sensed* as real. The failure to discriminate between that which is illusory and that which is real.	Experience. Experimental knowledge. A complete and deep division and mutual misunderstanding between four forms of knowledge—religion, philosophy, science and art.	The beginning of the development of forms of knowledge. Mystic knowledge. A new sensation of time. The sensation of infinity. The sensation of the unreality of the phenomenal, visible world. A knowledge of the hidden substance of things by their outer signs. Unfoldment of the "world of the wondrous." Co-ordination in a complete whole of religion, philosophy, science and art.

FORMS OF SCIENCE	An accumulation of "traces," from the produced reflexes. The appearance of instinct and the accumulation of simple instincts.	Personal knowledge. Impotence to communicate experience. The beginnings of the communication of experience in the training of the young.	Positive science. Positive philosophy. Materialism. Spiritualistic philosophy. Dogmatic religions. Spiritism and pseudo-occultism. Sectarianism. Dualism. Matter and spirit. Separation of different forms of science.	Idealistic philosophy. Mathematics of the infinite. *Tertium Organum.* Mystical religion. God and the Cosmos—one. The sensation of a living and conscious universe. The union of all sciences into one. Occultism. Understanding of "*Dharma*," i. e., of laws of relativity.
DIFFERENT BEINGS	The lower animal. Cells of the tissues and organs of the body. The one-dimensional being. *Vegetative or semi-vegetative life.*	The higher animal. The body of man. The two-dimensional being. The absence of duality, divisibility and disharmony. *Animal life.*	Man. A three-dimensional being *outwardly* and dual *inwardly.* Inner warfare. The impossibility of attaining inner harmony. The "soul" as the battlefield of the "spirit" and the "flesh." The kingdom of the personal. Unconscious automatism. The absence of personal immortality.	The beginnings of the transition to a new type, and a new sensation of space. Victory of consciousness. "Men of cosmical consciousness." Triumph of the super-personal principle. Conscious automatism. The attainment of inner unity, and harmony. The "soul" as the center of independent actions. The beginnings of personal immortality.

PETER DEMIANOVICH OUSPENSKY was born in Moscow in 1878. His first book, *The Fourth Dimension*, published in 1909, at once placed him in the ranks of important writers on abstract mathematical theory. It was followed by *Tertium Organum* in 1912, and by an extensive journey through England, France, Italy, Egypt, India, and Ceylon, undertaken, as Ouspensky put it, "to seek the miraculous." *A New Model of the Universe* followed and revealed his stature as a thinker and his deep preoccupation with the problems of man's existence.

Ouspensky's meeting with G. I. Gurdjieff in Moscow in 1915, on his return from his travels, marked a turning-point in his life. From that time on, his interest was centered on the practical study of methods for the development of consciousness in man.

Ouspensky lived in St. Petersburg, where his public lectures drew large audiences, until 1917. At the outbreak of the Revolution, he went to join Gurdjieff in the Caucasus. It was not until 1920 that they arrived in Constantinople. There he learned that interested friends abroad had searched for him without avail, that *Tertium Organum* had been published in the United States, where it had aroused great interest, and that, as a result, Viscountess Rothermere wished to invite him to visit England.

In London in 1921 Ouspensky began a series of lectures which eventually led to the establishment of study groups concerned with Gurdjieff's ideas. At the same time he assisted Gurdjieff in founding his Institute at Fontainebleau. Ouspensky continued his work in and near London until 1940. During this period, in which many influential English men and women attended his lectures—among them Aldous Huxley, Gerald Heard, J. D. Beresford, Algernon Blackwood, and A. R. Orage—Ouspensky worked on *In Search of the Miraculous* and *The Psychology of Man's Possible Evolution*, both published in 1947.

Finally, in 1940, Ouspensky came to the United States. Here, with some of his former London pupils and American audiences, he continued his lectures, discussions, and work, only returning to England shortly before his death in 1947.

VINTAGE WORKS OF SCIENCE
AND PSYCHOLOGY

A free catalogue of VINTAGE BOOKS *will be sent at your request. Write to* Vintage Books, 457 Madison Avenue, New York, New York 10022.

VINTAGE POLITICAL SCIENCE
AND SOCIAL CRITICISM

A free catalogue of VINTAGE BOOKS *will be sent at your request. Write to* Vintage Books, 457 Madison Avenue, New York, New York 10022.